Blue-Eyed Soul Brother

BLUE-EYED SOUL BROTHER

The **Versatile Football Life** of **Super Bill Bradley**

WILLIAM C. KASHATUS

Foreword by Ray Didinger

University of Nebraska Press -- Lincoln

The University of Nebraska Press is part of a land-grant institution with campuses and programs on the past, present, and future homelands of the Pawnee, Ponca, Otoe-Missouria, Omaha, Dakota, Lakota, Kaw, Cheyenne, and Arapaho Peoples, as well as those of the relocated Ho-Chunk, Sac and Fox, and Iowa Peoples.

∞

Library of Congress Cataloging-in-Publication Data
Names: Kashatus, William C., 1959– author. |
Didinger, Ray, writer of foreword.
Title: Blue-eyed soul brother: the versatile football life of super
Bill Bradley / William C. Kashatus, Foreword by Ray Didinger.
Description: Lincoln: University of Nebraska Press, [2024] |
Includes bibliographical references and index.
Identifiers: LCCN 2024004404
ISBN 9781496240422 (hardback)
ISBN 9781496241788 (epub)
ISBN 9781496241795 (pdf)
Subjects: LCSH: Bradley, Bill (Football player) | Football
players—United States—Biography. | Philadelphia Eagles
(Football team) | Football—United States—History—
20th century. | BISAC: SPORTS & RECREATION /
Football | BIOGRAPHY & AUTOBIOGRAPHY / Sports
Classification: LCC GV939.B676 K37 2024 | DDC
796.332092 [B]—dc23/eng/20240610
LC record available at https://lccn.loc.gov/2024004404

Designed and set in Minion Pro by L. Welch.

For the Bradley family—Bill, Susan, Carissa, Jon, Henry, Casey, Wyatt—and to the memories of Joe Hill, Mildred, May, Duffy, and Matthew

CONTENTS

ILLUSTRATIONS

FOREWORD

Ray Didinger

Deep in the heart of Texas beats a passion for the game of football. Oh sure, it is there in other places too. Ohio, Mississippi, Pennsylvania, Florida—they play the game there, but it is Texas where the Friday Night Lights glow brightest. It has been that way forever.

Football is part of the Texas identity going all the way back to Sammy Baugh in the 1930s, Doak Walker, Bobby Layne, and Kyle Rote; after that came Bob Lilly, Mean Joe Greene, and Earl Campbell. Their names are as much a part of Texas folklore as Sam Houston and Stephen F. Austin.

Bill Bradley is part of that history. He grew up in the small town of Palestine, the son of a railroad worker. He led his underdog high school team to the state championship in 1964, and he went on to star as a quarterback and safety at the University of Texas. Along the way, he picked up the nickname "Super Bill," and even now, decades later, you can't tell the story of Texas football without including him.

I met Bradley in Philadelphia in 1970, when he was a second-year player with the Eagles and I was a rookie sportswriter assigned to cover the team for the *Philadelphia Bulletin*. Billy had an air of confidence he brought with him from Palestine, along with his boots and blue jeans. During training camp, he would sit on the dormitory steps at night playing the harmonica. It was like a scene lifted out of an old Western—all that was missing was the campfire.

We didn't have much in common, but we hit it off. Of course, I knew his backstory, the high school state championship, the *Playboy* All-American spread at Texas, and the four-interception final game against Texas A&M.

I was surprised, frankly, when I saw him for the first time. He was smaller than I was, but he had an easy smile and a wry sense of humor that was welcome on an Eagles team that didn't win very often in those days.

Billy had not yet established himself as a star—that would come soon enough—but what impressed me was the way he carried himself. In the dining hall, where young players usually ate apart from the veterans and white players and Black players sat on opposite sides of the room, Bill would put his tray down at any table and join in any conversation. He was, indeed, everyone's Blue-Eyed Soul Brother.

When he played in the Big 33 game—an All-Star game matching the top high school players from Texas and Pennsylvania—Bill was the first white player to room with a Black player. His name was Jerry LeVias, and he was a star running back from Beaumont. He and Bill became friends during the Big 33 practices and decided to become roommates. It immediately made the newspapers: a racial barrier had come down in Texas. Bill couldn't understand the fuss. He still can't.

"Jerry and I were friends," he said. "We're still friends. What's the big deal?"

Most players who come from a small town are intimidated by the big city. Bill was just the opposite. When he came to Philadelphia, he chose to live in Center City. He embraced the city's culture and its history. He took up painting. He enjoyed hanging out with the rock music crowd at the Electric Factory. He knew his way around the Jersey Shore. Bill and I became friends partly because he knew places I didn't know—and I grew up here.

We would be riding through some unfamiliar neighborhood in South Philadelphia when he'd say, "Turn here."

I'd say, "Where are we going?"

He'd say, "You'll see."

At the end of the block would be a grungy bar that served something great—tacos maybe, burgers, wings—and a cute waitress was usually working the tables.

Once we were standing in line outside the Main Point, a folk music club in the suburbs, and I said, "We're friends, but if you screw up in a game,

I have to write about it. You know that, right?" Bill thought a moment and said, "Well then, I just won't screw up. Problem solved."

It was one of his typical wisecracks, but it proved to be largely true. I was the beat man covering the Eagles for seven years, and over that time, he was easily their best player. When he finally got a chance to play in 1971, he led the NFL with eleven pass interceptions. The next year, he again led the league with nine interceptions, becoming the first player ever to win the interception title in back-to-back seasons. He was the best free safety in the league, hands down.

Billy was also one of the most versatile players in the game. In addition to playing defense, he punted, returned punts and kickoffs, and held for placekicks. He was also the team's emergency quarterback. Coach Ed Khayat said, "If anything ever happened to Billy, it would take five players to replace him." He wasn't kidding.

The downside, of course, was the losing. Bill only knew success in high school and college, so the losing in Philadelphia frustrated him. The defense generally played well—and his play in the secondary was a big part of that—but the team never could figure it out on offense. In his eight seasons with the Eagles, the team went through four head coaches and six starting quarterbacks. They never finished with a winning record, not once. "Losing left me with an empty feeling, a feeling my career in Philadelphia wasn't complete," he once said. "It's like there is a final chapter that never got written.

"The personal stuff was nice—winning the interception titles and going to the Pro Bowl—but when you get right down to it, this is a team game, and that's where the real satisfaction is. We just couldn't put it together. I still have fond memories of those guys. They were part of an adventure I'll never forget. Whenever I see them now, it's like striking gold."

William Kashatus tells Bradley's story well in *Blue-Eyed Soul Brother*. It is a vivid portrait of a colorful character, one of a new breed of athletes who came out of the turbulent sixties, long haired and free spirited, and changed the face of professional football. The 1970s were the decade when the game exploded with *Monday Night Football* debuting on network TV and the Super Bowl becoming, in the words of *Time* magazine, "The

Great American Timeout." I think it was the best decade in NFL history and the most important, and this book brings it to life.

Bradley still holds the Eagles' records for interceptions in a season, most interception return yardage in a season (248 in 1971), and most interception return yardage in a career (536). Hall of Famer Brian Dawkins and Eric Allen tied him for the team record for career interceptions with thirty-four. When the Eagles named their all-time team, Billy was one of the safeties, along with Dawkins.

Bill Bradley certainly left his mark on the NFL, on the Eagles, and, yes, on me.

ACKNOWLEDGMENTS

The research and writing of *Blue-Eyed Soul Brother* have been very personal and, at times, emotionally challenging for me. In the process, I've met some of the finest people I know. At the top of the list are Bill and Susan Bradley, who gave me their full support and opened their home—and hearts—to me at a difficult time in their lives. Not only did they give me countless hours of their time, but they also reviewed the manuscript for factual accuracy and gave their permission to reprint photographs. For all those gifts, I am grateful. This book is dedicated to them and their family. Bill's lifelong friends also welcomed me with open arms (and an endless supply of rum and Coke) at one of their shindigs at Elkhart Lake in East Texas. As the evening unfolded and the libations increased, I learned about the on-field and off-field exploits of the Palestine Wildcats, winners of the Texas state high school football title in 1964. They were some of the most colorful and profane stories I had ever heard. Fortunately, Curtis Fitzgerald made sure I knew which anecdotes were tall tales and which were the God's honest truth. I am also grateful to Hal Sumrall, who warned me to stay out of the lake or become bait for the family of alligators who live in it.

Special thanks are due to all of Bill's family members, friends, teammates, and coaches who agreed to be interviewed for the book: Tommy Asaff, Bill Bergey, Norm Bulaich, John Bunting, Tom Campbell, Harold Carmichael, Carissa Carter, Jackie Cherry, Barry Chronister, Ted Cottrell, Ray Didinger, Mike Evans, Curtis Fitzgerald, Bill Hall, Mickey Hubert, Harold Jackson, Eddie Khayat, Ted Koy, Paul Kristynik, Jerry LeVias, Bob McKay, Larry Miller, Stephen Missildine, Wade Phillips, Kevin Reilly,

Corby Robertson, Cis Rundle, Billy Schott, Kurt Schulz, Jerry Sisemore, Bob Stephenson, Harold Sumrall, Dick Vermeil, Danny Westmoreland, Tom Woodeshick, and Steve Zabel.

I am also grateful to attorney Janet Fries of the Washington DC law firm of Faegre Drinker for vetting the manuscript and providing excellent legal counsel; Donna Jenkins and Jonathan Ryal of Palestine High School, who were invaluable resources on the history of the school's football program; Craig Westemeier of the University of Texas and Terre Heydari of Southern Methodist University for granting permission to reprint photos from those institutions; Ray Didinger, who wrote the foreword; and Bobby Hawthorne for reviewing and commenting on the manuscript and for endorsing the book, along with former Eagles John Bunting and Harold Carmichael. Special thanks are due to Rob Taylor and Sara Springsteen at the University of Nebraska Press for guiding the editorial process for the book and to Joseph Webb for his copyediting.

Finally, I owe a personal debt of gratitude to my late parents, William and Balbina, who passed when I was writing this book. Not only did they provide me with an education that few individuals enjoy, but they also supported my dream of becoming a writer. My wife, Jaqueline Butler, and our sons, Timothy, Peter, and Ben, are the light of my life. Few men admit to having heroes; I am truly fortunate to have been born to, married to, and fathered mine. My love for them is eternal.

Blue-Eyed Soul Brother

Introduction

Bill Bradley thought he was invincible. His football career had been an unbroken chain of success, starting in high school when he quarterbacked the Palestine Wildcats to the 1964 Texas 3A state championship, the only one in the school's history.[1] The next year he was named the Most Valuable Player of the Big 33 football game when he led the Texas All-Stars over their Pennsylvania rivals, 26–10.[2]

While Bradley's exceptional running and passing skills earned him high school All-American, his remarkable ability to throw the pigskin with either hand secured him the nickname "Super Bill." Supremely confident of his talent, Bradley could be cocky, but he also won over teammates and coaches with his winning smile and down-home charm. More important, he never missed an opportunity to acknowledge the contributions of his teammates. Bradley was no ass-kisser. He was as genuine as a Hill Country sunrise, and *everyone* knew it. That's why college recruiters from across the Lone Star State were knocking at his door until the Longhorns' Darrell Royal stole him away with the intention of capturing another national title.[3]

Bradley responded by leading Texas to a 7-4 record in 1966. He also led the Southwest Conference in rushing touchdowns (6) and captained a victory over Mississippi in the Bluebonnet Bowl.[4] The hype surrounding the boy wonder reached new heights when *Sports Illustrated* put his face on the cover of its September 11, 1967, college football preview edition.[5] It was as good as drawing a bull's-eye on Super Bill's jersey, as every defensive lineman in the Southwest Conference wanted a piece of him. Despite a 6-4 finish that year, Bradley was second in the conference in total touchdowns (14) and first in passing yards per attempt (7.7).[6] The reality check came the next season.

Bradley, now a senior tricaptain, knew that the fifth-ranked Longhorns needed to win from the jump in 1968. To kickstart the offense, Royal introduced the Wishbone formation, which emphasized the running game. The problem was that Super Bill was a running *and* passing quarterback. No matter how hard he tried, Bradley could not make the adjustment. UT opened the season with a 20–20 tie against eleventh-ranked Houston. That was unacceptable. But it got worse on September 28, when the Longhorns lost to archrival Texas Tech, 31–22. With a record of 0-1-1, the proverbial shit was rolling downhill.[7] No one was happy about it—not Governor John Connally, a UT alum; not Norman Hackerman, the university's president; and certainly not head coach Darrell Royal, who was taking the heat from both Connally and Hackerman, as well as the alumni. Something had to be done.

At 6:00 a.m. on Sunday morning, September 29, Joe Doenges, the UT manager, went to Bradley's dormitory and knocked on his door. Having crawled into bed a few hours earlier after the plane trip back from Lubbock, the quarterback stumbled to the door and opened it. "Hey, Joe, what do you want?" he asked. "I'm trying to get some sleep."

"Coach Royal wants to see you in his office right away," Doenges said, before he turned and walked away.

The first thing that crossed Bradley's mind was Royal's often repeated mantra that "three things can happen when you throw the ball, and two of 'em are bad."[8] Bill thought back to the previous season when he threw four interceptions against Texas A&M in the I formation. He had also turned the ball over six times in the first two contests of this season as he was trying to learn the new Wishbone offense, and now the Longhorns were 0-1-1. Whether Bradley liked it or not, the quarterback always got most of the credit for winning and most of the blame for losing, and he was going to have to answer for it.[9] Only God commanded more respect than Darrell Royal on UT's campus, and Bradley certainly didn't want to piss him off.

If Royal was summoning him to his office at that early hour, it was deadly serious. The quarterback threw on his clothes and ran across campus to Gregory Gymnasium where the head coach had his office. When he arrived, Bradley knocked on the door and was told to enter. Royal pointed to the chair across his desk, and the quarterback dutifully took his seat.

Super Bill knew the routine. It was not the first time he had been summoned to the office. He knew better than to say anything. Royal was partial to monologues, not conversations. But never in his wildest dreams could Bradley have predicted the nature of this one.

"Bill, we're going to make some changes around here," began the head coach, "and we're going to start with you. You are no longer my quarterback. Now, if you want to keep your scholarship, you can come out to practice today, and we'll try to find a spot for you. After all, you are still a captain."

The execution was short and quick. But it left Bradley in a stupor. There was nothing for him to say except, "Okay, coach." Then he got to his feet and left.

Unable to fully comprehend the decision, Bill went back to his dorm room and unburdened himself to his roommate, Bill Hall. After their discussion, Bradley realized that he had only two options. He could quit the team and go home, or he could remain on the team and try to help it win however he could. If Bill gave any further thought to quitting, it ended when he phoned his father back in Palestine.

"Dad, I think my football life here at UT is done," he began. "I was just told that I wasn't the quarterback anymore."

The silence was so thick, he could cut it with a knife.

"I'm going to hitch a ride home," he added.

If Super Bill was looking for sympathy, he had gone to the wrong place. Joe Hill Bradley knew a thing or two about competitive athletics. He was a hard-drinking railroad man who once played professional baseball and coached the sport for more than two decades.

"The hell you are!" he snapped. "The Bradleys don't quit. Your teammates voted you captain, so you go out there to practice and show 'em what you're made of. If you quit now, you don't have a home here!" Before Bill could utter another word, the elder Bradley hung up the phone.[10]

Bill didn't return to his dorm room. Instead, he walked around campus with tears in his eyes. He came to UT with the understanding that he would lead the Longhorns to a national title and restore glory to one of the best collegiate football programs in the country. He planned to build on that success as an NFL quarterback. It was his destiny. But now, in a split second, that opportunity had been taken from him. It was the first time in his life that he was told he had failed, that he could not lead, that he was not good enough. Now he had to ante up and show his head coach, his teammates, and his father what kind of a man he was.

Darrell Royal made five other position changes that day, but none received the attention of Bradley's demotion. News travels quickly when it's about Longhorns football. When he got to practice on Monday afternoon, there were sportswriters from every major newspaper and magazine, including *Sports Illustrated*, *Sport*, *Newsweek*, and *Time*. All of Texas—make that the nation—wanted to see how Bradley would respond to the demotion.

Although Super Bill was now the fourth-team wide receiver and punter, he was still a captain, and he had to act like one. Determined to break the tension among his teammates, he approached James Street, his replacement at quarterback, and asked him to throw a deep pass. Then he undid the strings of his sweatpants and sprinted downfield. As he dove for the ball, Super Bill's pants dropped to his ankles and he landed on the turf with nothing but the sun shining on his bare ass. When he got up, *everyone* was laughing—his teammates, the sportswriters, and even Coach Royal.[11] It was a stroke of genius. That was the moment Bill Bradley became a leader—when he learned how to deal with adversity.

Switching to defensive back, Super Bill recorded a Longhorns single-game record of four interceptions against rival Texas A&M. His defensive performance that season helped UT capture the Southwest Conference title and advance to the 1969 Cotton Bowl, where Texas defeated Tennessee, 36–13.[12]

Selected by the Philadelphia Eagles in the third round of the 1969 NFL draft, Bradley starred for losing teams from 1969 to 1976, a span in which the Birds went 35-72-5, never finishing a season above third place in the

NFC East.[13] While he spent the first two seasons in the league as a punter and returner, Bradley, in 1971, moved to defensive back, where he made an immediate impact in the Eagles' secondary. That year he led the NFL with eleven interceptions en route to earning his first All-Pro and Pro Bowl selections. His 248 interception return yards also led the NFL and set an Eagles record for return yards in a season. The gregarious Texan repeated as All-Pro and Pro Bowl selections in 1972, when he swiped another nine passes, becoming the first player in NFL history to lead the league in interceptions in consecutive seasons. He was selected to a third Pro Bowl in 1973.[14]

During his eight years in the City of Brotherly Love, Bradley set Eagles club records for most career interceptions (34), most interceptions in a season (11), most interception return yardage in a season (248), and most interception return yardage in a career (536).[15] Those statistics would have earned Super Bill induction into the Pro Football Hall of Fame if he had played on winning teams. Instead, he remains one of the most underrated defensive players in the history of the NFL. Bradley's gridiron success was only part of his story, though.

Bill Bradley was one of the most whimsical nonconformists in the National Football League during the transformative decade of the 1970s. Players began to assert their personal freedom by wearing their hair longer, engaging in more recreational activities, using illicit drugs, and demanding higher wages and more flexible terms for free agency.[16] Bradley did all that and more. He was not only a contradiction in a sport dominated by behemoth jocks, crewcuts, and violence but also a pioneer and product of the changes. Super Bill stood just under six feet tall and tipped the scales at a mere 180 pounds. A staunch believer in personal freedom, Bradley wore his woolly hair long and untamed and would've grown it "down to my ass" if the Eagles had let him. He favored tie-dyed shirts, bell-bottom blue jeans, and cowboy boots and drove a 1967 VW van he nicknamed the "Cottonmouth Blues Wagon." A sensitive human being who was unable to harm any living creature, Bradley opposed the Vietnam conflict, not from a political standpoint but because "folks [were] killing each other." At the same time, he considered two of his high school teammates his personal heroes because they went to war and nearly lost their lives in Southeast Asia. He probably would have gone himself if the draft board didn't give him a 4-F classification because of his bum knees.[17] Instead, the soft-spoken Texan competed in the NFL and spent his off-hours playing the blues on his harmonica, listening to country western music, people-watching at the local mall, and playing with children in the streets outside his South Philadelphia apartment.[18]

At the same time, Super Bill was a fierce competitor on the playing field and a savvy negotiator off it. During his first two years in the league, the Eagles limited his role to punting and returning. That is, until Bradley demanded—and earned—a starting position as a defensive back and, later, free safety. From that vantage point, he preyed on NFL quarterbacks, intercepting a few and as much as two times a game. Once he established himself as a multiple threat (defensive back, punter, returner, and holder), Super Bill demanded a salary increase. When the front office turned him down, Bradley, during training camp in 1972, went on a sixteen-day holdout until the Eagles agreed to a new three-year pact worth $145,000, more than doubling his original salary.[19] At the time, the free-spirited Texan told his teammates that the contract holdout "isn't just about me." That he was "protesting the paltry salaries all of us are making." To reinforce the point, Bradley agreed to allow teammate Tim Rossovich to join him in the holdout to secure "greater leverage."[20] If there was still any doubt about Super Bill's team commitment, he eliminated it two years later when he donned a T-shirt that read, "No Freedom, No Football" and refused to cross the picket line when the NFL Players Association went on strike to protest the "Rozelle rule" limiting free agency.[21] This was despite other Eagles players crossing the line a month into the strike.[22]

The football establishment dismissed Bradley as a hippie because of his idiosyncratic behavior. But it's difficult to find anyone else like him who was similarly stereotyped. To be sure, the NFL, beginning in the mid-1960s, employed nonconformists of virtually every ilk. There were activists like Dave Meggyesy, a linebacker for the St. Louis Cardinals, who participated in civil rights and antiwar demonstrations and later became a representative for the NFL Players Association. There were intellectuals like Pat Toomay, Blaine Nye, and Larry Cole, linemen for the Dallas Cowboys who were book smart and publicity shy. There were other free spirits who craved the limelight and became movie actors after their playing careers ended, like Tim Rossovich, Bradley's teammate with the Eagles, and Fred Dryer, a defensive end with the New York Giants. There was even a muckraking writer, Pete Gent, a wide receiver for the Dallas Cowboys, who exposed the NFL's hypocrisy regarding drug use in his novel *North Dallas Forty*. Bradley doesn't resemble any of them, though. He truly marched to the beat of his own drum.

Growing up in Northeast Philadelphia, I became a die-hard Eagles fan, and Bill Bradley was my hero. I admired not only the ferocity and passion with which he played defense but also the gracefulness of his interceptions, whether done with a backward vertical leap or a horizontal dive. Not until five years ago did I meet Bradley, at a suburban Philadelphia card show. I was struck by his friendliness and the ease with which he interacted with the fans. He seemed genuinely interested in each one and patiently listened to their memories of him as a player.

When I approached Bill, I became nervous, as if I was back in elementary school. Sensing my discomfort, he shook my hand and said, "How's it going, partner?" His warm smile, southern drawl, and easygoing manner made me immediately feel comfortable. When I told Bill how much he had meant to me as a youngster, he seemed moved. Then he pulled out a slip of paper; wrote down his address, cell-phone number, and email address; handed it to me; and said, "Please stay in touch."

Since then, Bill and I have become good friends. We've visited each other in his native Texas and in Philadelphia. We've attended Eagles games, gone pub-hopping, played harmless but juvenile pranks at airports, showed up at country western music concerts, kayaked the Guadalupe River in Texas and the Susquehanna in Northeast Pennsylvania, and visited Bill's family, teammates, and friends in Palestine, Austin, and Hill Country.

When Bill gave me permission to write his biography, I was concerned that he might lose interest, or worse, forget some of the most important events that shaped his life. He struggles with memory loss and fears that he will become a victim of chronic traumatic encephalopathy (CTE). Fortunately, neither of those concerns materialized. Instead, I discovered a truly exceptional human being.

People gravitate toward Bill because of his southern charm and laid-back manner. It's virtually impossible to find anyone who dislikes him. He does not speak ill of anybody else. Instead, Bill has a unique tendency to see the very best in others and bring it to the surface. Unsurprisingly, he is just as fiercely loyal to his family, friends, and teammates as they are to him. He also has a wonderful if not earthy sense of humor that sometimes borders on craziness, a quality we share that endears us to each other.

Blue-Eyed Soul Brother is a biography of my very first and only NFL hero. Although Jim Dent's *The Kids Got It Right: How the Texas All-Stars Kicked Down Racial Walls* (2013) highlighted Bradley's early life and stellar high school football career, it concentrates on his relationship with Jerry LeVias, an African American teammate, and the instrumental roles the two youngsters played in the integration of the Texas All-Stars at the 1965 Big 33 game at Hershey, Pennsylvania. *Blue-Eyed Soul Brother* offers a much more comprehensive treatment of Bradley's playing and coaching careers at the college and NFL levels, as well as his personal life after he retired from the game. Jerry LeVias inspired the title of the book. He was the one who, in the summer of 1965, nicknamed Bradley his "Blue-Eyed Soul Brother," due to his color blindness in matters of race, their close friendship, and a shared love of football and Motown music.[23]

Bradley's early life and high school and college careers are told in the broader contexts of Texas football and integration at the high school level, as well as the Longhorns' struggle to win another national championship after 1963 in the all-white Southwest Conference. The second part of the book details Bradley's experiences as a player and coach in the National Football League between 1969 and 2009, a transformative period in the strategy and culture of the game. It also explores Bill's personal life: his marriage to Susan Wright, a single mother; the love and support they gave each other in raising her children, Matt and Carissa; the heartbreaking death of Matt, a talented college quarterback, who made a heroic, eleven-year effort to regain the use of his voice and motor skills after a savage assault by a drunken college student; and Bill's current struggle with memory loss and other cognitive impairments.

Blue-Eyed Soul Brother is the inspirational story of a man whose contagious enthusiasm for life raised the spirits of those around him in both good and bad times. It is a story about the resilience of the human spirit in the face of professional and personal tragedy, a story to learn from and to remember when life appears to go awry.

1 Palestine

Palestine is one of the most charming small towns in East Texas. Located in the Piney Woods region of the Lone Star State, the town has surrounding forests abundant in pine and hardwood trees, expansive lakes, and white-tailed deer. Regal Victorian mansions once inhabited by railroad executives and oil barons grace the resplendent streets of the historic district, which beams with Southern charm. Antique shops, quaint hotels, and Eilenberger's, the oldest continually operating bakery in Texas, can still be found downtown. The stately Anderson County Courthouse, with its majestic silver dome, dominates center square, a reminder of a more prosperous time in the town's history. Just outside the city limits is Davey Dogwood Park, 254 acres of emerald greenery where locals can hike and bike along the many trails and enjoy the picturesque scenery. Springtime is breathtaking, as the park erupts with Texas wildflowers, including Indian blankets, bluebonnets, and pink evening primrose. Beyond the pastoral beauty of the town and the surrounding countryside, Palestine is best defined by its residents.

There are townies, farmers, ranchers, and even a few colorful rapscallions. Some are wealthy. Others run the gamut of the middle class. Still others compose the working poor who survive from paycheck to paycheck. Regardless of their ilk, Palestinians are a social bunch. If they like you, they like you hard and tend to organize a get-together on the flimsiest of excuses. If they grew up together, their loyalty is unconditional. They hold no grudges if you leave town to pursue bigger and better things, but only if you remember where you came from and return often enough to show it. Palestinians may have their political and cultural differences, but they all manage to coexist like one big family. It's always been that way, kind of like a historical fact.

Once the site of a frontier trading post, Palestine was founded in 1846 to serve as the seat for the newly established Anderson County. Legend holds that the town was named for Palestine, Illinois, by Daniel Parker, an elder of the Primitive Baptist Church. But the locals still debate that issue. Some claim that Micham Main, a Palestine, Illinois, migrant, chose the name when he was appointed by the Texas Legislature as one of three men to select a site for the Anderson County seat. Others insist that another legislative appointee, John Parker, also from Illinois's Palestine, chose the name.[1] What is certain is that by 1861 Palestine had grown to nearly two thousand residents and was connected to the rest of East Texas by a stagecoach that passed through the town every three weeks and serviced Huntsville, Crockett, and Nacogdoches as well.[2]

Plans for the construction of the Metropolitan Railroad between Texarkana and Austin, passing through Palestine, were interrupted by the Civil War. But an emerging timber industry led to the International Railroad and Great Northern Railroad's decision, in 1872, to build a line that connected Palestine to Longview, eighty-eight miles to the northeast.[3] When International and Great Northern Railroad (IGN) president Herbert M. Hoxie moved to Palestine in the mid-1870s, the town assumed a more important role in the railroad. A major depot was built in 1892 and a modern passenger coach shop in 1902.[4]

Between 1900 and 1909, the IGN hired its own workforce and used convict labor to extend the railroad. Inmates collected the iron ore from the surrounding woods and then smelt the ore in a blast furnace at Rusk Penitentiary thirty miles away. The finished rails were then transported to various building sites, where IGN employees laid and fastened the track. The IGN would eventually operate some 1,106 miles of track, and Palestine would become the center for the company's main workshops, where locomotives and passenger cars were constructed, overhauled, and repaired.[5]

Regularly scheduled train service to Palestine began in 1909 and continued until 1924, when the line was leased to various companies, including the Missouri Pacific Railroad (MoPac). The town was a hub for the southern branch of MoPac, linking Houston to St. Louis. Four years later, oil was discovered at Boggy Creek, just east of town. Palestine became a center for supplying and servicing oil wells in other producing fields later discovered in Anderson County.[6] But the railroad remained the biggest employer in Palestine. In fact, a county immigration society recruited railroad workers by publishing job advertisements in the *Palestine Daily Herald* and a dozen other newspapers across Texas. Thousands of unemployed men read those circulars and flocked to the Anderson County seat in search of work.[7] One of those men was Joe Hill Bradley.

Bradley and his wife, Helen, arrived in Palestine in 1927. Joe was just eighteen years old and his new bride, sixteen. With no prospects in their hometown of Dodge, Joe took a job with the Missouri Pacific as a telegraph operator and settled into the life of a railroad worker.[8] Life had not turned out the way he had planned. If Joe had had his druthers, he would be playing shortstop for the St. Louis Cardinals. But the Redbirds already had a shortstop, Rabbit Maranville, a future Hall of Famer, and Joe was only good enough to get a Class D contract. Money was the deciding factor. The railroad paid more than the Minors. Therefore, Joe worked for MoPac five days a week and played semipro ball on the weekends.[9]

When Bradley's marriage ended in divorce a few years later, he turned to carousing and liquor. In fact, the only thing he swore off was marriage. That was until 1943, when he wed Mildred Pauline Rainey, the daughter of Omega Thomas Rainey, a carpenter, and his wife, Rosemary, who ran a Houston boardinghouse.[10] Millie tried hard to make a sober and honest man of her husband. But theirs was an attraction of opposites. Joe, who was fourteen years older, was a binge drinker who favored bourbon and whiskey. Millie was a teetotaler. Joe was a "rounder," or a philanderer, who "ran around" with other women. Millie, on the other hand, was a devout member of the First United Methodist Church and wholly committed to the marriage.[11] Despite their differences, the couple somehow managed to coexist and raise a family that grew to include three children.

William Calvin Bradley was the couple's second child and eldest son. "Billy" was born on January 24, 1947, sandwiched between Rose May, who was four years older, and Ralph, who was four years younger. Billy inherited not only his paternal grandfather's name but also his father's passion for baseball. He had no choice in either matter. Every toy in his crib was a ball. When he was two years old, Joe discovered that his son was ambidextrous and encouraged him to throw with both hands. Shortly after, he began taking his son to the ballpark, where he would seat the toddler on the grass behind the backstop to watch Joe play with the Palestine Pals, the local semipro team. At age four, Billy was spending his afternoons in the backyard tossing a ball of aluminum foil in the air and hitting long flies with a plastic bat. A few years later, Joe would join his son after work to teach him the finer points of the game. By the time Billy joined up for Little League at age eight, he not only knew how to bunt, field grounders, and hit the cutoff man but also switch-hit. Under the demanding tutelage of his father, Billy became the stuff of legends.

"Billy and I played Little League against each other," recalled David Dickey, a boyhood friend. "Once I tried to steal home after he threw a wild pitch. The catcher retrieved the ball and threw it to Billy who was covering home plate. He took the throw and put his glove right above the plate. He didn't reach out to tag me. He just left the glove there and let me slide right into the tag. I remember thinking, *Who taught him to do that?*"[12]

Dickey would soon learn that Joe Hill Bradley taught his son everything he knew about baseball. In fact, Billy became so good at such a young age that he served as an assistant coach whenever his father conducted summer baseball camps for the local Little Leaguers. "I was my dad's guinea pig," recalled Bill. "Not only did he teach me the finer points of the game, but he [also] taught me to win. Nothing less was expected of me. I could go three-for-four with two home runs and five RBI in a game, and Dad would still be mad at me because I struck out the one time. He also expected me to know everything he was coaching the other kids, so it was a no-brainer for me to be his assistant coach."[13]

Joe also introduced his son to his favorite team, the St. Louis Cardinals. Since St. Louis was 728 miles to the northeast of Palestine, the only way the Bradleys could follow the Redbirds was through the daily box scores in the Palestine newspapers and on radio. While Harry Caray and Jack Buck stirred young Billy's imagination with their lively broadcasts, Joe knew there was nothing like being at the ballpark. One day he purchased a round-trip train ticket to St. Louis for his son and gave him enough money for bleacher seats at Sportsman's Park to see his hero Stan Musial play in person.

"Most parents wouldn't have sent a twelve-year-old kid that far on a train by himself," explained Bill. "But I knew the conductors, and it was a helluva lot of fun. In fact, it was one of the happiest days of my boyhood."[14]

By the time Billy entered junior high school, Joe was the chief dispatcher for MoPac. He was under tremendous pressure due to the overwhelming demands of the job, and he turned increasingly to the bottle. Despite his binge drinking, everyone on the railroad respected Bradley. In fact, they nicknamed him "Cephas," Christ's designation for the apostle Simon Peter as the rock of the church. So, too, was Joe Hill Bradley the rock, or foundation, of MoPac's southern branch. He was intimately familiar with not only the railroad territory within a one-hundred-mile radius of Palestine but also the idiosyncrasies of the engineers and the conductors who operated the trains. He could quote you the rule book and the timetables. Cephas could even move several trains across his assigned territory with minimal delay, no matter that most of the area was covered by single track. That meant aligning track switches in a split second so that trains could move into and out of sidings without having to stop and hand-throw switches.

When Joe began the job in the late 1920s, he communicated with engineers through Morse code. By the mid-1950s, the job became a bit easier with the introduction of two-way radios. However, Joe could not see the traffic he was directing, which meant that the slightest error could result in disaster, and sometimes those disasters were not his fault. "My Dad always covered for the engineers," explained Bill. "If there was a major wreck, especially on a passenger train, my dad would take the blame. That's just the way he was. He didn't want the engineers to get into trouble." Therefore, whenever a train wreck occurred, Bradley was fired by MoPac only to be rehired a few weeks later. The railroad simply could not afford to lose a dispatcher with his knowledge and experience. But each time he was fired, Joe was hurting for money and had to find another place for his family to live.[15]

The Bradleys might have weathered those financial storms if Cephas had saved any money. But his drinking eliminated that possibility. Because Palestine was a dry town, he had to buy his liquor from bootleggers. Then he would head over to the pinball hall and do his drinking there. Billy would have to go find his father and bring him home. "Aside from his drinking, our father was a real good dad," insisted Bill. "He loved all us kids. Rose May was daddy's little girl, but he treated Ralph and me like we were special too.

"Don't get me wrong, Dad was a disciplinarian when he had to be," Bill said. "His motto was 'spare the rod, spoil the child.' Our family was Methodist, but Dad sent me to a Catholic elementary school because the nuns there were strict disciplinarians and reinforced his motto. Dad was especially strict about being on time. God help you if you weren't home for supper because he'd come and find you, take his leather belt off and whip your butt. But like I said, all us kids felt loved by him."[16]

The Bradley children also created their own support system. Regardless of their age differences, they were extremely close. "My big sister, May-May, was a real lady and very smart," recalled Bill. "She taught me how to dance and introduced me to Motown and R&B. She was also the first person to go to college in our family, and I really respected her for that."

Ralph was at the other end of the spectrum. He contracted a severe fever shortly after birth, and it retarded his cognitive development. Today, he would probably be considered autistic, but the diagnosis did not exist in the 1950s. Nicknamed "Duffy," Ralph suffered from seizures and struggled to write and do simple arithmetic. "Duffy knew that he wasn't like the rest of us," said Bill. "Sometimes he'd get so mad about that fact that he'd slap himself across his face or on his body. He taught me sympathy for special-needs children. He also taught me that they, too, have certain abilities despite their handicap.

"Duffy was a musical genius. When he was a toddler, he had a small toy piano, and he could play anything. When Duffy got older, we got him a hand accordion, and all he had to do was hear a song once, and he could play it perfectly on that accordion. You name it, Hank Williams, Jimmy Dean, he could play any of their songs from memory."[17]

From an early age, Billy became his younger brother's protector. They slept in the same room together. If Duffy suffered a seizure, Billy woke him up, made sure he did not swallow his tongue, and placed a paper bag over his mouth so he could breathe. Since Duffy loved sports, Billy would take him along when he went to the local playground, and they would shoot baskets or throw a football around. He introduced his brother to his friends, who also accepted him into their peer group. When their father came home drunk, Billy shielded Duffy from his unpleasant behavior until Millie packed her three children into the family car and drove them to her parents' boarding house in Houston. They would spend a week there visiting with their grandparents while Cephas got himself back together, and then they'd return to Palestine. But after the second time Joe was dismissed from MoPac, Millie took a job at the local grocery store so the family could survive. She later opened a beauty parlor to insure the family's financial stability.[18]

Billy also had a close-knit group of friends who knew each other since elementary school. "We all grew up together and lived within a few blocks of each other on the poor side of town," recalled Harold Sumrall, the leader of the group. "We all came from broken homes. Our fathers worked for the railroad, and all of them were alcoholics. We became a support group for each other. Everybody gathered at my house. If you wanted to talk about a problem, you felt safe to talk about it there. If not, you could just hang out."[19]

The boys led a Tom Sawyer–Huckleberry Finn–like existence growing up in Palestine, which had a population of twelve thousand in the 1950s. They shared a contagious desire to create mischief. Playing hooky from school to go fishing at a nearby lake and shooting rabbits with a shotgun were among their favorite pastimes. Sumrall, who was a few years older than the others, not only led the mischief but also made sure his friends got away with it. The grown-ups trusted Hal because he was older and seemingly responsible, and the kids admired him because he was shrewd.

Sumrall used these assets to his advantage. For example, when he was fourteen years old, the parents put him in charge of the concession stand at the Palestine High School football games. Unbeknownst to the fans, Hal was charging his own inflated prices and giving minimal change. He pocketed between $300 and $500 a game that season and split the profit among his friends. He would later parlay his entrepreneurial skills to make a fortune in the oil business.[20]

"Sports is what really brought us all together though," insists Curtis Fitzgerald, another member of the gang whose father spent more time in jail than at his job working on an oil rig off the Galveston coast. "I hardly ever saw my dad, and my step-dad would come home drunk and beat the shit out of me when I was younger. I hung around mostly with Bill, Eddie Bentley, and Jerry Reeder. All our fathers drank, so we became a support group for each other. We also found an outlet in sports, especially in junior high school. You name it, we played it, and we played it hard."[21]

While Bradley and Fitzgerald were the best all-around athletes in the clique, the others were talented in a specific sport. Danny Westmoreland and Barrett Broyles were exceptional baseball players. Jimmy Groh and Mickey Hubert were outstanding basketball players and Eddie Bentley, David Dickey, and Jerry Reeder remarkable football players.

"We began playing together at the YMCA in fourth grade and competed with or against each other in Pee Wee League football, basketball, baseball, and track," said Sumrall. "It continued that way all the way through junior high. In fact, we went from the sixth grade through the eighth without losing hardly any games at all." At the end of eighth grade, Jack Graves, the principal of Reagan Junior High School, presented Bradley, Fitzgerald, Groh, and Sumrall with the Dennis Bratton Award for athletic leadership.[22]

The athletic prowess resulted in a special camaraderie. "We were like brothers," said Bradley. "There was peer pressure, but it was a good kind of peer pressure because it built determination and a healthy sense of competition."[23]

Life was not all fun and games for the youngsters, though. By sixth grade they were all working various jobs, mostly hauling hay and digging ditches. One summer, Billy worked on his uncle's dairy farm in nearby Tyler and learned how to tend the livestock and milk cows. "I started paying Social Security when I was twelve years old," said Bradley. "I only got twenty-five dollars a week, and they still withheld Social Security. I wasn't the only one either."[24] Those jobs taught the boys that nothing in life was handed to them. They had to earn it. As a result, they would later become some of the toughest kids in East Texas on and off the football field.

While Bradley and his friends provided each other with emotional support, they still needed an adult to help them channel their competitive drive in a constructive way. That adult was Bob Knight, the junior high physical education teacher who doubled as a basketball and football coach. Born in Iredell, Bosque County, Texas, in 1909, Robert "Bob" Knight was the youngest of eight children of William and Jane Hand Knight. His mother died when he was three years old. Unable to provide for the family, William placed all his children in the state orphans' home at Corsicana. At the state school, young Bobby distinguished himself as class president and captain of the football and basketball teams.

Matriculating to Sam Houston State Teachers College in Huntsville, Knight was a standout fullback on the 1930 football team that captured the Texas Intercollegiate Athletic Association championship with an undefeated record. In 1937 Knight began his career in the Palestine schools, where he taught physical education at the junior high, coached basketball and volleyball, and organized a summer baseball league. After a stint in the navy during World War II, Knight returned to Palestine, married Wilda Virginia West, and resumed his career as a teacher-coach. Over the next three decades, he distinguished himself as an exceptional football coach and a mentor to dozens of student athletes.[25]

"Coach Knight was our first and biggest father figure," said Sumrall. "He was also the best coach we ever had. Every college in Texas wanted to hire him to coach football, but he wanted to stay at the junior high level and teach the fundamentals of the game to young kids."[26]

"Coach Knight and his wife didn't have any kids," noted Danny Westmoreland, "so he treated us all as if we were his kids. He really cared about us, and he taught us to care about each other. He instilled in us the idea that we were all like brothers and must treat each other like we were brothers."[27] Similarly, Bradley remembered his junior high coach as a "very kind soul" but someone who "didn't take any bullshit."

Knight could have easily passed as a Marine drill sergeant. He was a short, stocky man with a bald head. He dressed in tennis shoes, sweatpants and a T-shirt and favored partially smoked cigars as evidenced by the ever-present stogie protruding from the corner of his mouth. Like a drill sergeant, Knight was a strict disciplinarian. God help the youngster who crossed him. "If you started trash-talking with another player, Coach Knight would call a time-out and get out the boxing gloves," Bradley explained. "The two offenders had to put those gloves on and slug it out. There was no more pissin' contest after that!"[28]

Bob Stephenson remembers a basketball game where he got into a scuffle with Bradley. "There was some pushing and shoving going on," he explained. "Bill and I were both extremely competitive. I liked to win. He liked to win. So, it's not unusual for an altercation like that to happen. Coach Knight took us into the locker room, got the gloves out and told us to settle it because we were going to be teammates the next year and would have to get along." Bradley and Stephenson worked out their differences and became close friends in high school.[29]

Knight also liked to use dodge ball as a method of discipline. If someone was causing trouble, he put the culprit up against the wall, gave the other players a bunch of rubber balls, and let them pummel the miscreant. But the coach's favorite punishment, according to Fitzgerald, was "whooping your ass with the size 15 tennis shoe he carried around in his hip pocket."[30] "When he retired, we threw him a party and gave him a size 15 bronze tennis shoe," recalled Sumrall, chuckling at the memory.[31]

Knight also preached the same hard-nosed philosophy as Joe Hill Bradley. Both men expected to win and instilled that desire in the youngsters they coached. Even when their teams won, the two men focused on the mistakes made by the players. "Like my dad, Coach Knight was a perfectionist," recalled Bill. "Nothing we did was ever good enough for either one of them. Winning was an obsession with them. They told us if we were really winners then we wouldn't have made any mistakes. That was their philosophy, and it became mine as well."[32]

"Today, parents would consider that child abuse. Kids get trophies just to participate in sports. That's why they're soft. They don't earn their positions on a team. It's just handed to them. When I was growing up, sports were all about developing character. That meant you earned whatever you got. You took hard knocks not only from your opponents but also from your coaches and learned how to rise above it. That's what winning is about, preparing yourself to rise above the hard times you'll face later in your life."[33]

At the end of Bill's seventh-grade year, Knight organized an intramural basketball tournament. Each of the seventh-grade homerooms and each of the eighth-grade homerooms competed against each other, and the winners of each grade competed in a championship game. Bradley's and Fitzgerald's homeroom prevailed among the seventh graders and were scheduled to play an exceptionally tall team of eight graders for the championship. Billy took one look at the competition and instructed his teammates, "We're going to stall 'em. We're not going to shoot the ball unless we get a layup. We're just going to dribble and pass."[34]

Bradley had seen the so-called four corners offense on television watching the North Carolina Tarheels, whose coach, Dean Smith, introduced the tactic to the college game. The five seventh graders executed the strategy perfectly and beat the eighth graders by a single point, 8–7.[35]

"I knew then that Bill was running on a different fuel than the rest of us," said Fitzgerald. "He was an old pro when he was just a little kid."[36]

Bob Stephenson also attributed Bradley's success to a knack for finding an edge and exploiting it. Stephenson, already 6 feet 1 as an eighth grader, was the center on that basketball team. "I'd always look for Bill when I took jump balls," he said. "I knew that Bradley would be holding the pants of the closest opponent so he could beat him to the ball. Bill did whatever he could to win and, just as important, never got caught."[37]

To be sure, Bradley, at just 5 feet 6 and barely 90 pounds, needed to find an edge on the competition. He was still small when he entered high school in the fall of 1961. Although Bill had already quarterbacked a few seasons of Pee Wee League football, his mother refused to let him play in high school because the boys were much heavier than he was, and the chance of injury was much greater.

"When Mrs. Bradley made a decision about something it was pretty hard to change her mind," said Fitzgerald. Nevertheless, he rounded up the entire ninth-grade football team and walked the six blocks to the Bradley home on Inwood Drive. When they arrived, Mildred knew exactly what they wanted. She ushered the twenty youngsters into her living room and told them her decision was final.

"You boys might as well go back to school," she said with her arms crossed. "Bill is not playing any more football until he gets bigger. And since he's not growing very fast, I doubt he will ever play the sport again."

"Please, Mrs. Bradley," begged Fitzgerald. "Just hear us out."

"You've got fifteen minutes, Curtis," she said.

For the next two hours, Fitzgerald and the other boys pled their case. "If Bill quarterbacks our team in high school, we've got a chance to make it all the way to states," they insisted. "Without him, we've got no chance. Up until now, we've never made it past the first round of the playoffs. In fact, we haven't won a district football title since 1958."

Mildred finally relented. "But Curtis, I'm going hold you responsible," she said. "If Bill gets hurt, I'm going to tan your hide."[38]

It would have been difficult to find a more talented or more popular athlete at Palestine High School than Bill Bradley in the early to mid-1960s. "He was the most complete athlete that I ever saw," said David Dickey, who was a year older. "Bill was the field general in baseball, football and basketball."[39]

Teammates were in awe of Bradley's talent. Even in track, Bill set records in pole-vaulting, high-jumping, and the hurdles. At one meet he competed in the pole vault and cleared 6 feet 4 to win the state Amateur Athletic Association (AAA) event for two straight years.[40] Bradley, a point guard on the basketball team, could dunk the ball as a freshman. Two years later, he was averaging 25 points a game.[41]

"Bill didn't even play on the high school tennis team, but he challenged the coach to a match," recalled Mickey Hubert, another one of

Bradley's football teammates. "Bill had on a pair of Bermuda shorts and cowboy boots and still beat him, badly."[42] But Bradley's best sport—and first love—was baseball. "He was like a man among boys out there," said Barrett Broyles, an outfielder on Palestine's freshman team. "Bill could do everything—hit, field, and pitch. Once, our coach, Jesse Williams, tried to hit off him. Bill made him look ridiculous."[43] Bradley's natural position was shortstop. "Bill had great range and great instinct and could get a jump on the ball," said Danny Westmoreland, who was an outstanding high school catcher. "That allowed him to make a play deep in the hole and still throw out the runner. I saw him make plays no one else could possibly make."[44]

Bradley and Westmoreland were, at age fifteen, playing varsity baseball for Palestine High School in the spring and semipro baseball for the Palestine Pals in the summer. The two sophomores were the youngest members of the team and, because of their amateur status, the only players who didn't get paid. The rest of the team was comprised of college players who returned home for the summer and former Minor Leaguers, mostly in their thirties and forties.

"By our senior year of high school Bill was such an outstanding athlete that his reputation preceded him," recalled Westmoreland. "I remember one game against Henderson. They had this young, loud-mouthed coach who kept on antagonizing Bill. Well, Bill got on base, stole second, then stole third. It really pissed off their coach, who started screaming, 'Why don't you steal home, Bradley?' On the next pitch, Bill broke for home and slid in safe. He got up, brushed off his pants and tipped his cap to their coach. Boy if that didn't piss the guy off."[45]

Bradley's prowess in the other sports enabled him to shine on the gridiron. As a sophomore he started at quarterback and defensive back, in addition to punting and kicking. He also returned kickoffs and punts. Together with David Dickey, Bill formed the best backfield in District 7-AAA until the second game of the season, when Dickey broke his wrist, ending whatever hopes the Wildcats had for making the playoffs.[46]

Palestine had not seen a quarterback with Bradley's talent since 1958, the year James Saxton, arguably the best high school quarterback in the

Lone Star State, led the Wildcats to their last district title. The next year Saxton was the No. 1 recruit of Coach Darrell Royal at Texas. Royal made him his primary halfback in the Wing-T formation, and Saxton responded brilliantly. He won All-American honors in 1961 and finished third in the voting for the Heisman Trophy behind Ernie Davis of Syracuse and Bob Ferguson of Ohio State.[47]

"Saxton was my very first football hero," recalled Bradley. "I watched him play when I was a kid. He was a high school senior when I was in ninth grade. I worked out with him in the summers when he came home to Palestine. I wanted to be just like him."[48] Little did Bill realize that he would be *better* than his hero by the time he graduated.

In 1963 Bradley and Dickey teamed up again. After losing the first two games of the season to Lufkin, a bigger school, and Corsicana, 27–7, the Wildcats hit their stride. Playing Nacogdoches in the third game, Bill was forced to carry the offense because Dickey was double-teamed. Bradley scored all four of Palestine's touchdowns, throwing for two and rushing for two, in the 28–14 victory. It was the beginning of a seven-game winning streak that culminated in the District 7-AAA title game against Jacksonville, Palestine's archrival. Although Jacksonville jumped out to a 6–0 lead, the Wildcats prevailed when Dickey returned a punt 75 yards for a touchdown to tie the game. Bradley kicked the extra point, giving Palestine the 7–6 victory and its first district title since 1958.[49]

Palestine's opponent in the first round of state championships was Corsicana, which defeated the Wildcats at the beginning of the season. It looked as if history would repeat itself when Jim Hagle, Corsicana's All-State running back, returned the opening kickoff 90 yards for a touchdown. On the next kickoff, Jerry Reeder fumbled the ball on the Wildcats' 20-yard line, and Corsicana scored again to extend its lead to 14–0.

Palestine fought back to tie the game at 14–14 on rushing touchdowns by Bradley and Dickey. Corsicana scored another touchdown midway through the fourth quarter to regain the lead, 21–14. With minutes left in the game, Bradley intercepted a pass and ran 26 yards into the end zone to pull within one point of Corsicana, but the touchdown was voided when he was called for pass interference. Palestine turned the ball over on downs, and Corsican ran out the clock for the victory.[50]

Dickey is still confounded by the call. "It was a clean interception all the way," he remembered. "Besides, how could there be pass interference when you intercept the ball?"[51]

Danny Westmoreland was more diplomatic. "At best, the referee made a questionable call," he said. "But it's difficult not to blame the official for the loss."[52]

However, Dickey and Westmoreland agree that if Palestine had won the game, the team would have captured the state title that year. Instead, Corsicana cruised to the state title game and defeated Pharr–San Juan–Alamo, 7–0. "If we had not lost the coin toss, we would have won the state championship," Dickey insisted. "Hagle beat us with that kickoff return to start the game."[53]

Westmoreland believed that despite Corsicana's quick start, the Wildcats had the momentum by the third quarter. "What broke us was the pass interference call," he said. "If Bill's touchdown counted, we would've gone for the 2-point conversion, and I know we would've won the game, 22–21. And with Bradley and Dickey playing as well as they did that season, I think we would have had no trouble winning the state title."[54]

Unfortunately, speculation never trumps history. The fact remains that Corsicana—not Palestine—won the Texas state football title in 1963. The harder pill to swallow was that '63 was Dickey's last football season at Palestine. Recruited by the University of Arkansas, Dickey went on to have a successful career for the Razorbacks, earning First-Team All–Southwest Conference honors in both 1966 and 1967 and leading in several school, SWC, and national offensive categories.[55]

Without Dickey, the Wildcats' prospects of capturing that elusive state championship looked dim in the eyes of Palestine fans. But Bradley had other plans.

2 Friday Night Lights

Bill Bradley lived for Friday nights. He thrived on the competition, speed, and ferocity of high school football. The scrappy quarterback got a huge adrenaline rush whenever he dropped back from center, found a receiver 60 yards downfield, and led him into the end zone for a touchdown with a Hail Mary pass. He was truly a gifted signal caller. Anyone who watched him play quickly saw that he was a surefire Division I prospect. Bill also loved the brute physicality of the sport. Going helmet-to-helmet on a tackle or driving an unsuspecting receiver to the ground with a body block made the youngster feel invincible. Naturally, he reveled in the glory he earned on the gridiron. Yes, Bradley was good—damn good. And he knew it too.

But Bradley was no prima donna. He was the first one downfield on a kickoff. He sacrificed his body to make an interception. And he *always* blocked for his halfbacks. What mattered most to Bill was the intimate bond the game forged between himself and his teammates. It was a brotherhood that would endure for the rest of their lives. Indeed, the game was an inextricable part of his identity as a player, teammate, and brother. But it was only part of his attraction to football.

Bradley also treasured the pageantry of the sport. He basked in the glow of the giant floodlights high above Palestine's Luckett Kolstad Field with its packed bleachers and boisterous student section. He became energized whenever he heard the marching band strike up the school's fight song. He got even more excited when the cheerleaders appeared. Dressed in short skirts and maroon-and-white sweaters that accentuated their budding womanhood, the girls represented some of the best eye candy in East Texas when they flaunted themselves in front of the Wildcats' bench doing their high leg kicks and shaking their pom-poms.[1]

To be sure, the same spectacle unfolds every Friday night on hundreds of gridirons across the Lone Star State, from Marshall on the eastern edge of Texas to Wichita Falls on the northern rim and from McAllen at the southern corner to El Paso on the western edge. High school football is the bright spot in every one of those towns. It's a phenomenon that has come to be known as Friday night lights.[2] Nowhere else in the country does the term mean more than it does in Texas, thanks to James Perkins Richardson, widely considered the father of high school football in the state.

Richardson learned to play the sport at Yale. After graduating in 1891 he spent a year as a secondary school teacher in Stamford, Connecticut, and New York City. In 1892 Richardson relocated to Galveston to teach modern languages at Ball High School. He also established and captained the first high school football team there as a form of physical education.[3] On December 24, 1892, Ball played the Rugbys, a local team, in the very first game of schoolboy football in Texas. Played at the Denver Resurvey grounds on Galveston Island, the contest attracted "a large concourse of people" and was "mainly an exhibition of brute force," according to the *Galveston Daily News*.[4] The game was crude and unsophisticated compared to today's version. The emphasis was on running the ball. Passing was illegal. The teams did not huddle either. After the ball was snapped, the play moved immediately and directly forward.[5] The Rugbys won, 14–0, no doubt due to their players being an average age of nineteen and much stronger compared to Richardson's squad with an average age of sixteen.[6]

The following year, Galveston established a three-team league consisting of Ball High School, the Rugbys, and a YMCA team. Over an eight-week period, a total of nine games were played between the three squads. Ball extended its winless streak, losing to the Rugbys, 12–10, before falling to the YMCA team, 8–0. Not until the following year did Ball record its first victory, a 24–0 rout against another local squad called the Impromptus. A few days later, on November 29, 1894, Ball lost to the Aggies, 14–6, in a contest that marked the debut of football at Texas A&M. Ball would add the University of Texas to its schedule in 1895 and play a rematch against the Aggies in 1896.[7]

Although Galveston's early games received the most complete coverage from the local newspaper, football developed elsewhere in Texas in the late 1890s and early 1900s. Arthur L. Livermore founded a rugby team at Sam Houston High School in 1889, which was playing American football rules by 1901, when it played Ball High on Thanksgiving Day. Houston won, 23–6, in a game that required police intervention to break up a series of fights, something that eventually brought an end to the contest. The first recorded games involving school-sponsored teams in the Dallas area occurred on October 12, 1900, when St. Matthew's grammar school played the Wall School of Honey Grove, located just south of the Texas-Oklahoma border. Honey Grove won the contest, 5–0.[8]

While high school football was developing in these larger cities, smaller towns were only beginning to establish public secondary schools. Palestine High School, founded in 1888, did not field a football team until 1908. That initial squad posted a season record of 2-1-0. The program struggled to play .500 ball for the next four decades. The only bright spots came 1922 and 1948, when the Wildcats won district titles, and 1937, when Russ Cotton, a crafty 6-foot-2, 180-pound quarterback, led the team to an 8-1-1 record. Cotton would go on to play at the University of Texas at El Paso until the Pittsburgh Steelers drafted him in 1942.

The Wildcats' fortunes changed for the better in the 1950s under head coach Weldon Bynum. During his eight years at the helm, Bynum's teams compiled a win-loss-tie record of 51-23-4, for a winning percentage of .654. They also captured a third district championship in 1954, thanks to the talents of an exceptional sophomore quarterback by the name of James Saxton, who became Bradley's hero.[9] Unfortunately, Bynum's most talented players graduated in 1959, and he decided to step down. The new head coach, Luke Thornton, was forced to rebuild with a squad that went 1-9-0.

Thornton was a strong but humble leader. During World War II, he served as a paratrooper in the U.S. Army, receiving several medals for his courage on the battlefield. After graduating from East Texas State Teachers College, Thornton embarked on a long and distinguished career as a coach, athletic director, and principal in several Texas school districts. He came to Palestine in 1959 with nine years of head-coaching experience, most of it at Rockwell High School and Wilmer-Hutchins High School in Dallas, where he compiled a cumulative record of 46-42-5. Thornton was particularly successful at Wilmer-Hutchins, a 2A school, where his Eagles teams captured back-to-back district titles in 1956 and 1957, the latter squad making it all the way to the Texas state quarterfinals.[10]

Thornton initially struggled at 3A Palestine, where he assumed the multiple roles of athletic director, head football coach, and history teacher. During his first four years at the school, his teams never won more than four games in a season. To his credit, the Wildcats' coach persevered. He joined forces with Bob Knight, who cultivated the players at the junior high level. Knight taught the fundamentals and Thornton, the finer points of the game. The two coaches constantly consulted with each other. They watched each other's practices and determined which kids were best suited for which position both on offense and defense. They compared notes on how to motivate and discipline the players. Knight built an extremely successful junior high football program, one that went undefeated for two straight years. Then he turned the kids over to Thornton.

Luke was a handsome man with a soft smile and deep brown eyes filled with reassurance. Because he was a history teacher, he became familiar with his players' academic performances as well as their football abilities. That knowledge enabled Thornton to develop a close relationship with them. "No doubt about it," said Bradley. "Luke was another father figure to us, just like Bobby Knight was for us in junior high school."[11]

Thornton genuinely cared about his student athletes. He exercised such a strong influence on some of his players that they returned to Palestine after college to become teacher-coaches themselves. One of them was Jackie Cherry. "Luke was a people person, a real motivator," recalled Cherry. "He knew that every kid was different, and he learned as much as he could about each player in order to find the best way to motivate him." Cherry had the great misfortune to serve as Bradley's backup at quarterback. There were times when he despaired that he'd never see the playing field. "Although I was a backup, Coach Thornton made me believe that I was important to the team," he explained. "I would have run through a brick wall for Luke."[12] Not only did Cherry return to Palestine as a teacher-coach, but he also later became the principal of another local high school.

Another acolyte was Danny Westmoreland, who doubled as a linebacker and wide receiver on the '64 team. "I think Coach Thornton saw something special in each one of us kids, and it wasn't just for football either," said Westmoreland, who became a phys ed teacher and football coach at Palestine after graduating from Sam Houston State Teachers College. "If your grades weren't up to snuff, he'd pull you aside and make you understand the importance of school. He wouldn't raise his voice, but you got the message. I also think he saw something special in us as football players when we were freshmen, and he groomed us for a state championship."[13]

By 1963 Thornton had the nucleus of an exceptionally strong team in Bradley, Dickey, Fitzgerald, Reeder, Stephenson, and Westmoreland. That squad captured Palestine's fourth district title, but it was eliminated from state competition in the first round by Corsicana. Although Thornton lost Dickey, his star fullback, to graduation, he still had a star-studded senior class led by Bradley.[14] What's more, the head coach believed that the 1964 squad could capture a state title.

"My boys are tough," he told the *Palestine Herald-Press* that August. "I really don't believe there is a tougher group of players pound-for-pound anywhere else in Texas."[15] To reinforce the point, Thornton placed a sign above the locker room door that read, "THROUGH THIS DOOR PASS THE TOUGHEST BOYS IN THE STATE OF TEXAS."[16]

"The previous season, that sign read, 'THE TOUGHEST BOYS IN DISTRICT 7-AAA,'" recalled Mickey Hubert, a junior tight end on the '64 squad. "That really meant something, because the toughest teams in Texas came out of 3A. In fact, Coach Thornton told us that if we could win our district, there's no telling how far we could go in states. Well, we won the district in '63, and he was convinced that the '64 squad was even tougher, so he had the sign changed to read, 'TOUGHEST IN THE STATE OF TEXAS.'"[17]

Before every game that season, the Wildcats would slap the sign on their way out the field, whether it was for practice or a game. It became not only a tradition but also a firmly embedded superstition that the players truly believed brought them good luck.[18]

When the Wildcats defeated Rusk, 30–0, in a preseason scrimmage, fan enthusiasm reached fever pitch. Rusk wasn't just any run-of-the-mill opponent. It captured the district title two years earlier, posted a 7-2-1 record in '63, and was poised to go deep into state competition in '64. But the Wildcats' offense managed to score seven times against the Eagles, while Palestine's defense held them scoreless. What made the victory even more impressive is that the 'Cats' offensive and defensive linemen were an average of 25 pounds lighter than their opponents.

"We have a wealth of returning players who hustle and who know what to do," noted Thornton after the scrimmage. "Our offense looked real good, and I was also pleased with the defense, which is further along this year than it's ever been since I've been here." But the head coach tempered his enthusiasm. "We're going to need those advantages because we're too small to set up and just knock heads with the opponent," he added.[19]

Thornton was right to be cautious. The Associated Press selected Palestine as the No. 1 AAA team in Texas in 1964.[20] Expectations were extremely high. So was the pressure on the players to perform, something that led the coaches to tinker a little too much with the lineup. Concerned about the weight differential between bigger opponents and the smaller but faster Wildcats, Thornton and his staff made some key position changes before the first regular-season game. Danny Westmoreland, a middle linebacker, was moved to the outside. Jerry Reeder, who was bigger and faster, replaced him inside. The problem with that move was that Reeder could not locate the football quickly, enabling an opposing fullback to elude him. Another change had tight end Bob Stephenson moving to offensive tackle, where his 6-foot-3, 185-pound physique would help, but his exceptional blocking skills were limited.[21]

First-ranked Palestine opened the regular season on Friday night, September 11, on the road against fifth-ranked Athens. The Hornets featured Danny Tidmore, a highly recruited quarterback, and a senior-dominated offense that led the team to a 7-5 record the previous year. Although Athens lost Tidmore to injury the week before, his backup, Larry Taylor, proved to be every bit as capable, throwing for three touchdowns. Bradley, on the other hand, completed only two passes for 12 yards. He turned the ball over three times, twice on interceptions and a third time on a fumble. The Wildcats were humiliated by Athens, 28–7. The loss dropped Palestine to seventh in the statewide polls.[22]

Wildcats lineman Mickey Hubert attributed the loss to overconfidence. "We were picked to win the AAA state title," he explained. "The whole town came out to watch us. Just imagine what that did to a seventeen-year-old kid's ego! Then we go out against Athens and lay an egg. How embarrassing was that? That defeat gave us a much-needed dose of humility."[23] But Danny Westmoreland saw it differently. "There were at least four of us who were playing out of position," he insisted. "The changes made no sense and, I believe, cost us that game. After we lost to Athens, the coaches moved us right back to our regular positions."[24]

Bob Stephenson was one of the Wildcats who was playing out of position. Usually a tight end, Stephenson was switched to offensive tackle. "We played an unbalanced line," he explained. "There were four linemen on the right side of the center, and two on the left. The coaches had me set up as the outside tackle on the strong side where I was an ineligible receiver because there was a flanker on the line of scrimmage. I never understood why they did that, but I was switched back to my regular position after that game." Stephenson also believes that the Wildcats lost because the players "got a big head after reading that we were the No. 1 ranked 3A team in the state."[25]

The overconfidence of the players and the personnel changes seem equally to blame for the loss. Regardless, the Wildcats' poor play is what ultimately cost them the game. And that was unacceptable to the coaches. Two days later, Thornton and his staff met with the captains—seniors Eddie Bentley, Bradley, Reeder, Stephenson, and Westmoreland—and told them that they failed to demonstrate the necessary leadership to win the game. "They chewed our asses good," remembers Bradley. "They berated us for everything—a lack of leadership, attitude, you name it.

We deserved it too."[26] But the ass-chewing session is not what turned things around for the 'Cats. That motivation came from another coach.

After the game, Athens' head coach Bill Hamrick walked into the visitors' locker room and told the Wildcats, "If you guys work hard enough, maybe you'll win your district, and we'll play again." It was like rubbing salt into a wound. Not only was Hamrick being arrogant, but his remark was also intended as an insult. The 'Cats would remember it too.[27] Payback would come two and a half months later, when Palestine defeated Athens in the bidistrict final.

The next opponent was Terrell. Palestine had beaten that team handily the previous two seasons by scores of 12–0 in 1962 and 19–6 in 1963. Despite that, the Tigers were confident that they could beat the Wildcats. Terrell had a senior-laden team and had won their opener against a strong Greenville squad, 41–0, the week before.[28] Bradley proved them wrong. Orchestrating a three-touchdown outburst in the second quarter, Bill added another score in the third period, for the 26–8 victory. He connected on seven of eleven pass attempts and teamed up with fullbacks Jerry Reeder and Mike Myers for a total of 300 yards, while the 'Cat defense limited Terrell to just 130 yards.[29] The victory gave the Wildcats the momentum they needed to crush their next opponent, Ennis, 34–6, on October 2.[30]

Although the victories against Terrell and Ennis were impressive, they were nondistrict opponents. The most important games began on October 9, when Palestine faced the undefeated Henderson Lions in the District 7-AAA opener. Crippled by mistakes, the 'Cats fell behind early, 6–0. Henderson controlled the first half, limiting Palestine to just three first downs while collecting nine. Fortunately, the Wildcats' defense was able to turn back two of the Lions' scoring threats. Palestine came to life early in the third quarter when Curtis Fitzgerald intercepted a pass and scored on a 75-yard run, only to have the touchdown nullified on a clipping penalty. It was one of nine miscues that prevented the Wildcats from taking advantage of other hard-fought scoring opportunities.

With twenty-five seconds remaining in the third quarter, Bradley hit tight end Bob Stephenson with a 7-yard pass to tie the contest at 6–6.

Palestine began another offensive drive midway through the fourth quarter from its own 17. A 48-yard run by Jerry Reeder accounted for most of the yardage. Bradley kept the drive alive with a fourth-down pass to Stephenson, who ran 18 yards to the Lions' 12. The Wildcats' quarterback gained 2 more yards on a keeper, then rifled a masterfully executed pass to Stephenson to take the lead, 12–6. Bill kept the ball to run for the 2-point conversion, giving Palestine a 14–6 lead. The Wildcats' defense held the Lions after the ensuing kickoff, and Bradley ran out the clock for the victory.[31]

Palestine was now 3-1-0, with its first district win under its belts, and was living up to the expectations of a top-ranked team. The town fell deeply and passionately for the 'Cats. Businesses closed their doors on Friday nights, as residents flocked to Luckett Kolstad Field to watch the game. Older folks sat in the bleachers reminiscing about the star players they had seen in the past. Younger, more energetic fans gathered on the playing field and formed two lines beginning outside the Wildcats' locker room and extending to the team's bench. Every game the players ran between those two lines onto the gridiron. When the Wildcats played away, a caravan of two dozen cars followed the team school bus to the opponent's field.[32]

Three thousand Palestinians traveled to Carthage for the next district contest on October 16. After the Bulldogs recovered an onside kick, the Wildcats' defense held them to four downs. Bradley, hampered by an ankle sprain, began the 'Cats' first scoring drive late in the first quarter on his own 46. Alternating the pass and the run, Bill marched the offense to the Carthage 8-yard line before connecting with Stephenson in the end zone. Bradley kept the ball to run for the 2-point conversion, and Palestine took the lead, 8–0. That's all it would score until the fourth quarter. With his offense struggling, Bradley decided to call his own plays. Between downs, an angry Thornton would scream, "Damn it, Bradley! Stop changing my plays!" In the huddle, Fitzgerald gave his teammate the permission to continue. "Pay no mind to him, Billy," he said with a sly grin. "Your plays are working. His aren't."[33]

Palestine's only other touchdown came in the first two minutes of the fourth quarter on an 80-yard drive. Bradley ran the last 22 yards for the score, behind exceptional blocks from halfback David Farrow at the line of scrimmage and Stephenson in the open field. Fitzgerald ran the ball into the end zone for the conversion points, giving the Wildcats a 16–0 lead. Carthage's only touchdown came with a minute and four seconds remaining in the game on a 20-yard pass from quarterback Lynn Poss to end Bill Harrigan. But the Wildcats' defense stymied the Bulldogs' attempt to run for the conversion.[34] The 16–6 victory helped Palestine advance from the seventh spot in the 3A statewide football polls to fifth.[35]

Now the 'Cats were on a roll. Playing at home against the Center High School Rough Riders, Palestine took the opening kickoff and marched 69 yards downfield in ten plays, with Bradley scrambling the last 18 yards for the touchdown before pitching the ball to Farrow for the extra 2 points.

Bill stepped up the offensive attack in the second quarter, scoring three times for a 26–0 halftime lead. He caught Center napping in the third quarter when he located Fitzgerald down the right sideline and threw the ball cross-field on a dime about 30 yards. The flanker caught the pass in stride for a 52-yard touchdown. The Wildcats' defense was just as impressive. It so thoroughly dominated the Rough Riders that they were only able to gain 11 rushing yards the entire first half. Center collected another 71 rushing yards in the second half, but most of it came against Palestine's reserves, who finished off the 34–0 whitewashing for the 'Cats' third straight district win.[36]

Bradley was a god in Palestine. Not only was he the Wildcats' starting quarterback—and everyone in town knew who the quarterback was—but he also enjoyed the novelty of dating the prettiest cheerleader and having his picture in the local paper every week. By mid-October, Bill's gridiron feats were also being covered in Dallas, a hundred miles away. Blackie Sherrod, a legendary sportswriter at the *Dallas Times Herald*, became one of Bradley's biggest promoters. Sherrod, also one of Longhorns head coach Darrell Royal's closest friends, promoted the University of Texas as Bill's "best choice for college."[37] On most football teams, a player getting that kind of publicity would create jealousy, if not animosity, among his teammates. But that wasn't the case with the Wildcats. Bill's teammates loved and respected him.

Stephen Missildine, who doubled as an offensive and defensive lineman, said that Bradley was like all quarterbacks in that he was a "natural leader with a lot of confidence." "What set Bill apart was his charisma and humility," explained Missildine. "It's very rare to find that kind of combination of traits in a gifted athlete."[38] Mickey Hubert echoed those sentiments. "Bill's just a super nice guy, and for all his talent, he's always been very humble," said Hubert. "He'd be the first to tell you that our football success was a *team* effort."[39] Jackie Cherry, Bradley's backup, had more reason than anyone to be envious. "Sure, it was tough being Bill's backup," he admitted years later. "But I never begrudged him his success because he was always very humble. He was a year older, but he never treated me any different than the guys in his class. I think he knew how difficult it was for me."[40]

Bradley would be the first to admit that he was very confident as an athlete. But he also knew that he owed a lot of his success to his teammates. "Was I proud of my accomplishments?" he asked rhetorically. "Hell, yeah! But when I talked about it, I also made sure to mention my teammates. Without them, I wouldn't have been successful. We were all taught by our coaches to be humble. If someone bragged about his accomplishments, the coach would make everyone else run while the braggart stood and watched. Problem solved—no more bragging."[41]

"Billy was one of us," insists Curtis Fitzgerald, one of Bradley's closest high school buddies. "He never carried himself like a slapped dick, like he was better than everyone else. We all got into mischief together, and we all had each other's backs."[42]

If ever a high school athlete embodied his hometown, he was Bill Bradley. Like Palestine, Billy B. was small town, blue collar, a little country, a little bullshit, and a whole lot of balls. If there was mischief to be found, Bradley and his buddies found it. When Bill turned sixteen, his uncle, "Booger Red" Douthit, a dairy farmer from nearby Elkhart, bought him a 1950 Mercury four-door with a flathead V-8 engine for $600. The very same day, Bradley and Fitzgerald drove to the Knox Glass Bottle Company plant on the outskirts of town, where the high school kids did their drag racing on a quarter mile stretch of flat road. Bill bet he could beat any son-of-a-bitch who challenged him to a race. He did—and walked away with $25 in his pocket.[43] If they got bored with drag racing, Bradley and Fitzgerald would take some of the air out of the tires of that '50 Mercury and ride the rails of the nearby train tracks.[44]

Once, the two miscreants spent the day baling hay and loading it onto a flatbed. Afterward, they climbed inside the truck and drove around the field with a 12-gauge shotgun shooting rabbits. Two teens in a '57 Chevrolet heard the gunshots and drove out to confront them. "If you don't stop that shooting, we're going to whip your ass," said one of the teens to Fitzgerald, who was holding the shotgun.

Bradley, tired out from a hard day's work, was in the driver's seat drinking a beer and was in no hurry to enter the fray. Nor was Curtis going to take an ass-whipping by himself.

"Well, I'm not fightin' both of ya at the same time," he said, assessing the situation. "That's bullshit! But I'll fight each one of you separately."

One of the teens accepted the challenge and took a step forward. "Put that gun down, and we'll see about that!" he barked.

Meanwhile, the other teen reached for the shotgun. When Fitzgerald recoiled, the gun went off, blowing a twelve-inch hole in the roof of the '57 Chevy. "Next shot might hit you!" laughed Curtis. "Now, get the hell out of here!" Not wanting to tempt fate, the two teens got into their car and sped off.[45]

Bradley and Fitzgerald were not selfish. They made sure to include teammates in their shenanigans whenever possible. Once, near the end of the school year, Bill teamed up with Eddie Bentley, a lineman and another hopeless prankster, to have school closed. "Hell, no one wanted to be there anyway," said Bill, defending himself.

There had been a thunderstorm that morning, which provided the two culprits with the ideal circumstances to do their dirty work. In the past, the high school principal, Mr. Lennie Lee Davis, was known to dismiss school if the storm was especially bad. His decision was often based on the effect of lightning and thunder on the school's lighting, which flickered on and off during a bad storm. Realizing this, Bradley and Bentley snuck downstairs into the basement of the school shortly after first period classes had begun. They located the electrical boxes that controlled the lighting and went to work.

"Eddie, you go over to that box," directed Bill. "That one controls the lights on the first floor. When you pull the switch down, I'll leave the switch up in this box 'cause it controls the lighting on the second floor. Then, when I throw my switch down, you pull yours up. We'll keep doin' that and see if ol' Davis falls for it!"

Within ten minutes, the plan seemed to work. Davis went on the classroom speakers and announced, "Boys and girls, there's a bad thunderstorm, and it looks like it's pretty dangerous because our lights are going on and off. School is out for the rest of the day."

Unfortunately for Bradley and Bentley, they could not hear the announcement down in the basement. Instead, they simply continued to throw the light switches. "We were having all kinds of fun," recalled Bill. "We were hootin' and hollerin' just having a good ol' time for ourselves."

Suddenly, Principal Davis appeared. When he saw the two pranksters, he grabbed each one by an ear, marched them up to his office, and paddled their behinds with the so-called board of education.

"We got three licks each," recalled Bradley. "Next day, I woke up and my ass was purple!"

Years later, Bill found out that Davis, a former lineman for the Palestine Wildcats back in the day, was quite a jokester himself. In fact, the old guy secretly admired the stunt so much that he joked about it for the rest of his life.[46]

On another occasion, Mickey Hubert and Danny Westmoreland joined Bill to pick up a teammate who didn't have a ride to a weekend practice. The only problem was that they stole a school bus to do it.[47]

Harold Sumrall was even more ballsy. One Saturday night, Sumrall, Fitzgerald, and Bradley came across a Dr. Pepper soda truck. They noticed that the driver-side door was unlocked and that there was a full tank of gas. Sumrall jumped inside and hot-wired the vehicle, and the three culprits took turns driving it to Longview, a hundred miles away. Bill took the first shift, and as the trio was leaving town, head coach Luke

Thornton and his wife passed by in their car. Bradley threw the truck into reverse so fast that he almost blew the transmission.

"Yeah, that was a close one," remembered Bill. "But we had one hell of a good time. We drank our fill of soda that night, so much that we had to pull off the road to take a piss every few miles or so," he recounted. "But we made sure to fill the tank back up when we got to Palestine. I just can't remember how we got the money to do that."

Of course, Thornton didn't say anything about the incident when they all got back to school on Monday. After all, Bradley was the one he saw driving the truck, and he certainly couldn't afford to lose his star quarterback when the Wildcats were smack in the middle of the district schedule.[48]

Palestine continued its winning ways in November, defeating district opponents Kilgore, 28–16, and Nacogdoches, 26–8. Those two victories gave the Wildcats a perfect 5-0 record in the district and moved them into a dead heat with Jacksonville, the only other undefeated team, for the District 7-AAA lead.[49]

Next up was Pine Tree, which held third place in the district. But the Wildcats came out flat. The contest was a scoreless tie until the fourth quarter. With three minutes remaining in the game, Bradley went rogue. Ignoring Thornton's play calls, Bill engineered a 43-yard march against Pine Tree's stubborn defense. Midway through the drive, the Wildcats' signal caller jammed his right hand against an opposing player's helmet. The hand was badly swollen, but he still ran the final 10 yards for the only touchdown of the game.

Thornton sent Jackie Cherry in for the 2-point conversion. "Coach told me to go to tailback and have Bradley pitch me the ball," recalled the backup. "I was supposed to run 27 sweep left and throw the ball to David Farrow."[50]

But when given the instructions, Bradley, true to form, changed the play. "I got a better idea," said Bill to his backup. "You go to quarterback, and I'm going to tailback." The last thing Cherry was going to do was argue with Bradley. He did as he was told. He pitched to Bill at tailback who threw the ball *left-handed* to Farrow, who caught it for the two points. It was the Wildcats' eighth straight win (seventh straight in district play) and second shutout in three weeks. The 8–0 victory also set the stage for a showdown between fifth-ranked Palestine and tenth-ranked Jacksonville, which remained undefeated in district play.[51]

"The Pine Tree game was a perfect example of Bill's ability to lead," said tight end Bob Stephenson. "When he started calling his own plays, it wasn't a matter of going rogue as much as his confidence to do the right thing. He knew the offense and the capabilities of his backs and receivers just as well if not better than the coaches. Every Sunday afternoon, Bill met with Luke Thornton to prepare for our next opponent. So, Bill had a pretty good idea of what the head coach wanted and took it from there."[52]

The showdown against Jacksonville was played on November 20. Again, the Wildcats' offense had trouble finding its rhythm in the first quarter, as two of its early drives were foiled by a pass interception and a tough Indians defense. Midway through the second quarter, Jacksonville took advantage of a Bradley fumble, recovering the ball at the Palestine 40. Indian quarterback Richie Robertson engineered a five-play drive, capping it with a 13-yard touchdown pass to tight end Jimmy Caveness. After converting the point-after attempt, Jacksonville held a 7–0 lead, which held up late into the fourth quarter.

With four minutes left in the game, Bradley returned a Jacksonville punt to the Wildcats' 29 and then began a do-or-die drive. Bill milked the clock, alternating screen passes to Fitzgerald with short bursts by Jerry Reeder. With less than a minute to play, Reeder powered into the end zone, cutting Jacksonville's lead to one point.

Throughout the season, the Wildcats opted to go with the 2-point conversion instead of the traditional extra-point kick and had been successful with it most of the time. Bradley's favorite target was his 6-foot-3, 185-pound tight end Bob Stephenson, who could pull down an alley-oop pass while being triple-teamed.

When Bradley got into the huddle, he told Stephenson to be ready for the hook-up. But this time, Stephenson refused. "No, Bill, give the ball to the man who got us here. Give it to Jerry."[53]

On the final play of the game, Bradley handed off to Reeder at right tackle, who broke through the defensive line to score the 2 points. Palestine won, 8–7, and captured its second straight District 7-AAA title and the fourth in the football program's history.[54] The come-from-behind victory allowed the Wildcats to move up in the state poll to No. 4, behind Dumas, Vidor, and Andrews.[55]

Athens, the only team to defeat the Wildcats, would be Palestine's opponent in the bidistrict final. Thornton and his players wanted revenge, but that wouldn't be an easy task. The Wildcats' linemen were outweighed by an average of thirty-five pounds per player compared to the Hornets' linemen. But assistant coach Jim Yeager insisted that the weight difference didn't matter. "We are in better shape and more polished than we were at the beginning of the season when we played them," he said. "The most outstanding thing about our line is its ability to minimize mistakes."[56]

To ensure the defense was prepared, Yeager ran them especially hard at practice the week before the game. "Yeager was the bad-guy coach," recalled Fitzgerald. "He was a hard-nosed prick, but he got the very best out of us." By all accounts, Yeager was an ornery son-of-a-bitch. Bradley compared him to a "rodeo bull with a rope wrapped tight around his balls. . . . It was as if he went through life trying to buck someone off his back to get that damn rope off his nuts. He was just plain mean," said Bill. According to Cherry, Yeager would "break you down until you got so frustrated that you wanted to quit. . . . Only then would he build you up," explained the backup signal caller. "He wasn't going to change his ways for anybody either—not even for Luke Thornton."[57]

Nevertheless, Yeager's remarks were prophetic. Despite Athens's significant weight advantage, the Wildcats held the team to two first downs, one of them coming on a penalty. Palestine played conservatively. "We felt that if we scored our defense would come through," explained head coach Luke Thornton. "So we weren't going to gamble by putting the ball in the air a lot."[58]

The only score of the game came with fifty-five seconds of playing time remaining in the first half. Bradley engineered the touchdown from both sides of the ball. First, he set up the score when he returned a punt all the way back to the Hornets' 3-yard line with the help of two tremendous blocks. Then, taking over at quarterback, he gained another yard on a sneak and, on second down, tossed a pitchout to Ronnie Jones, who powered into the end zone. Electing to go for two points, Bradley rifled a pass to Bob Stephenson on a tackle-eligible play to make it 8–0. That's all that Palestine needed to avenge its only defeat of the season and win its first-ever bidistrict championship.[59]

However, the true hero of the game was the Wildcats' defensive line, which completely shut down the Hornet offense. "Although the score was only 8–0, we dominated Athens," insisted Steve Missildine, a defensive tackle. "They only crossed the 50-yard line three times the entire game." Missildine was especially impressive, holding the Hornets' star fullback Bull Kirksy to just 12 yards.[60]

After the game, when asked about his team's chances to make it to states, Thornton replied, "There are only eight teams left now. We're going to take this one game at a time. We play Bonham next and we're going to have to be better and tougher to beat them."[61]

The 'Cats' head coach remained on an even keel. To his credit, Thornton never looked further than the next game, a point he also emphasized with his players. "Our routine never changed," recalled Westmoreland. "The coaches ran us like dogs before every single game we played. There was no letup. After practice drills ended, they kept us on the field to run wind sprints. We never stopped. It was that way through the regular season and stayed that way during the playoffs. The players wanted it that way too."[62]

"We were just plain tough and had a lot of heart," added Hubert. "There was no gloating either, no drawing attention to yourself after you scored a touchdown or made a big play, no showboating like they do today. If we'd have done that, Coach Thornton would have put us on the bench."[63]

If nothing else, the Wildcats were consistent, right down to their pregame rituals. Prior to each away game, the Wildcats filled a small container full of dirt from the 50-yard line of their home field and sprinkled it across their opponent's gridiron.[64] They would do the same when they faced Bonham in the state quarterfinals at Abilene on December 4.

The 'Cats scored their first touchdown early in the second quarter on a 6-yard pass from Bradley to David Farrow, capping a 47-yard drive in which the Wildcats' field general picked up 29 yards himself. Unfortunately, the 2-point conversion was unsuccessful, and Palestine's lead was 6–0 going into the half.

In the third quarter, Bradley intercepted a Bonham pass at the Palestine 47 and returned it to the Warriors' 30-yard line. A few plays later, Bill connected with Bob Stephenson for the score. The same combination produced the two extra points, and the Wildcats led 14–0. Minutes later, Jerry Reeder intercepted the ball and returned it 65 yards for the final touchdown. Cherry tacked on the two points with a quick pass to John McDonald to make the final score, 22–0.[65]

Up next was Hirschi High School, from Wichita Falls, in the semifinals. Hirschi had defied the odds simply by making it that far. The Huskies played in the long shadow of Wichita Falls High School, a program that was established in 1903. The Coyotes had won twenty-two district titles and five state championships, the most recent coming in 1961 with a perfect 14-0 record. Hirschi, on the other hand, began its football program just three years earlier. Most start-ups take at least five seasons to establish a successful program. But head coach Jesse Stiles somehow managed to compile a record of 23-10-1 during those three seasons.[66] Although 1964 was Hirschi's first season as a AAA team, it was 9-3 entering the semifinals, and it was bigger, tougher, and much faster than the 'Cats. That fact was not lost on Harold Ratliff of the Associated Press, who predicted that the Huskies would upset Palestine.[67]

The contest was played on Saturday afternoon, December 12, at Arlington before a frenzied crowd of nine thousand. A lot was riding on the game for both teams, but especially for Bradley. The Longhorns' legendary coach Darrell Royal and his recruiting coordinator, Russell Coffee, had traveled the two hundred miles from Austin to scout the boy wonder. Seated in the press box, the UT coaches were disappointed in what they saw. Bradley failed to complete a single pass in four attempts during the first half, while the Wildcats' offense could only muster 48 yards on the ground. Also, the offensive line did not give him much protection. Guard

Stephen Missildine got blindsided on a punt return and continued to play with a concussion. He was so dazed he had to ask center Eddie Bently to remind him of his assignment on virtually every play. Thus, the first half belonged to Hirschi, as the Huskies' speedy backfield rolled up 239 offensive yards and a 16-point lead.[68]

"Nothing went our way in the first half," said Danny Westmoreland, who doubled as a flanker and middle linebacker. "We couldn't get the offense going. If we made a big play and picked up a first down, it was called back on a penalty. We kept shooting ourselves in the foot."[69]

Even worse, Palestine's Curtis Fitzgerald, Bradley's go-to receiver, appeared to suffer a season-ending injury. "Right before the half, Ronnie Faulkner, Hirschi's quarterback, threw a long pass, and I tried to knock it away from their receiver with my left arm," recalled Fitzgerald. "At the same time, Mike Meyer, our other defensive back, moved in for the tackle. His face mask caught my left arm, which was already extended as far as it could go, and I could hear the bone pop. I felt this sharp pain, and I knew something wasn't right."[70]

By the time Fitzgerald reached the locker room at halftime, his upper arm was swollen and turning purple. Team physician Dr. Robert Burns quickly determined that Fitzgerald fractured the humerus bone.

"You need to go straight to the hospital," said the physician.

"But Doc, I want to stay around and watch the rest of the game," protested the youngster.

Burns thought a moment. "Well, okay," he relented. "But you go straight to the hospital when you get back to Palestine."[71]

There was stone-cold silence in the Wildcats' locker room. The coaches went into the showers to have a smoke, while the players sat on the benches stunned. No one said a word. It remained that way until the officials knocked on the door to get the team back out to the field for the second half. At that point, Thornton gathered his players around him and said, "Hey guys, everything that can go wrong on a football field has gone wrong. Nothing's worked for us. But if you want to win this ballgame, you can still win it. They scored 16 points in a half. We sure as hell can score more than that. Let's go!"[72]

The game didn't get much better for the Wildcats in the second half. Hirschi, with 4:33 left in the third quarter, scored its third touchdown to extend its lead to 23–0. Darrell Royal had seen enough. With Palestine down by more than three touchdowns, the Longhorns' head coach and his assistant left the press box at the beginning of the fourth quarter to beat the traffic out of Arlington.[73]

Fitzgerald was standing on the sidelines watching the debacle unfold when another physician, Dr. Leroy Mathis, came down from the stands. "Curtis, how come you're not at the hospital?" asked Mathis, who suspected that the hard-nosed youngster was going to try to get back into the game.

"I just want to watch the second half," replied Fitzgerald.

"Let's go have a look at it," said Mathis as he escorted the fullback to the locker room.

When the physician removed the air cast and examined the arm, he knew there was a serious problem. "I think you might have a compound fracture," he said.

"But it's not broken, right?" a hopeful Fitzgerald asked.

"No, but it might be fractured," repeated the physician. "You will need to go to the hospital to get it X-rayed. I'll be waiting for you at Palestine Methodist. When the bus gets back, I want to see you there. And dammit, Curtis, don't you try to go back into the game!"

"Okay," mumbled Fitzgerald hanging his head in a mock display of disappointment. But as soon as Mathis left the locker room, he sprinted back out to the field, intent on reentering the game.[74]

Meanwhile, Bradley had gone to work. After a 15-yard kick return, the Wildcats' field general began an eight-play, 63-yard drive from his own 37. The most sensational play of the drive was a 32-yard pass and run from Bradley to Ronnie Jones. Bill uncorked another dart to Jones, who picked up another 18 yards before he was felled at the Huskies' 4. From there, Bradley kept the ball to skirt around the end, fighting off two defenders, and bulled into the end zone for the touchdown. Electing to go for two points, Bill lofted the ball to Stephenson to hit paydirt, and the Wildcats made the score 23–8.[75]

Fitzgerald returned to the field in time to see Stephenson score the 2-point conversion. He proceeded to trail Thornton up and down the Wildcats' sideline, trying to make himself as conspicuous as possible.[76] Eleven minutes remained on the clock. On its next possession, Hirschi was forced to punt. Faulkner, who doubled as the Huskies' punter, booted a high spiral that rolled into the Palestine end zone for a touchback. Bradley marched the Wildcats down the field 80 yards in four plays, ending it with a 29-yard pass to John McDonald to cut Hirschi's lead to 23–14. Bill then connected with Stephenson for another 2-point conversion, making the score 23–16.[77]

"The coaches believed that Bill and I could get those two points from the very beginning of the season," said Stephenson. "By the time we hit the postseason, we had all the confidence in the world that we'd make those conversions. I'd just run into the end zone and find a hole, and Bill would throw me the ball, or Bill would find the hole and lob the ball up there, and I'd go to it. I think those 2-point scores were instrumental in creating the momentum we needed to beat Hirschi."[78]

Hirschi took over with 7:32 left to play. But a 15-yard penalty forced the team to punt on fourth down. Bradley made a 10-yard return to his own 35. On the first scrimmage play, he handed off to Jerry Reeder, who skirted the left side, ran over two defenders, and sprinted down the sideline for a 65-yard touchdown. The 2-point conversion was batted away, and the score stood at 23–22.

Just 3:56 remained on the clock, and Hirschi had the ball. Huskies fans were already celebrating the victory. Then a sterling defensive effort by the 'Cats put Hirschi in a fourth-and-two at its own 46-yard line. Instead of punting, the Huskies' head coach rolled the dice and decided to go for it, hoping to keep the ball out of Bradley's hands.[79] "We couldn't believe it," recalled Bradley, nearly sixty years later. "I made the call for the defensive backs and line backers to walk up to the line of scrimmage. If they'd thrown a pass, the receiver would've been behind us, and the game would've been over."[80] But the Huskies tried to force the run and were stopped dead by the Wildcats defense.

Now Palestine had the ball with 2:09 remaining in the game and no time outs left. With 54 yards to go for a score, it needed every second of it too. Reeder lost a yard on the first scrimmage play. Jackie Cherry came in at the quarterback slot and pitched to Bradley, who threw a 12-yard pass to Stephenson at the Wildcats' 42-yard line for a first down. The tight end carried two defenders out of bounds with him to stop the clock. A personal foul by the Huskies moved the ball all the way to the 29 with 1:08 left in the game. After throwing an incompletion, Bradley hit a diving Bill Heidelberg at the 19 for another first down. It was a brilliant one-handed catch. Nine times out of ten, a pass like that would be tipped away. If Heidelberg hadn't caught that ball, the game would've been over for the Wildcats. On the next play, Reeder gained another three yards.[81]

Wildcats fans were going crazy. Heading into the huddle, Bradley saw Darrell Royal standing in the end zone, stomping his feet and clapping his hands for Palestine, a show of emotion that was completely out of character for the Longhorns' coach. After leaving the game early in the fourth quarter, Royal continued to listen to the game on radio. When Bradley launched the Wildcats' comeback, the head coach turned the car around and returned to the stadium. It was all the motivation Bill needed to snatch victory from the jaws of defeat. At that very moment, Bradley knew that "there was no way [Palestine] was going to lose." "No fucking way," he added, "not as long as I was on that field."[82]

Thornton, pacing up and down the sideline, finally noticed that Fitzgerald had returned. He made a beeline for his halfback. "Are you okay?" he asked in desperation.

"My arm's not broken," said Curtis, tearing off the air cast.

"That means you can play," barked the head coach. "Get in there!"[83]

Bradley couldn't believe it when he saw his best friend running onto the field. "What the hell are you doing out here, Fitz?" he blurted out.

"It's okay, Bill, the doc cleared me to play," replied Curtis.

Bradley was nobody's fool. Growing up in East Texas, he could smell bullshit whenever it was blowing up- or downwind. "That's a lot of shit!" he chuckled.

"Well, he didn't clear me," admitted Fitzgerald, "but coach thinks he did!"

That's all the quarterback had to hear. Stepping back into the huddle, he said, "The call is X-right, V-slant. Curtis, look for the ball quick. It's going to you."[84]

Bradley threw down the middle to Fitzgerald, who caught the ball at the 10 and went down with twelve seconds and counting. The Wildcats were out of timeouts. Bradley hurried his teammates to the line of scrimmage.

On third down and a yard to go for a first down, Bill found Fitzgerald open on the sideline. He rifled the pass to his flanker at the 5-yard line as two Hirschi defenders converged. Somehow, Fitzgerald fought his way out of bounds to stop the clock at 00:03. Stumbling back to the huddle, the Wildcats were exhausted and dehydrated, but mustered the strength for one last play.

"I've got to throw the ball in the end zone," Bradley shouted over the deafening crowd noise. "Curtis, get open. I'll buy you as much time as I can."

After three straight catches, the entire Huskies defense knew that the ball was going to Fitzgerald and tracked him into the end zone. With just seconds left, Bradley dropped back and rolled left, retreated, and rolled left again. As the clock ticked to 00:00, Bill lobbed a toss high into the Hirschi end zone.

"As soon as I let go of the ball I was tackled," recalled Bradley. "As I was going down, I could see Curtis going up for the catch between two defenders. But I never saw if he came down with the ball."[85]

Fitzgerald was good to his word. He pulled down the ball and secured it as he was tackled in the end zone. Palestine had pulled off a miracle 28–23 victory.

No sooner had the officials pulled the Hirschi players off Fitzgerald then his Wildcats teammates piled on top of him. Thornton and his assistants led the charge from the sidelines as some four thousand Palestine fans stormed the field. Hoisting Bradley on their shoulders, the fans began stuffing five-, ten-, and twenty-dollar bills inside his pants. They did the same with his teammates. The Wildcats were heading to the state title game.[86]

Down on the field, Blackie Sherrod of the *Dallas Times Herald* buttonholed his friend Darrell Royal and asked for a quote. "It was the greatest effort I ever saw on a football field—high school, college or pro," said the Longhorns' coach. "We are really looking forward to Bill Bradley playing football for us in Austin."[87]

James Saxton, Bradley's football hero as a kid, was also at the game. "Bill's definitely the coolest quarterback I've seen in a long, long time," he said of the effort. "He's also the best all-around athlete to come from Palestine in quite a while."[88] For Bill, it was the highest praise he had ever received. But after the game, the boy wonder gave all the credit to his teammates.

"Shoot, Curtis Fitzgerald is the boy who made the big play," he insisted. "It was a poor pass on my part. But Curtis turned it into a great play. I won't ever forget it.

"Bob Stephenson and Jerry Reeder also played a great game," Bradley added. "I thought we could win after Jerry got loose on that 65-yard touchdown run that made it 23–22. Stephenson came up big plenty of times, too. Those guys deserve all the credit."[89]

To be sure, the Wildcats offense came up big. But there's more than sheer talent involved when a team overcomes a 23-point deficit at the end of the third quarter to pull out a come-from-behind victory. "In a game like that most teams just give up," explained Bob Stephenson. "We simply refused to do that. We were a tough bunch of kids, and not just physically but also mentally tough. At the same time, we were also lucky. To come from that far back and win was nothing short of a miracle. I think our luck came when Hirschi's coach decided to go for a first down instead of punting with two minutes left in the game. That really sealed the deal for us. Bradley had a hot hand by that point in the game, and if anyone could pull out a victory with two minutes left, it was Bill."[90]

The 3A state title game was played on December 18 in subfreezing temperatures and on a frosted turf at Kyle Field, home of the Texas A&M Aggies. But after the upset against Hirschi, the final against San Marcos would be anticlimactic. On the Rattlers' first possession, Bradley intercepted quarterback Rox Goodwine on the San Marcos 36 and returned the ball to their 11 before he was stopped. Two plays later, Bradley, at quarterback, found Fitzgerald in the end zone, but the point-after attempt failed.

On the Rattlers' next possession, San Marcos marched 58 yards in ten plays for its first touchdown. Goodwine, who carried six times for 47 yards, completed the drive with a 2-yard dash. The Rattlers' extra-point kick was successful, and San Marco led, 7–6.

Early in the second quarter, Jerry Reeder picked off a Goodwine pass to set up the second Palestine touchdown, a 14-yard pass from Bradley to Stephenson to regain the lead, 12–7. A missed 2-point conversion followed. The Maroon and White's third touchdown came in the third quarter, when Bradley piloted the Wildcats 62 yards on seven plays. Bill picked up the touchdown with a right-end sweep after tricking the Rattlers with two fake handoffs.

The fourth and final Wildcats touchdown came late in the fourth quarter after a Bob Stephenson interception. Bradley engineered an eight-play drive that climaxed with a 1-yard run by Jerry Reeder. Another blown 2-point conversion left the score at 24–7. Although San Marcos scored with minutes left, Palestine had already put the game on ice. The 24–15 victory made Palestine AAA state champions for the first time in the school's history.[91]

Bill was one of seven Wildcats to earn All-District honors that season, and his performance in the playoffs solidified his case for All-State honors and High School All-American. In four postseason games he threw eighteen touchdown passes, ran for another sixteen scores, and punted for a 40.1 average.[92]

Bradley was an athletic prodigy. He could do things on a football field that other players could only imagine, because of his talent, intelligence, and intuition. There were no limits to his potential, no ceiling to what he could achieve. That is why his best gridiron performance was yet to come.

3 Blue-Eyed Soul Brother

Bill Bradley never saw himself as a trailblazer for the integration of Texas high school football. But for a white kid growing up in Palestine, he certainly had the background and experience to be a pretty effective one—not that Palestine was a utopia of racial integration.

With the exception of a few affluent Black families who resided in the blocks northeast of the courthouse square, African Americans lived on the other side of the railroad tracks, to the south of Spring Street, which cut through the middle of town and served as a boundary line between Blacks and whites. That's where the MoPac Railroad built yellow-painted cottages for the Blacks they employed as laborers and porters. Nicknamed "Yellow Basket," the neighborhood would later become one of two ghettoes. The other one was known as "Tin Cup Alley," located to the southeast of Yellow Basket near the lumber mill that supplied MoPac with railroad ties.[1]

Segregation became formalized in the 1880s with the creation of the public schools. The railroad workers wanted compulsory, tax-supported schools for all children, both Black and white. But the much wealthier white professionals and businessmen were resistant to the idea of integration because education was considered the key to economic success and upward mobility. The matter was resolved with the establishment of separate white and Black schools, which remained segregated until the mid-1960s.[2] Public facilities were also segregated. Blacks had to sit in the balcony of the local Ritz movie theater on Main Street. They ate in separate restaurants. There were separate drinking fountains and separate restrooms. But that did not prevent the families of the railroad workers, both Black and white, from associating with each other.[3] Poverty is a great equalizer, and most all of Palestine's railroad workers were poor.

"I credit my parents for teaching us to respect Black people," said Bradley. "My mom's family, the Raineys, had a Black maid who was like family to us. My dad played baseball against Negro League teams when he was younger and quickly learned to respect their playing abilities. He also worked as a railroad car porter for a while, and most of the folks he worked with were Black. So, we weren't allowed to use the N-word in our house. We were taught that Blacks were entitled to the very same respect, rights, and privileges as whites."[4]

May-May Bradley echoed her brother's sentiments. "We learned from my father never to pass judgement on other people," she said. "My daddy was kind to everyone he met, and he loved his friends, both Black and white."[5]

Today, when our society is especially race conscious, it seems naive to say that the Bradleys were color-blind, as Bill insists. But their actions certainly appear to reinforce the claim. "My sister May-May introduced me to Motown and rhythm and blues," he said. "We listened to James Brown, Otis Redding, the Four Tops, and Bo Didley on KLIF Radio out of Dallas. R&B is still my favorite music."[6]

Bill was so enamored with soul music that once he talked his buddy, Curtis Fitzgerald, into selling a set of wheel covers for thirty bucks to buy tickets to a Bo Didley concert in Tyler. "We were the only two white faces in the crowd," Bradley remembered. "It didn't matter, though. Everyone was having a good time. I don't think anybody even noticed us."[7]

Another time, Bill, Curtis, and a few of their buddies were walking the streets of downtown Palestine and came across two drinking fountains, one designated "WHITES ONLY" and the other "COLORED ONLY." Bradley, who relished any opportunity to challenge the status quo, dashed over to the colored fountain, bent over and took a long drink for himself.

"Now, look here fellas," he said. "The water coming out of this faucet is as clear as any I've seen. It tastes good, just like the water coming out of the white fountain. So, what's the big deal? Why can't we all drink from the same water fountain? I'll never understand that."[8]

While Bill's friends might not have been as ballsy, none of them saw anything wrong with playing pick-up basketball with and against the Black kids. "We might not have been bosom buddies with the Blacks," Bradley explained, "but we hung out together. Hell, we even supported each other's football teams. It's just a shame we couldn't have all played on the same team. With their talent and our talent, we could have won state every year."[9]

On Thursday nights in the fall, Bradley and his Wildcats teammates crossed the railroad tracks to watch the players from the all-Black A. M. Story High School compete. The following evening, the Black football players would hike over to Palestine's Luckett Kolstad Field and stand outside the fence, watching the Wildcats play.[10] Although that doesn't sound like such a big deal today, it was huge in the 1960s, especially in Texas, where segregation was strictly enforced. Despite that fact, A. M. Story, which opened in 1953, was a better, more modern facility than Palestine High, which dated to 1918. With an enrollment of just 450 students, A. M. Story was half the size of the town's white high school and enjoyed a higher teacher-to-student ratio.[11] Not until the mid-1960s were the Black and white high schools integrated.[12]

According to Robert D. Jacobus, author of *Black Man in the Huddle: Stories from the Integration of Texas Football*, school integration in the Lone Star State was "mostly geographic, and somewhat demographic, in nature."[13] Whereas East Texas, Dallas–Fort Worth, and the Greater Houston area remained segregated until the mid-1960s, the Coastal Bend area of South Texas, the Rio Grande Valley, and the San Antonio area integrated in 1955, about a year after the Supreme Court's landmark decision in *Brown v. Board of Education*, which declared segregation unconstitutional. On the other hand, integration in the Texas Panhandle, Central Texas, and West Texas varied from town to town and city to city.[14]

Demographics also influenced the integration of Texas high school football. The process of integration began in the mid-1950s in areas like the Coastal Bend and the Rio Grande Valley, where the Black population was small and white resistance to integration was slight. However, integration took much longer in places like East Texas, where towns had a significantly higher Black population, some as high as 50 percent.[15] Here, Black high school football players had to deal with strict segregation, both de facto and de jure, until 1967, when the University Interscholastic League (UIL), which was founded in 1910 and consisted only of white schools, absorbed teams from the Prairie View Interscholastic League (PVIL), which represented the state's Black schools.[16] Considering the rigid segregation of the high schools and small towns, Bradley, his family, and his teammates were extremely progressive in their attitudes on race.

When Bill was selected to play for the Texas All-Stars in the annual Big 33 game at Hershey, Pennsylvania, he would "stand out like tits on a bull because of [his] close friendship with Jerry LeVias," one of the first African American players from the Lone Star State to compete in that contest.[17] Jim Dent recounts the poignant story of these two Texas high school football players at the 1965 Big 33 game in his bestselling book *The Kids Got It Right: How the Texas All-Stars Kicked Down Racial Walls.* Dent shows how Bradley and LeVias challenged the racism that had existed for more than half a century in the Lone Star State. In the process, the two teammates made integration not only more palatable for white Texans but also easier for high school football programs in more segregated areas of the state to assimilate Black talent.

The Big 33 Football Classic was founded in 1957 by Al Clark, sports editor of the *Harrisburg Patriot-News*, and was named after the best thirty-three graduating high school football players in the Keystone State.[18] Because the contest was sponsored by the M. S. Hershey Foundation to raise funds for its boarding school, the game was held each August at Hershey in central Pennsylvania and *always* featured an All-Star team from that state. Widely considered the Super Bowl of high school football, the game was allegedly played to determine which state in the nation had the best high school football players.[19] Between 1957 and 1964, Pennsylvania's teams dominated the game. In fact, no opponent had ever scored a touchdown against them, which led Pennsylvanians to claim that their football players were the best in the country—that is, until 1964, when Texas was invited to play in the showcase.[20] Pennsylvania won the first meeting, 12–6, which prompted *Sports Illustrated* to proclaim that the "extraordinary bone bruiser" had indeed "erased any doubts about who possessed the toughest teenagers in America."[21] But Texas had been forced to split its All-Stars between the intrastate North and South All-Star Game played in Dallas and the Big 33 because both contests were played on the same weekend.[22]

Pro Football Hall of Fame quarterback Bobby Layne, who coached the Texas Big 33 All-Stars, considered the defeat nothing less than blasphemy in a state where football was an all-consuming passion. Infuriated, Layne and his assistant coach, Doak Walker, took their case all the way up to Governor John Connally, who changed the date of Texas's sacred North and South All-Star Game so that all of the state's top players could participate in the 1965 Big 33 contest. To ensure a victory over the Pennsylvania All-Stars, Layne also asked permission to recruit African American players for the game, as Texas was flush with Black gridiron talent.[23]

When Bradley was selected to play safety and punt in the Big 33 All-Star Game, he didn't know much about it. "I was honored to be chosen for the Big 33," he explained years later. "But the North-South All-Star Game was much more prestigious for a Texas high school football player. That game drew thirty thousand–some people every year. We also had the Oil City Bowl in Texas, which was a third All-Star game played after the Big 33. And to be honest with you, [the] Oil City Bowl was also considered more prestigious than the Pennsylvania All-Star game."[24]

Bill lucked out in the summer of 1965. He was able to compete in all three All-Star games due to the schedule change. Prior to the Big 33, Bill starred in the North-South game, quarterbacking the North to a 12–6 victory before an estimated crowd of 39,100 spectators at the Cotton Bowl in Dallas. The South scored first. Running back Chris Gilbert of Spring Branch set up the touchdown with a 43-yard run. Charlie Riggs, the Galena Park signal caller, followed with a 3-yard pass to John Lerma of Rio Grande City for the 6–0 lead. The North tied the game in the second quarter when Bradley scored on a 3-yard run after a fumble recovery by Danny Abbott, an Amarillo's Tascosa High School guard. The North's second tally came in the fourth quarter after Don King of Wichita's Hirschi High recovered a fumble on the South's 19-yard line.

Bradley scored again, racing over left tackle for seven yards and the winning touchdown. The following week, Bradley and most of the other players who participated in the North and South All-Star Game headed to Hershey for the Big 33 game. Their numbers included James Harris of Brownwood High School, the only Black player to be selected to the intrastate contest.[25]

Having been snubbed by the Texas high school football coaches who comprised the selection committee, Jerry LeVias did not play in the North and South All-Star Game.[26] However, he was one of three Black players chosen by Texas sportswriter Fred Cervelli, the one-man committee who selected the Texas high school players for the Big 33 game. Unlike James Harris and George Danford, another Black flanker from Waco's Moore High School, however, LeVias would capture national headlines with his performance in Hershey.[27]

Born in Beaumont, Texas, Jerry LeVias contracted polio at age seven and spent two years in heavy metal leg braces.[28] With the help of his grandmother and two older cousins, Mel and Miller Farr, future NFL Pro Bowlers, Jerry not only overcame the disease but also became lightning fast in touch football.[29] When LeVias was twelve, Clifton Ozen, the African American football coach at all-Black Hebert High School, hired him as a water boy for the Panthers.[30] But after watching the youngster tear up the field in flag football, Ozen recruited the fleet-footed LeVias for his team. Jerry went on to play quarterback and defensive back and return punts and kicks for the Panthers. In his senior year, LeVias scored twenty-two touchdowns against opponents in the all-Black Prairie View League and gained more than 1,000 yards in all three major categories—running, passing, and receiving.[31]

Although Jerry received more than one hundred scholarship offers, none came from the historically Black college football powerhouses where he wanted to go. Schools like Grambling, Southern, Prairie View, and Alcorn State believed that his 5-foot-7, 140-pound stature was too small. But Coach Hayden Fry of Southern Methodist University saw that LeVias made up for his slight size with remarkable speed and recruited him in the spring of 1965 to break the color line in the Southwest Conference.[32] Later that summer, Jerry teamed up with Bradley at the Big 33 game to make some high school football history of their own.

LeVias and Bradley were an unlikely pair: one Black, the other white; one religiously devout, the other a free spirit; one a shy wide receiver, the other a cocky quarterback. But that summer they became the closest of friends and the best of teammates. The big-hearted, gregarious, and free-spirited Bradley had LeVias's back on a team of predominantly white Texas schoolboys who had never suited up with, let alone competed against, a Black player. Some of their fathers were members of the Ku Klux Klan, but all of their families taught them that the mixing of the races was a sin. For his part, LeVias was not too enthusiastic about playing on a team full of whites.

Having grown up in an all-Black neighborhood, Jerry had had little contact with whites and certainly had never played with or against any white football players. "We were aware of segregation growing up," said LeVias. "We knew what the so-called rules were in the South. You had to be across the tracks by 5:00 p.m. You could only ride in the back of a bus and had to use a colored bathroom and drink from a colored water fountain." At the same time, Jerry's father cultivated a sense of pride and self-esteem in his son that would enable him to withstand the discrimination he would face later in his life. "My daddy wouldn't let us sit in the back of the bus," he recalled. "I never drank out of colored water fountain or used a colored bathroom because my daddy wouldn't allow it. If I had to go to the bathroom, I did it before I left home. My dad would not allow me to be treated like a second-class citizen."[33]

At Hershey, LeVias would have to face several obstacles. The first major hurdle came on the day the Texas All-Stars arrived in central Pennsylvania and roommates were assigned at the boarding school's dormitory. Because Layne had already assigned James Harris and George Danford—the other two Black players on the team—to the same room, Jerry was the odd man out. Layne took a chance and told his equipment manager to pair LeVias with Bradley.

When Bill checked in, the short, bald-headed manager handed him the key to his room. "Thanks, fella," said Bill as he grabbed the key and turned to leave.

"Hold on there, Hoss," said the man. "You ever heard of a boy named Jerry LeVias?"

"Can't say that I have," replied Bradley, knowing absolutely nothing about the Beaumont football star. "But I'm from Palestine, and news doesn't travel too quickly out in East Texas."

"Well, you should know that Jerry LeVias is a little n——. And I was just wondering if you would mind rooming with him."

Bradley grimaced when he heard the word *n——*, but he kept his cool. Instead, he asked, "Well, can he play football?"

"Of course, he can!"

"Then I don't see any problem," said Bill, as he picked up his suitcase and headed for the stairs.[34]

When Bradley reached his dorm room, he threw his bag on the bed, pulled out a transistor radio, and switched stations until he found an Isley Brothers song. Then he began swaying to the music and singing, "It's your thing, do what you want to do. I can't tell you who to sock it to."

Nearly sixty years later, Jerry LeVias still remembers the sight. "I looked at this white guy dancing around the room and singing the Isley Brothers, and I'm saying to myself, *What's wrong with this white boy?*" he said. "And he knew all the words to the song too! Well, I'd always heard that white boys couldn't dance. Whoever said that certainly hadn't met Bill Bradley! We introduced ourselves, and immediately he started talking trash. He was a wild one! But I could also see that he was different from what I had heard about white folks. Since Grandma raised us to believe that we are all God's children, no matter the color of our skin, I gave Bill the benefit of the doubt. I found out that he was a really genuine person."[35]

The next morning, Bradley found out just how good a football player his new roommate was. So did their head coach, who had called for the first practice at 8:00 a.m.

Bobby Layne was one of the most successful quarterbacks ever to play for the Texas Longhorns. Selected to four straight All–Southwest Conference teams from 1944 to 1947, he was a consensus All-American in his senior year. The Pittsburgh Steelers made him their first pick in the 1948 NFL draft. But Layne did not want to play for the Steelers, so his rights were quickly traded to the Chicago Bears, where he became the third-string quarterback behind Sid Luckman and Johnny Lujack in 1948.

Consequently, the Texan refused to return in 1949 and was traded to the New York Bulldogs for their first-round pick in the 1950 draft and $50,000 cash. With Layne at quarterback, the Bulldogs won only one game and lost eleven, but he played extremely well for the soon-to-be-defunct Bulldogs. In 1950 the journeyman signal caller was traded to the Detroit Lions, where he was reunited with his close friend and Highland Park High School teammate Doak Walker, the 1948 Heisman Trophy winner. Together, Layne and Walker led the Lions to their first NFL championship in seventeen years in 1952 and then did so again in 1953 for back-to-back league titles. During his eight seasons in Detroit, the Lions won three NFL championships, and Layne played in four Pro Bowls and made first team All-Pro twice.[36] When he retired after the 1962 season, Layne owned the NFL records for passing attempts (3,700), completions (1,814), touchdowns (196), yards (26,768), and interceptions (243).[37]

In his younger days, Layne was well known for his late-night barhopping. Not only did he drink six days a week and play football on Sunday, but he occasionally imbibed during games too.[38] He did not believe in a whole lot of rules either. Layne's reputation had preceded him among some of the Texas All-Stars. Seated in the wooden bleachers at the Hershey practice field, the youngsters waited for their head coach to arrive.

"I hear he's crazier that a shithouse rat," Bradley told Norm Bulaich, a fast, hard-running halfback from La Marque High School, near Galveston. "My daddy said he drank all night and played his best games with horrendous hangovers."

"Hell, I heard he drank at halftime," said Bulaich.

"But, by God, he won," Bradley said. "I remember when I was a little kid watching him play for Detroit on our TV. I saw him firing those wobbly ducks to Doak Walker. He won two championships for the Lions and would've won a third if not for breaking his leg."[39]

A few minutes later, Layne appeared on the practice field. Although he walked with a limp and was slightly overweight, the former Pro Bowler still possessed the boyish face and thick blonde hair he sported in his midtwenties. Puffing on a Marlboro, the Texas coach removed the cigarette from his lips and began his speech.

"Okay, boys, you know why you're here," he began. "Hershey is a long way from home. We're going to be here for a while. But we're also going to have some fun. We're going to practice a little. I'm going to give you some time to chase the girls around town. I know they're a plenty, and they look almost as good as Texas girls."

Layne barely completed the last sentence when a hearty cheer erupted in the stands. In seconds, he had won over the players. Then, just as quickly, he became dead serious.

"I don't care what you do with your free time," Layne said. "I don't care if you drink or smoke. Just put the butts in the ashtray and the beer cans in the trash. In my book, there's not much you can do wrong around here after dark. But if you lose this game to these Pennsylvania hillbillies, don't *ever* talk to me again!"

There was absolute silence. Then Layne chucked and said, "Okay, you knuckleheads. I believe you're going to win, so get up off your butts and go to work!"[40]

George "Lefty" James, who coached the Pennsylvania All-Stars, was already working his players out on a field about one-hundred yards away. They had been banging helmets for over an hour before the Texans showed up. After lunch, these sons of coal miners and steel mill workers would be at it again for another three hours. James, who had been the head coach at Cornell in the 1950s, would work them like rented mules for the entire week leading up to the Saturday night game. Such grueling practices were common for Pennsylvania's hard-nosed high school players. In fact, their unofficial nickname was the Coal Crackers, which they wore with great pride. Layne could not care less. His players took the practice field in shorts and T-shirts. He did not plan on conducting hitting drills all week, as he realized that most of his players had participated in the North and South All-Star Game and that they had endured two-a-day practices for five straight days prior to that contest. Layne knew his players were in game condition. Instead of warming up with the usual calisthenics, the Texans divided up on either side of the goal posts and batted a football back and forth over the cross bar.[41]

When Bradley saw a few of the Coal Crackers laughing, he shouted, "Laugh all you want to. Come Friday night, we're going to kick your asses!"

But Lefty James and most of his players saw the Texans horsing around and considered it an insult. While they were busting their asses in full pads and helmets doing "Crab crawls" and sleigh drills in the heat and humidity, the Texans dared to have fun. "We were going through boot camp that summer," recalled Terry Hanratty, the Pennsylvania quarterback who would go on to star at Notre Dame and later play in the NFL with the Pittsburgh Steelers. "Lefty thought it was totally wrong that Bobby Layne was letting the Texas guys cut up and have fun."[42]

It was exactly the appearance of nonchalance that Layne wanted to create in order to gain a psychological advantage over the opponent. By giving the appearance that his players were not taking them seriously, the Coal Crackers would either become so angry that they would physically exhaust themselves in their practices and have less energy for the big game or become so overconfident that the Texans would take them by surprise. But Bradley insists that there was another reason for engaging in the gridiron form of volleyball.

"You gotta remember, we all came from different parts of Texas," Bill explained. "We didn't know each other when we showed up in Hershey. Playing volleyball with a football loosened us up. It broke the ice for a lot of us. It was an excellent way to build team chemistry. We just went out there and had a good ol' time for ourselves."[43]

Regardless of his intentions, Bobby Layne was still fuming over the previous year's defeat. He was intent on kicking some Pennsylvania ass. His secret weapon was the shotgun formation that the San Francisco 49ers had introduced to the NFL a few years earlier, an offense that relied on speed. Four of his players ran the 100-yard dash in 9.8 seconds or less, and the entire backfield covered that distance in 10.0 seconds or less.

Layne also realized that several of his kids would be playing out of position, including Bradley and LeVias. Both of them were quarterbacks, but Layne intended to play Bill at safety on defense and punting on offense, and Jerry would play wide receiver. Rusty Clark, a 6-foot-3 200-pounder from Houston's Westbury High School, would handle the signal calling for the Texans. Not only could Clark throw with exceptional accuracy, but he also had a rifle for an arm. LeVias, on the other hand, was totally unfamiliar with the wide receiver position. On the few occasions he lined up at halfback in high school he was taught to take off at full speed and keep going. Doak Walker, wanting to alternate that pattern, taught him the comeback route and how to then spin off the defensive back to gain more yardage. Since Bradley was the backup quarterback, LeVias took reps with him and Clark. In no time, Bill and Jerry developed a unique chemistry.

On one play from scrimmage, Layne had LeVias line up to Bradley's right as the split receiver. When Bill took the snap, Jerry came back to his left and Bradley pitched him the ball on a reverse. LeVias rolled around left end, stopped, and threw back across the field to Bradley, who was wide open. It was executed beautifully, like poetry in motion. Layne filed the play away, one of many weapons in the arsenal he planned to use in the game.[44]

"Bill and I made an immediate connection during that first practice," LeVias recalled. "I thought he was just as good as any of the Black ballplayers I played against, and not just in high school. During my summers in Beaumont, I had the opportunity to play touch football in the park against Willie Ray Smith and Gayle Sayres. Bradley was every bit as good."[45]

After the practice, Layne gathered his players and said, "Good work, boys. . . . Now go enjoy yourselves. There's something waiting for you over there in the farmhouse."

The farmhouse was designated as a recreation area for the Texas All-Stars, where they could do as they pleased without any adult supervision. When they arrived, the players discovered a cooler full of Rolling Rock beer waiting for them, compliments of their head coach. In no time, Bradley cracked open a bottle and quenched his thirst.

"Here, Jerry, take a swig!" he said, offering the bottle to his roommate.

LeVias, who belonged to the Church of Christ, didn't curse or gamble, let alone drink alcohol, customs that were second nature to Bill. But to be polite, Jerry took a sip of the Rolling Rock and, when Bradley wasn't looking, spit it out. Then he returned the bottle to Bill, who continued drinking out of the same bottle.

"That's what told me Bill was different than most white people," explained LeVias. "After I drank from that bottle, he wouldn't wipe the top off or anything like that. He wasn't afraid that he might catch something from me. He just kept drinking out of the same bottle without a second thought. I never saw a white person do anything like that to that point in my life and can't remember if I saw anything like it since."[46]

While the players were enjoying their libations, Bradley introduced Jerry to a few of their white teammates. One of them, Corby Robertson, the best linebacker in the Texas, had chosen to attend one of Houston's public high schools instead of a private academy, although his family was wealthy. Robertson was a genuine kid who judged others on their character, not their race.

"I just want to tell you how happy I am that you're on the team," said Robertson, extending his hand to LeVias. "I heard all about the great things you did in Beaumont, and I'm excited to be your teammate."

"That makes me feel good," said a smiling LeVias. "I can't tell you how happy I am to be here."[47]

Running back Chris Gilbert congratulated Jerry on a "great practice" and said that the Coal Crackers "are going to have problems catching up to you." Norm Bulaich, another running back, was just as welcoming. Bulaich, a high school All-American, was the only unanimous selection on the *Dallas Times Herald*'s blue-chip list of the twenty-three most highly coveted high school seniors in Texas, according to the eight Southwest Conference head coaches.[48] He also had 9.9 sprinter's speed and immediately connected with LeVias once he saw the swiftness and agility with which Jerry eluded defenders at practice.

"Since high school football wasn't integrated in Texas back then, it was kind of a novelty for me to play on the same team with Jerry, James Harris, and George Danford," recalled Bulaich in a recent interview. "I think it was a novelty for all of us on the Texas All-Stars. I say that because the Black players were treated well by the white players. We all knew they had outstanding ability, but we found out pretty quickly that they were great guys too. I know Bobby [Layne] didn't care about race either. All he cared about was winning that All-Star game, and he knew those three guys could help us do that."[49]

"Those fellas are pretty doggone nice," LeVias told Bradley. "Are all the guys that nice?"

"Don't fool yourself, Jerry," replied Bill. "Robertson, Gilbert, and Bulaich are Texas blue-chippers. Not only are they great players, but they come from good families, and they're smart. But some of the guys on our team are just rawboned country boys. They're real good football players, but they're also real dumbasses. Those rednecks will be going to schools like Texas Tech, A&M, and TCU, where the fans will call you 'n——' and 'spook' and 'monkey.'"[50]

Bradley's remark hit LeVias like a ton of bricks. He had already committed to Southern Methodist University (SMU) and believed that only the very best high school players attended the schools in the Southwest Conference. But he didn't realize that there was a distinction between "best players" and "best people." At least he didn't have to worry about the rednecks on the Texas All-Stars. Apparently, they watched him run pass routes with Bradley and were impressed by what they saw. Because Bill had already earned their respect and he was fine playing with LeVias, there was no reason for the other Texas All-Stars to reject the Beaumont star, even if he was Black.[51]

Although LeVias might not have been popular with his white teammates, he did capture the interest of UCLA's head coach Tommy Prothro, who was actively recruiting him for his fourth-ranked Bruins. Jerry had already committed to Hayden Fry at SMU, but that didn't stop Prothro, who showed up in Hershey intending to sign the blue-chipper. Fry had sent his assistant Chuck Curtis to shoo away predators like Prothro, who tried to steal highly touted prospects once they had already committed to another school. But Bobby Layne, one of Fry's best friends, prevailed by threatening to "beat the shit out of" Prothro unless he "got out of Hershey."[52]

Prothro wasn't the only coach who came to Hershey to shanghai players. That's why many head coaches who already signed highly prized recruits sent bodyguards to "babysit" their blue-chip freshmen. Royal, concerned that Bradley, Corby Robertson, and Chris Gilbert might be tempted by another offer, dispatched his assistant Russell Coffee to scare off the vultures. Coffee relished the assignment. "If I see you talking to one of my players," he told a coach known for his shady tactics, "I will personally kick your ass. In fact, I should just go ahead and kick your ass right now because I know you're a cheater!"[53] If that didn't scare him off, Coffee could count on Layne to impose his will on the culprit.

"I don't know exactly what Russell Coffee was supposed to do at the Big 33," confessed Corby Robertson in a recent interview, "but I do know his principal role was to keep the alcohol pouring for Bobby Layne and Doak Walker. I assume he kept those two coaches pretty happy!"[54]

While Layne was out drinking, Bradley managed to do some partying of his own—not that there was much to do in Hershey. Located one hundred miles to the northwest of Philadelphia and two hundred miles to the southeast of Pittsburgh, the sleepy little town of twelve thousand was known as "Chocolate Town, U.S.A." due to founding father Milton S. Hershey's decision to build a chocolate factory there in 1903. Aside from chocolate, Hershey was best known for its amusement park and its wooden roller coaster, which gave riders an adrenaline rush like no other.

One other novelty captured the interest of the frisky young footballers: the Big 66, a collection of local teenaged girls who would serve as "dates" for the Texas and Pennsylvania players at a dance scheduled for Thursday night at the Hershey Country Club. To be selected as a Big 66 girl was considered a great honor in the town, and few of them waited for Thursday night to introduce themselves to the football players.[55] Bradley was counting on early introductions.

He had already met two of the Big 66 debutantes—Mary Jane and Pam—at the amusement park on his first night in Hershey. Naturally, they were taken with Bill's good looks, southern charm, and sweet-talking ways and were eager for a reunion. The next night, after their teammates turned in, Bill snuck out of the dormitory with LeVias in tow and met the two girls behind the farmhouse. Pam was waiting with Mary Jane in her cherry red Mustang. Both girls had conveniently told their parents that they were going to spend the night at a friend's house. There was no need to worry about their boyfriends either. The Pennsylvania players were saddled with a 9:00 p.m. curfew, thanks to Lefty James, their drill sergeant of a coach.[56]

Free of all obstacles, the party of four climbed into the mustang—Bradley and Mary Jane in the front and Jerry and Pam in the back—and went in search of a nice, quiet place to park.

They drove outside of town to the state game lands, where they found a small bluff overlooking the picturesque Susquehanna River. No sooner had they parked than Bill and Mary Jane "went at it" in the front seat, "smooching and petting like a couple of horny jack rabbits."[57] In the back, Jerry, petrified at the thought of being discovered kissing a white girl, sat with his hands in his pockets while Pam tried to snuggle with him.

Bradley, caught up in the throes of passion, came up for air and noticed that there was no action in the backseat.

"Jerry, what the hell are ya doin'?" he cried. "We didn't come all the way out here for you to sit with your hands in your pockets! If you don't kiss her, I'm coming back there, and I'm goin' to do it!"[58]

Having been granted permission, Jerry loosened up and yielded to Pam's advances.

"Whenever I went out with Bill, I didn't know what was going to happen," said LeVias. "It was a real education for me, especially since I didn't drink, gamble, or *ever* kiss a white girl. Of course, Bill did all that, and he did them all pretty well.

"Bobby Layne, our coach, just looked the other way. As long as we were ready to practice and win the game, he didn't care what we did off the field. That was unheard of at Beaumont. I mean, my high school coach, Cliff Ozen, was a strict disciplinarian. He set a curfew at 10:00 p.m., and he enforced it. He'd be driving around the streets of the town. If you were out there, he'd take a two-by-four to your rear end! But Layne let

Bill and the other guys do a lot of hell raising. He even bought us beer for after practice!"[59]

At the same time, LeVias appreciated Bradley's efforts to bond with him. The two of them went *everywhere* together that week. It was clear to Jerry that Bill wasn't patronizing him, that he respected his playing ability, and that he genuinely liked him as a person. "Up to that time in my life, I never knew *anybody*—white or Black—like Bill," admitted LeVias. "He treated people the way they'd want to be treated. He looked beyond skin color—the way it should be."[60]

Two nights later, at the Big 33 dance, the two roommates hooked up with Mary Jane and Pam again. When Bill spotted Mary Jane, he swaggered across the dance floor to greet her. But this time her boyfriend was standing beside her. "Well, hello, Mary Jane!" said Bill, with a toothy smile. "Seems we haven't seen each other for at least six hours. Are you going to take me for a spin in that hot little Mustang of yours tonight?"

Infuriated by the remark, the boyfriend reared back to take a swing at Bradley, but one of his teammates, a big strapping lineman, grabbed him from behind before he could deliver the blow. At that moment, the band struck up "Johnny B. Goode."

"Mary Jane, would you like to dance?" asked Bill, oblivious to the tension he was causing.

"Why, of course I would, Bill," she replied, with a devious grin.

Since the Big 33 host committee invited six Black girls to the dance—equal to the number of Black players on both teams—LeVias had his pick. He quickly found a partner and joined Bradley on the dance floor.

After the band played "I Can't Help Myself," Bradley turned to LeVias and said, "Hey, roomie, it's okay to dance with the white girls too. If the Coal Crackers give us any trouble, we'll kick their asses!"[61]

That night when they got back to their dorm room, Jerry confided, "You know Bill, I was wondering what you would think about me dancing with a white girl, let alone kissing one."

"What?" replied Bill. "Don't think I haven't kissed a Black girl."

Jerry put his arm around his roommate's shoulder. "You know, Bill Bradley," he said, "you are my blue-eyed soul brother."

"I think that's the best compliment anyone ever gave me," replied Bill, placing his arm around his friend's shoulder. "I always figured I had some Black in me," he added. "Hell, I can dance and dunk a basketball just as good as any of you fellas!"[62]

Years later, LeVias recalled the inspiration for the nickname he gave Bradley that night. "Whenever you found a white guy who could sing Motown, talk smack, and especially dance to Black music," he explained, "you'd call him a 'blue-eyed soul brother.' 'Blue-eyed' because he was white, and 'soul brother' because he could do everything else as well as a Black guy."[63]

Although Bradley didn't realize it, his night was not quite over. At about 2:00 a.m. he was awakened by a knock on the door. When he opened it, Bobby Layne was standing there with a quarter of scotch in one hand and a shit-eating grin on his face. "Hey, Billy Boy!" he chirped. "How 'bout a night cap?" Apparently, the bars in town closed an hour earlier, and Layne wasn't quite through with his drinking.

Bill, never one to turn down an invitation, agreed. Player and coach ambled over to the farmhouse, where they enjoyed a couple of beers. When they arrived, Bradley was surprised to find that Robertson and Gilbert were already there waiting for them. Layne had already extended the invitation to the Longhorns' other two prized recruits.

"I'd never had an experience like that up to that point in my life," recalled Robertson. "I'd known coaches to look the other way when they knew their players were drinking. Heck, Layne even supplied the beer for us that week. But we never drank in his presence, let alone competed against him in a drinking game!"[64]

Layne proceeded to teach the three teens how to play Cardinal Puff, a drinking game popular in the military during World War II. Bradley was the first victim. Seated at a table with a pint of beer in front of him, he said, "I drink to the health of Cardinal Puff for the first time." After he took a sip of beer, he began a sequence of rituals: tapping a finger once above table, once under table, stamping left foot, stamping right foot, standing up, and banging the glass on the table before toasting Cardinal Puff. When he completed the ritual successfully, he said, "I drink to the health of Cardinal Puff for the second time." Bill then performed the same sequence again, but this time twice. If he made a mistake, he had to quickly drink the rest of the beer and start again with a fresh pint. Robertson and Gilbert watched very closely, while Layne greeted the slightest mistake with a sarcastic remark. Of course, Layne won the contest hands down.[65]

Realizing that his other players would be getting back late from the Thursday night dance, Layne did not schedule a practice for Friday morning. But when he walked past the boarding school's gymnasium at 8:00 a.m., he was surprised to see Bradley and Robertson on the basketball court competing against LeVias and another teammate, Ken Spain, in a dunking contest. He couldn't believe his eyes. There were Bradley and Robertson just hours later, on a basketball court.[66]

More astounding was that Bradley, at 5 feet 10, and LeVias, at 5 feet 9, were the smallest players on his team, and yet they could dunk a basketball. Spain, at 6 feet 10, was a full foot taller than Jerry. He would go on to play center in the American Basketball Association for the Pittsburgh Condors. But that didn't stop LeVias from betting Spain $10 that he could dunk the ball with two hands standing flat-footed. Spain took the bet and lost.[67]

After Spain and Robertson left, Layne ambled over to the court and placed his right arm across Bradley's shoulders and his left across LeVias's. "You are two of the best football players I've ever seen in my life," said the coach. "We're going to kick some Coal Cracker ass tomorrow night. Just make damn sure you don't break an arm or a leg dunking the damn basketball. I need both of you."

Layne started to walk away but then stopped and turned to face the two boys. "Y'all are also two of the best fellas I've ever met," he added. "Bradley, you've done a great job of making Jerry feel at home. Jerry, I couldn't be more proud of you if I'd been your own daddy. I'm going to miss both of you after tomorrow night. And I'm going to watch both of you play college and pro football every chance I get. You boys are going to be two of the best to ever hit the big time."[68]

Bobby Layne was not only a great coach but also a prophet.

The 1965 Big 33 All-Star Game was played on Saturday night, August 14. The game had been sold out for months. Hershey Stadium was packed with a crowd of 25,893 spectators, mostly from Pennsylvania. Sportswriters and college recruiters hoping to discover a future Heisman Trophy winner squeezed into the press box. The only significant presence from Texas were the Kilgore Rangerettes who arrived that morning. Outfitted in midthigh skirts that showed more leg than a New York City hooker on a Saturday night, the Rangerettes kicked for the sky as one of the bands played "Deep in the Heart of Texas." Bradley noticed them right away. Then he looked into the west stands, where he spotted his proud parents, Joe and Millie, who had driven 1,500 miles from Palestine in their 1958 Oldsmobile to watch their son play. Directly behind them was Bill's future head coach, Darrell Royal, who was disappointed to learn that his incoming quarterback would not be handling the signal calling duties that evening.[69]

Unfortunately, Texas governor John Connally could not attend the game. But Pennsylvania's chief executive William Scranton was there. The previous year, Scranton cashed in on a bet with Connally when the Coal Crackers defeated the Texans, winning a set of silver spurs and a ten-gallon hat. Confident that Pennsylvania's high school All-Stars would win again, Scranton was pondering how he would distribute the 2,122 Texas pecans he would collect from Connally after this year's contest.[70]

The game was billed as "Texas speed vs. Pennsylvania brawn." Layne's advantage came with three players who could run the 100-yard dash in less than 10.0 seconds, including James Harris (9.4), LeVias (9.5), and Norm Bulaich (9.6).[71] Conversely, Lefty James was betting that the performances of fullbacks Mike Reid, a 235-pounder, and John Helton, a 225-pounder, and linebacker Jerry Ruccio, a rugged 200-pounder, would prevail.[72] "Those Pennsylvania guys were gigantic," remembered running back Norm Bulaich. "I mean, all their players looked like they were 220 [pounds] or more. I'll tell ya, I didn't relish the thought of going up against some of those guys, especially Reid, who doubled as a middle linebacker."[73] Regardless of size, the starting lineups of both squads were replete with future college—and NFL—talent.[74]

Of the nineteen starters (three played on both side of the ball), the Texans had fourteen players who went on to compete in the fiercely competitive Southwest Conference and ten who were later selected in the NFL or Canadian Football League drafts.

Similarly, the Pennsylvania All-Stars had thirteen players who chose to remain in state with Division I powerhouses. Six signed with Penn State and four with Pitt. Others were nabbed by out-of-state schools like Arizona State, Minnesota, and Notre Dame. Seven of the Coal Crackers would later be selected in the 1969 NFL draft.

From the start of the game, the Coal Crackers knew they were in trouble. *Sports Illustrated*'s John Underwood wrote that the Texas linemen drove the "heavier Pennsylvanians back a yard before they could react" and that their defensive backs "moved as if they were wearing Army boots."[75] The Coal Crackers still managed to score first on a 32-yard field goal by Mike Reid.

Down 3–0, Layne became anxious. He realized that his quarterback, Rusty Clark, was having difficulty finding his receivers because the offensive line wasn't giving him the necessary protection. LeVias had already lobbied the head coach to go with Bradley because he felt Clark couldn't throw far enough to reach him downfield. Turning to his line coach, Harley Sewell, Layne barked, "Harley, round up your lineman and show those farts how to block. We're not going anywhere until Clark gets some time to throw!" But it was clear to the head coach that Clark was losing confidence with each failed pass.[76]

With minutes remaining in the first quarter, Clark, hurried again by a collapsing line, threw an interception. Layne had seen enough and inserted Bradley at quarterback. In the huddle, Bill looked his teammates in the eyes and said, "Boys, if you think I'm worried about losing this game, think again! I've been in deeper shit than this. Believe me, we're going to win this fucker!"

Turning to LeVias, Bradley continued, "Jerry, go deep. Just take off—no fake, no nothing."

"Yessir, roomie," replied LeVias. "Just heave it, and I'll catch it."

Texas All-Stars starting line-up

OFFENSE	POS.	HIGH SCHOOL	COLLEGE	NFL/CFL DRAFT
Ash, Gilbert	TE	Galena Park		
Bell, Ronnie	OG	McKinney	SMU	
Bulaich, Norman	RB	La Marque	TCU	Baltimore Colts
Clark, Rusty	QB	Houston Westbury	Baylor	San Francisco 49ers
Cloud, Bill	OT	Galena Park	Houston	
Gilbert, Chris	RB	Spring Branch	Texas	New York Jets
Harris, James	WR	Brownwood	Houston	Washington Redskins
King, Don	OG	Dallas Kimball	SMU	
Krueger, Rolf	OT	Austin	Texas A&M	St. Louis Cardinals
LeVias, Jerry	WR	Beaumont Hebert	SMU	Houston Oilers
Spruill, Skippy	C	Odessa	Houston	Calgary Stampeders (CFL)

DEFENSE	POS.	HIGH SCHOOL	COLLEGE	NFL/CFL DRAFT
Abbott, Danny	LB	Amarillo Tascos	Texas	
Bradley, Bill	S	Palestine	Texas	Philadelphia Eagles
Cloud, Bill	DT	Galena Park	Houston	
Harris, James	CB	Brownwood	Houston	Washington Redskins
Housely, Wendell	CB	Richardson	Texas A&M	Minnesota Vikings
Krueger, Rolf	DT	Austin	Texas A&M	St. Louis Cardinals
Montgomery, Ross	LB	Midland	TCU	Chicago Bears
Phillips, Terry Don	DE	Longview	Arkansas	
Robertson, Corby	LB	Houston Lamar	Texas	
Smith, Glenn	S			
Winston, Leland	DE	Lake Jackson	Rice	Kansas City Chiefs

Pennsylvania All-Stars starting line-up

OFFENSE	POS.	HIGH SCHOOL	COLLEGE	NFL DRAFT
Constantine, Rich	G	Uniontown	Virginia	
Helton, John	RB	Mount Union	Arizona State	Buffalo Bills
Kane, Jim	T	Dunmore	Bloomsburg	
Kwalick, Ted	TE	Pittsburgh Montour	Penn State	San Francisco 49ers
Miloszewski, John	E	Beaver Falls		
Naponic, Bill	QB	Hempfield	Illinois	
Orszulak, Harry	WR	Pittsburgh W. Mifflin	Pittsburgh	San Diego Chargers
Pherson, Ellis	C	Hempfield		
Reid, Mike	RB	Altoona	Penn State	Cincinnati Bengals
Urbanik, Bill	T	Donora	Ohio State	
Waite, Burt	G	Chambersburg	William & Mary	

DEFENSE	POS.	HIGH SCHOOL	COLLEGE	NFL DRAFT
Bradley, David	E	Chief Logan	Penn State	Green Bay Packers
Duncan, Jeff	S	Hanover		
Edwards, Steve	CB	Pittsburgh Duquesne	West Virginia	
Hanratty, Terry	CB	Butler	Notre Dame	Pittsburgh Steelers
Hetrick, John	S	Hershey	Maryland	
Kamzelski, Ron	T	Ambridge	Minnesota	Cleveland Browns
McCune, Jay	G	Ringgold		
Reid, Mike	LB	Altoona	Penn State	Cincinnati Bengals
Ruccio, Jerry	LB	Allentown Dieruff	Syracuse	
Salerno, Gene	LB	Bishop McDevitt		
Sabastianelli, Ted	E	Blakesly	Penn State	

Before breaking, Norm Bulaich asked, "What should the rest of us do, Bill?"

"Block," replied Bradley.[77]

On the first play from scrimmage, Bill dropped back, planted his right foot, and let the ball fly. It was a high pass that looked more like a spiraling punt than a throw, but it easily reached its target. LeVias beat his coverage, reached out, and caught the ball squarely in his palms. The 49-yard reception marked one of the first times in the history of Texas high school football that a Black player caught a ball thrown by a white teammate.

Penn's defensive backs retreated deeper into the secondary, concerned about being beaten again. Bill saw the adjustment and handed off to Bulaich for an 8-yard gain. Chris Gilbert tacked on another 7 yards on a run-pass option. Surprisingly, the Coal Crackers' defensive backs made no adjustment, so Bradley continued the rushing game. This time he ran a bootleg and sprinted 13 yards down the right sideline to the Pennsylvania 7.[78]

In the huddle, Bill instructed LeVias to "run to the back line, then cut back about three yards." "Be looking for the ball all the way, Jerry," he added.

By the time LeVias got into the end zone, the pass was already in flight. Bradley had rifled a perfect strike to the Black receiver, who caught the ball chest high. "Touchdown, Texas!" roared Layne from the sidelines. "Way to go Jerry! Way to go my blue-eyed soul brother," he added, giving a nod to both LeVias and Bradley.

Those six points represented the first time that Pennsylvania had surrendered a touchdown against an out-of-state team in the history of the Big 33 game. LeVias kicked the extra point, and Texas grabbed a 7–3 lead.[79]

The next score came with just three minutes remaining in the first half. Bradley scrambled in and out of the pocket, eluding Coal Cracker linemen to orchestrate a 72-yard drive that ended with a second touchdown pass to LeVias. *Sports Illustrated*'s John Underwood wrote that Bill performed like a "Fred Astaire, who obviously didn't want to dance with any sweaty fat ladies."[80] But the highlight of the drive was the quarterback-receiver tandem of Bradley and LeVias, both of whom were ambidextrous.

On the first possession, Bill called a reverse, pitched the ball to Jerry, and sprinted 20 yards downfield to catch the pass from the *left-handed*-throwing LeVias. Not to be outdone, Bradley, three plays later, threw a left-handed strike to LeVias in the end zone to increase the Texas lead to 14–3.[81]

"Bill was a better athlete than a quarterback," said Bulaich. "I was just in awe when I saw him throw that *left-handed* pass to Jerry. And Bill was a righty! That really takes some kind of athletic ability. I also know how competitive Bill was, and not just against opponents. When LeVias, who was also a righty, threw him a left-handed pass three plays earlier, Bill was going to show Jerry that he had nothing on him!"[82]

By that point, the Coal Crackers didn't know what hit them. Their linemen were breathing like spent racehorses, and their cornerbacks appeared to be just as exhausted. To their credit, the Pennsylvanians came fighting back. Quarterback Bob Naponic teamed up with wide receiver Ted Kwalick, who made a string of leaping catches and then hand-fought two Texas defenders in the end zone for a 34-yard touchdown pass. The extra point narrowed the score to 14–10. Altogether, Kwalick caught eight of the fourteen passes the Coal Crackers completed, mostly in the first half. After that, the "swarming Texas defense shut him down."[83]

The Texans completely dominated the second half. In the third quarter their defense held the Pennsylvanians to just eight offensive plays. For some unknown reason, Lefty James chose to stay with Naponic at quarterback instead of replacing him with Terry Hanratty, considered by many the best high school passer in the country. Instead, Hanratty spent the night as a defensive back trying to chase down Jerry LeVias. Midway through the quarter, Bradley conducted a 90-yard drive, which began with a fake draw and a 22-yard pass to LeVias. On the next play, Jerry ran a straight fly pattern, and Bill connected with him for another 32 yards. On the third play from scrimmage, Bradley, out of the shotgun, threw a screen pass to James Harris, who picked up another 12 yards. Bill gained an additional 7 on a keeper and six more on a run by Bulaich. Harris completed the drive on a 1-yard touchdown plunge, increasing the Texas lead to 20–10.[84]

In the fourth quarter, Bradley, who was later named Most Valuable Player, teamed up with running back Ronnie Scoggins, who accounted for 69 yards of an 80-yard drive. Scoggins put the game away on a 15-yard touchdown run to seal the Texans' 26–10 victory.[85]

At the end of the contest, assistant coach Doak Walker walked over to Bradley and said, "Hey, Billy! I need to look under that jersey of yours to see if you have a big *S* on your chest." From that point on, Bradley was called "Super Bill."[86] The moniker would be a blessing . . . and a curse.

4

Longhorns

If football is a religion in Texas, the biggest cathedral is in Austin. Since 1893, when the University of Texas began playing the sport, the Longhorns have captured four national championships and thirty-two Southwest Conference titles. That amounts to more than nine hundred wins and still counting.[1] Although the sun doesn't shine on the same dog's ass every day, odds are that it shines on the Longhorns every Saturday in the fall. You can also bet that UT will continue to hold bragging rights over the Lone Star State's other Division I gridiron programs well into the future. That was Darrell Royal's objective when he arrived as head coach in 1957.

Royal was a firm believer in field-position football, which emphasized the importance of being in the opponent's territory more than possessing the ball itself. "If the other team can't score on you," he theorized, "then you can't lose."[2] During the 1960s, Royal's Longhorns rarely lost, forging a gridiron dynasty on defense and pride. The players were gritty, lean, fanatical, quick-hitting Texans who tackled in swarms and sprinted to the scrimmage line. Bill Bradley lived that philosophy. After getting a taste of the national limelight at the Big 33 game, he wanted to attend a university that would allow him to bask in it. Just as important, that university had to be in his native state of Texas. Despite dozens of letters Bradley received from Division I programs, he made only two recruiting visits in his senior year of high school. His first visit was to Texas A&M in College Station on the same day as Barry Stone, a highly touted recruit from Kilgore. Neither of them knew what to expect from Gene Stallings, who had just been hired as the Aggies' head coach.

What Bradley and Stone did know was that A&M hadn't won a national championship since 1939, when Homer Norton's Aggies went 11-0 and defeated Tulane in the Sugar Bowl. They also knew that the last time A&M won a Southwest Conference title was nearly a decade before in 1956, when Bear Bryant's team went 9-0-1. Stallings was a member of the famed Junction Boys who helped the Aggies to the '56 conference title. Two years later, he was reunited with Bryant, then head coach at the University of Alabama, as a defensive assistant. He was also on hand for two of Alabama's national championship seasons in 1961 and 1964.[3] Stallings had now returned to his alma mater with visions of capturing a national title of his own. What he lacked in experience as a head coach he made up for in enthusiasm, though his recruiting techniques left something to be desired.

When Stone opened the door to Stallings's office, the Aggie head coach jumped over his desk, grabbed the unsuspecting recruit by the shoulders and pushed him up against the wall. "You wanna be an Aggie, don't ya?" he barked just inches from Stone's face.

Bradley, who managed to elude Stallings' grasp, stood there dumbfounded. "It scared the shit out of me," he admitted years later. "Right then and there I decided I wanted no part of A&M."[4]

Bradley's second visit was to the University of Texas at Austin. "I knew I wanted to be a Longhorn," admitted the blue-chip quarterback. "There was no question in my mind. Coach Royal played quarterback at Oklahoma and held a lot of their records, so he knew the position, and he knew it damn well. He also took a strong interest in me when I was in high school and promised me that I had a future with UT football."[5]

Darrell Royal certainly had more experience than Stallings as a head coach. Prior to being hired at UT in 1957, Royal had already been head coach of the Mississippi State Bulldogs (1954–55) and the University of Washington Huskies (1956). In his first seven years at UT, Royal captured four Southwest Conference titles and a national championship in 1963. The key to his success was the ability to hire talented coaches, delegate responsibility, and, like the chief operating officer of a business corporation, oversee a program that was one of the largest and most successful in Division I football. By the time Royal retired in 1976, he was the winningest head coach in Longhorns football history, with a record of 167-47-5. For many, he was also considered the patron saint of college football in the Lone Star State, having captured at total of eleven Southwest Conference championships and three national championship titles (1963, 1969, 1970).[6]

"Coach Royal was amazing," said Bradley in a recent interview. "He was probably the greatest coach I ever knew. He paid attention to detail, and he made you pay attention to detail. He'd run a play over and over again until it was perfect. He also told it like it was—never sugar-coated anything, not surprising for someone who grew up during the Great Depression. He had a command of his team like no other coach."[7]

Royal was much more than a football coach, though. He was an educator who cultivated a strong sense of self-respect in his players. "Personal appearance was important to him," noted James Street, who succeeded Bradley at quarterback in 1968. "Coach Royal made sure our hair was cut, that our shoes were shined and that our fingernails were clipped. Sounds basic, right? But it was important to him because we were representing ourselves, our families and our school."[8]

Royal also believed that his players were student-athletes who should be active in the daily life of the school, that they weren't at UT simply to play football. He insisted that all of them live in the dorms with other students, not in fraternity houses or their own dormitory. For Royal, living in the dorms was an important part of the college experience because it allowed a student-athlete to meet students with other interests and abilities than sports and to be exposed to the culture of the campus itself.[9] It also strengthened the team dynamic.

"I really believe the dorm made our team," recalled Bob McKay, an All-American tackle for the 1969 Longhorns. "We were there all the time. We lived with each other 24-7, and when you do that, you knew who was going to work hard and who wasn't going to work at all—at anything. If a player quit in the dorm, he'd quit on the football field, too."[10]

At the same time, Royal appears to have had some reservations about his policy of having players live in the dorms. A recently released memo dated November 10, 1959, indicates that the head coach discouraged not only the racial integration of the dormitories, which began on May 9, 1956, but also the recruitment of Black athletes at UT. According to the memo, Royal, who coached Black athletes at the University of Washington, "says that negro students cause problems" and that "white players particularly resent Negro boys coming into their [dormitory] rooms and lounging on their beds." The memo also states that Royal was "quite pronounced in not wanting any Negroes on his team until other Southwest Conference teams admit them and until the housing problem is solved or conditions change."[11]

The memo confirms what detractors had been saying about UT for decades, specifically that Blacks were not welcomed there in the classroom or on the playing field, that the university used standardized testing to slow the process of integration, that Texas fielded the last all-white national championship football team as late as 1969, and that Royal was racist and would never start a Black player over an equally talented white player.[12]

"That's all bullshit," Bradley snapped when reminded of the allegations of racism. "UT's rivals have been saying that crap for years, and not a word of it is true. I can tell you that Coach Royal did not have a prejudice bone in his body. If he did, why would he offer Julius Whittier [the first Black student-athlete to play for the Longhorns] a scholarship in 1969?"[13]

Bob McKay also insisted that Royal would play with "whoever showed up for tryouts and made the cut, Black or white." "I was still at UT when Whittier was playing on the freshmen team," said McKay. "I never heard anything bad about him. I think the fact that Coach Royal gave him a scholarship tells you that he didn't have an issue with Blacks."[14]

Bradley and McKay have a point. In fact, Royal's first scholarship offer to an African American player at UT was not to Julius Whittier, but to Leon O'Neal, a tight end from Killeen. O'Neal received a full football scholarship a year earlier than Whittier in 1968, but he never made it past the freshman squad due to an ankle injury. O'Neal lost his football scholarship when he went on academic probation and transferred to Southwest Texas State University (now Texas State).[15] But the O'Neal and

Whittier scholarships do not absolve Royal from allegations of racism if the timing of those offers is considered.

Although UT began admitting Black students in 1956 and opened the athletic program to Blacks in 1963, O'Neal was not offered the scholarship until 1968, and Whittier a year later. Even then, Whittier did not make his debut on the varsity gridiron until 1970 because NCAA rules at the time did not allow freshmen to play varsity football. Thus, it is true that the 1969 Longhorns football team was the last all-white national-title team in college football history.[16] That doesn't mean that Royal condoned institutional discrimination or the slow pace of racial integration at UT, though. In fact, he was appointed the university's athletic director in 1962 and in that capacity oversaw the integration of African Americans into all of UT's athletic programs.[17] Royal was also known for recruiting Black players during his brief tenure at the University of Washington in 1956.

Tom Campbell, a defensive back who played for the 1968 and '69 Longhorns, insists that Royal "never had a problem with Black players." Campbell, whose father, Mike, was an assistant coach and the defensive coordinator for Royal both at Washington and Texas, noted that "the Huskies were already recruiting Blacks in 1956, but that was in the North. . . . When Coach Royal and Dad came to UT in 1957, they were in the Deep South, and it was segregated," he explained. "They had to change their recruiting policies." Instead, Campbell contends that Frank Erwin Jr., the chairman of UT's Board of Regents in the 1960s, "made it clear to Coach Royal that if he recruited any Black player, he'd be fired."[18]

Erwin was the most powerful figure at the University of Texas in the 1960s. Having earned a law degree at UT in 1948, he opened his own practice and soon developed friendships with many leading figures within the conservative faction of the Democratic Party in Texas. In 1963 those connections got him elected chairman of the party's state Executive Committee as well as a seat on the University of Texas System Board of Regents, a body he chaired from 1966 to 1971. Working closely with his political allies in the state legislature, Erwin increased university appropriations from $40.4 million to $349.7 million during that span. Most of the money was allocated to expanding the university's physical plant, which included more than sixteen million square feet of new indoor space. Under Erwin's leadership, UT also increased its enrollment from forty-seven thousand in 1965 to sixty-seven thousand in 1971, an increase of 43 percent. By the time he stepped down from the Board of Regents, the University of Texas consisted of twelve component institutions and was one of the nation's leading state-supported systems of higher education.[19]

However, Erwin's tenure was marked by controversy. He firmly believed in his own authority to shape the university in the image he chose. Accordingly, he often displayed an intolerance of opposing views, especially those of the left-leaning and civil rights movements emerging on college campuses across the nation in the 1960s. Determined to stifle the emerging counterculture, Erwin attempted to close campus facilities to such organizations as Students for a Democratic Society and the Young Socialist Alliance and worked behind the scenes to remove professors whose politics he considered unpatriotic. At the height of anti–Vietnam War protests in 1967, Erwin hosted a birthday party for President Lyndon Johnson in the school auditorium at Austin. When Johnson was met with angry demonstrators, Erwin unleashed three hundred armed policemen on the dissidents and condemned them as "a bunch of dirty nothings" who think they can "disrupt the workings of a great university in the name of academic freedom." His epithet, "dirty nothings," was quickly adopted by student radicals at the university, who soon sported pins identifying themselves by that name.

After the shootings at Kent State University in Ohio in May 1970, Erwin and the regents successfully fought student and faculty initiatives to cancel classes to protest the shootings and the Vietnam War, and later Erwin adopted a policy prohibiting administrators from negotiating with student demonstrators under any circumstances. Although these iron-fisted policies alienated many students, Erwin, who was derided as the "Emperor of UT" by students, was widely praised in the conservative Texas legislature, which continued to increase university allocations.[20]

Considering these circumstances, the process of integration at UT in general, and Longhorns football in particular, was much slower than at other Division I schools. That doesn't mean that Royal agreed with the discriminatory policies that had long existed at the university before or even after he arrived there. He even conceded in a December 23, 2005, *New York Times* interview that "things they [were] a-changing" in the 1960s on college campuses across the nation, "but that they weren't changing that quickly around here [at UT] at the time."[21]

Perhaps the best evidence that Royal did not discriminate against his Black players came from Julius Whittier himself. "The treatment a black football player received from the Texas athletic program had as much to do with individual character, personality and athletic skills as with race," Whittier wrote many years later. "In my opinion, the winning combination for matriculating at Texas includes a strong, well-developed character and personality and above-average skills at what one does best. In keeping with the frontier spirit of the state, the university holds no one's hand. If you are not an aggressive self-starter, you are not cut out for Texas."[22] In other words, Royal, who was not permitted by UT to recruit a Black athlete until 1968, was as close to color neutral as any football coach in the Southwest Conference.

Bradley spent the fall of 1965 on the freshmen team, better known as the Shorthorns. He was not only the starting quarterback and a defensive back for a squad that was loaded with talent but also arguably the best player on a team that included future All-Americans Chris Gilbert (Spring Branch) and Corby Robertson (Houston-Lamar). "Bill was the best athlete I'd ever seen when he hit UT's campus," insists Robertson, who doubled as a tight end. "He could do things on a football field that nobody else could do. He could punt with either foot. He could throw with either hand. He was just unbelievable!"

Robertson recalled one play where Bradley was at safety and he was at linebacker. "Bill got beat about five yards on a deep rout, and the quarterback throws the ball to the receiver who beat him," he said. "Bill still got a hand on the ball to bat it away from the receiver. I swear that when he jumped his feet were up at my chest when he knocked the ball down."[23]

One of the reasons for Bradley's success was his creative instinct. He had the ability to quickly identify a problem in the offense and correct it on the fly. Against A&M that year, the Longhorns were having trouble with the running game. Every time tailback Chris Gilbert got the ball, the Aggies' defensive end was tackling him behind the line of scrimmage. Bradley got his teammates together in the huddle and said, "Chris, I'm going to fake to you, but I'm keeping the ball. Corby, you block the DE instead of the tackle."

The strategy gave Bradley a huge opening down the end line, and he ran for an 80-yard gain. "That call wasn't even in our playbook," said Robertson. "But it shows you how well Bill could improvise."[24]

Bradley's best performance came against Texas Christian in mid-October, when he threw two touchdown passes, ran for a third, and collected three interceptions. Two of those pickoffs were intended for Norm Bulaich, a teammate of Bradley's on the Texas Big 33 All-Stars.

"I was frustrated as hell," recalled Bulaich in a recent interview. "So, later in the game when I caught a screen pass and Bradley got in my way, I knocked him on his ass real good."

Bill got even in the fourth quarter, though. Bulaich was en route to a 30-yard kick-off return when Bradley blindsided him with a forearm shiver. Shaken up on the play, Bulaich took his time getting up.

"That was a cheap shot, your motherfucker!" he snapped.

"No worse than what you gave me last quarter, you son of a bitch," laughed Bradley before helping Bulaich back to his feet.[25]

Bill also played baseball in his freshman year. In high school he was such a good hitter and shortstop that the Detroit Tigers selected him in the seventh round of the 1965 draft and offered him a $20,000 bonus to sign. Instead, Bill, on his father's advice, chose to attend Texas on a football scholarship. But Joe Bradley also made sure that his son secured an oral commitment from Royal to allow Bill to play baseball at the school. Not only was Bradley the starting shortstop on UT's freshman team, but he also competed on the freshman track team. Recruited by the track coach to compete in the regionals at Rice University, Bill finished second in three events with a 6-foot-2 high jump, a 23-foot-6 broad jump, and a 13-foot-6 pole vault.[26] Bradley's exceptional timing, speed, and fundamental skill set enabled him to excel at any sport he chose. And Royal knew it too.

But the Longhorns' football coach wasn't impressed by Bradley because he was an exceptional athlete. There were probably a hundred kids in Texas who fit that description, and most of them played quarterback. No, Royal was impressed by Bill because he possessed a competitive fire that burned white-hot when he was on the gridiron and because the kid truly believed that he was the very best signal caller in the Lone Star State. But even that didn't stop Royal from courting other high school quarterbacks.

When James Street, a scrawny signal caller from Longview High School, was being recruited by UT, he attended a freshman game and sat in the press box with Royal. "Bill Bradley was the quarterback, and he was unbelievable," recalled Street. "Coach Royal told me he figured other schools would throw Bradley up to me to discourage me from coming to UT. And then he said, 'If you go somewhere else, you'll never know whether you could have played with the best and competed for a position against the best.' I remember thinking, *I think I can play with these guys*. But, boy, that Bradley was awful good."[27] The following year, Street, who became one of Bradley's best friends, would replace Bill as the quarterback of the freshman team.

Bradley's first season as the Longhorns' starting quarterback was 1966. It wasn't supposed to be that way, though. Royal had recruited another blue-chip quarterback by the name of Greg Lott two years earlier. Lott was a 6-foot, 175-pound football prodigy at Lubbock High School, where he was an all-around athlete. He had speed, quickness, tremendous balance, and a razor focus that allowed him to seize control of a game. He could also play defensive halfback just as effectively as quarterback. In fact, after Royal signed Lott, he told a Longhorns alumnus that he "found a kid in West Texas who could change the game on either side of the ball."[28]

Like Bradley, Lott had an impressive freshman season. He was the Shorthorns' leading rusher with 222 yards at 8.9 yards per carry, alternating between quarterback and tailback. Named to the 1964 Freshman All-Southwest Conference Team, Lott not only survived Royal's grueling spring practices replete with a gauntlet of hellacious blocking drills the following year, but excelled as a passer, rusher, and blocker. Royal was so impressed he told one of his coaches that Lott "can really shift gears" and that he was "the first one who can round the corner since Duke [Carlisle]," the legendary Longhorns quarterback of the 1963 national championship team. Even the Texas sportswriters predicted that Lott was "maturing so quickly" that he would "start for the Longhorns in '65 and go on to become the first great Royal quarterback."[29]

Instead, Royal stayed with his policy of not starting sophomores until their junior or senior year, believing they needed more experience to adjust to the speed, physicality, and pressure of the game at the varsity level. As a result, Lott served as a back-up to veteran quarterback Marvin Kristynik. Unfortunately, UT finished the 1965 season with a mediocre 6-4 record. That was unacceptable to Royal, who was accustomed to undefeated or one-loss seasons. Desperate to get back on track in 1966, the head coach broke with his policy of not starting sophomores and made Bradley his starting quarterback, to capitalize on his passing ability, and slotted Lott into the wingback position, to exploit his explosive speed.[30] While Bill's displacement of Greg as the Longhorns' signal caller could easily have caused ill feelings between the two, they became roommates and good friends that season.[31]

Texas opened the 1966 campaign on September 17 at home against ninth-ranked University of Southern California. Unfortunately, the 'Horns were outplayed and outsmarted by the Trojans during the first half. USC limited Texas to just eighteen offensive plays and scored all their points in the first thirty minutes of the game for a 10–0 lead at halftime. Bradley finally rallied the offense early in the fourth quarter when he began a 91-yard drive that culminated with a fake handoff to running back Chris Gilbert, while he jogged around right end to score UT's only touchdown. The Longhorns went for two points on the conversion, but Bill's quick pass over the middle was intercepted by the Trojan defense.[32]

While he might not have lived up to his "Super Bill" moniker, Bradley did manage to gain 43 yards on fourteen carries for the game, complete three of seven passes for 42 yards, and catch one pass from wingback Greg Lott for 13 yards.[33] After the game, Royal told Fred Sanner of the

Austin American-Statesman that his sophomore quarterback "needed some rest from the pressure of over-publicity."

"Bill's a fine athlete and he's going to be a great one," explained the UT head coach, "but you just don't jump out there as a sophomore and succeed. He needs to grow into the position."[34]

On September 24 UT traveled to Lubbock to open the Southwest Conference schedule against Texas Tech. A record crowd of 48,155 packed Jones Stadium, expecting to see a wild one between the two conference rivals. Instead, Raiders' fans were forced to endure the gridiron feats of Super Bill Bradley, who led the Longhorns' offense to a 31–21 victory. UT controlled the game from the start when junior wingback Greg Lott fielded the opening kickoff and returned it 88 yards for a quick 6. With that momentum, the 'Horns were off and running.

Bradley paced the Texas offense, collecting 62 yards on fourteen carries and connecting on five of six passes for 38 more. Tailbacks Jimmy Helms and Chris Gilbert rushed for 52 yards each, and Lott contributed another 41 yards. Bradley scored on a quarterback sneak in the first quarter and ran for another touchdown in the second to increase the 'Horns' lead to 21–0. When Bill wasn't leading the offense, he thwarted the Tech attack, uncorking an 80-yard punt to the lip of the Raiders' goal line early in the second quarter. By halftime, the Longhorns held a commanding 31–8 lead and never looked back.[35]

But there was no celebrating in UT's dressing room after the game. When asked about his impressive punt, Bradley responded with humility, "Yes, I guess it was the longest I ever made. Shoot, I just got the wind behind it."[36] The answer was carefully worded, based on Darrell Royal's advice to "place the team above personal achievement" and to "talk to the press, but don't tell them anything."[37]

At the other end of the locker room, Royal bemoaned the loss of three key starters. "This is the worst I've ever felt after a win," he confessed to Carlton Stowers of the *Austin American-Statesman*. "It looks like we lost [center] Ken Gidney with a bad knee, [offensive lineman] Ronny Landry with a bad elbow and [defensive lineman] D. H. Martin with a badly sprained ankle. I don't know how much longer this can go on. We've been hurt every game for the last year and a half."[38]

Injuries continued to plague the Longhorns the following week, when Bradley went down in a 35–0 rout of Indiana University. Bill hurt his right knee cutting on a sprint out early in the second quarter.[39] "I was being pressured by a [defensive] lineman and managed to get out of the pocket," he recalled many years later. "But when I planted my right leg to throw, I hyperextended my knee and tore some cartilage." Still, Bradley returned to quarterback on the next offensive series to connect with tailback Greg Lott for the game's second touchdown. "I wanted to stay in the game after that, but the team doctor, Stan Casner, examined my knee and insisted that I go to the Student Health Center to get X-rays."[40]

Backup Andy White entered the game with a 14-point cushion and responded by quarterbacking the Longhorns to their final three touchdowns with six completions in eight passes for 65 yards. "I thought Andy played remarkably well," said Royal after the game. "His passing was terrific. He showed he's capable, and we all have confidence in him. Andy will be our quarterback until Bill returns."[41]

With Bradley out, Texas lost to Oklahoma, an 8-point underdog, 18–9, at the Cotton Bowl on October 8.[42] The Longhorns did not do much better the following week when they returned to Memorial Stadium to play Arkansas. Bradley, with a heavily taped right knee, was back in the starting lineup against the Razorbacks. It was a sloppy affair, with both teams combining to commit thirteen fumbles and four interceptions. Still, the Longhorns held a razor-thin 7–6 lead midway in the third quarter. With 4:28 remaining in the third period, Arkansas quarterback Jon Brittenum threw a strike to split end Tommy Burnett, who ran the ball into the end zone to take a 12–7 lead. Although a series of Razorback fumbles and interceptions gave the Longhorns many chances to pull out the game, Texas was unable to capitalize. UT got the ball back one more time with ten seconds left to play.

"Hold 'em one more time and we'll win it," cried the Razorback bench as the Arkansas fans let loose with their "Sooie Pigs" chant. They got their wish when Texas fumbled on the first play from scrimmage and

Arkansas recovered the ball to ice the game. An anguished Darrell Royal fell to his knees and pounded the ground while the Longhorns' offense quietly walked off the field.[43]

Worse, Greg Lott, Bill's roommate, suffered a devastating injury to his right knee and was out for the season. Lott had been playing well, making long runs and scoring touchdowns, and looked as if he had a future in the NFL as a receiver. But in the third quarter as he was running downfield on a kickoff, Lott took a violent shot to the knee and crumpled to the ground in pain. Despite several surgeries, the knee never healed properly, and by 1968 Lott's football career was over.[44]

While Bradley might've bested Lott for the starting quarterback position, Lott won the competition for the most beautiful girl on campus. Bill, who attracted a fair share of female attention, was a serial monogamist, dating several co-eds during his time at UT.[45] But Greg had captured the most desirable female on campus—Farrah Fawcett. Farrah, a native of Corpus Christi, Texas, enrolled at UT in the fall of 1965. She had planned to major in microbiology but changed to the fine arts and demonstrated an exceptional talent for sculpting. Voted one of the ten most beautiful girls on campus—a rare honor for a freshman—Fawcett's photograph found its way into the hands of a Los Angeles business publicist who encouraged her to come to Hollywood. Instead, she decided to stay at UT, where she joined the Tri-Delta sorority, played a lot of tennis, and developed a group of close friends.[46]

"Farrah was the most stunning creature I had ever seen," recalled Lott of their first meeting in a 2009 interview. "She was a very sensual woman. She never wore make-up at home. She had no airs. That's what I loved about her. She looked like a million dollars without doing anything."

But Lott played hard-to-get. "I didn't chase her," he admitted. "I think she liked that. I saw her at a party a few weeks later and she asked, 'Why did you disappear on me?'"[47]

Greg, an All-American type with a muscular build, deep voice, and effervescent smile, was exactly the kind of male Farrah preferred—"good guys with handsome, round faces who played sports and were comfortable in the world of other good guys, men who were not unlike her own father,

Jim Fawcett, an oil field contractor."[48] Bradley, who also fit the same mold, might've dated Farrah if his roommate hadn't won her affections earlier. Instead, Bill joined her wide circle of friends and admirers.

"Farrah was not only drop-dead beautiful, but she was the complete package: gorgeous, intelligent, and athletic," recalled Bradley in a recent interview. "But she was already dating Greg when I met her. They were lovers and best friends, and I respected that. No way would I try to impose myself on her. She knew that, and that's why she trusted me. That's why we were friends 'til the day she died."[49]

Fawcett left UT for Hollywood in 1968 to pursue a career in acting. However, Lott stayed on at the university to complete his degree in marketing. Sadly, his life went into a downward spiral after he became addicted to alcohol and drugs. The couple split in 1970 but rekindled their love affair in 1998 after Lott became clean and established successful businesses in Austin and Lubbock. They stayed together until Farrah's death from cancer in 2009.[50]

On October 22 Texas returned to its winning ways against Rice. Royal limited Bradley to handing the ball off or running it himself, as the Longhorns put on their most crunching rushing attack of the season. Tailback Chris Gilbert ran for 116 yards on twenty-five carries, while fullback Linus Baer chipped in another 44 yards on six carries, and Bradley ran for 54 yards on seven rush attempts. Still, the 'Horns offense could only muster one touchdown, and that one came in the first quarter. Texas scored its only other touchdown on a 90-yard pass interception by Mike Robuck, a lanky defensive tackle, in the second quarter.[51] Instead, the Longhorns relied on a tough defense whenever Rice managed to enter the red zone and came away with a 14–6 Southwest Conference victory.[52]

Texas closed out October at home against Southern Methodist University in a game that made Darrell Royal regret that he hadn't recruited Jerry LeVias, Bradley's go-to receiver at the Big 33 All-Star Game a year earlier. In fact, Royal was given the first opportunity to sign the running back by his coach Clifton Ozen at all-Black Hebert High School in Beaumont. Ozen tried to secure a scholarship to Texas for LeVias in his senior year and called the Longhorns' coach. When he told Royal that he had "an exceptional Negro—a player qualified both academically and athletically for the Southwest Conference," the 'Horns' coach asked LeVias's size. Ozen replied "about 153 pounds," which was 13 pounds heavier than LeVias's actual weight. Royal said that Jerry "wasn't big enough for the league."[53]

During the game, the Longhorns kicked and punched LeVias after a tackle and showered him with racist epithets, despite Bradley's constant pleas: "Stop calling him a n——! Jerry's a good guy. I know him."[54]

LeVias kept SMU in the game that afternoon catching seven passes for 68 yards and scoring a critical touchdown. With three minutes left to play and the Longhorns sitting on a 2-point lead, Bradley fumbled on a quarterback sneak at the SMU 33. Mac White, the Mustangs' fiery red-headed quarterback, launched a dramatic comeback, marching SMU 51 yards to the Texas 16 before Dennis Partee kicked a 22-yard, game-winning field goal. The heartbreaking 13–12 loss left the Longhorns for dead with a 2-2 record in the Southwest Conference, while SMU improved its conference record to a perfect 3-0.[55]

After the game, Bill approached Jerry to shake his hand and apologize for the crass behavior of his teammates. "I'm sorry, roomie. Sometimes these guys just don't know what they're saying."

"Don't worry about me Super Bill," replied LeVias. "I hear this stuff everywhere I go."[56]

At the end of the season, when LeVias led SMU to a Southwest Conference title and a berth in the Cotton Bowl against fourth-ranked Georgia, Ozen called Royal again and reminded him that Jerry was "the little ol' boy you wouldn't take."

"Well, he didn't sound very big then when you described him," replied the Longhorns' coach. "But he looks plenty big to me now."[57]

UT improved its standing in the conference on November 5, when it traveled to Baylor. Chris Gilbert paced the Longhorns to a 26–14 victory with a 55-yard run to set up one touchdown and then a 65-yard touchdown run to nail down the win. Those two runs helped Gilbert establish a single-game school record of 237 yards on twenty-four carries. Bradley was still lacking the elusiveness he demonstrated at the beginning of the season, but he ran with more abandon than in any other game since injuring his right knee against Indiana. Bill scored with five minutes elapsed in the first quarter when he nosed into the end zone from the 1-yard line on a quarterback sneak. Three plays after Gilbert's 55-yard run, Bradley whirled around right end on a 5-yard sprint out to score a second touchdown. The 26–14 victory pulled the Longhorns back up to 4-4 for the season and 3-2 in the Southwest Conference, in third place behind SMU (4-0) and Arkansas (4-1).[58]

Gilbert and Bradley continued their stellar performances against Texas Christian University on November 12. Gilbert carried the ball thirty-two times for 117 yards, the fifth time that season he had gone over the 100-yard mark. Bradley was the Longhorns' second leading rusher with 48 yards on sixteen carries. He also connected on four of ten passes for 44 yards and a touchdown to Ed Small. But Bill was at his best punting, as he went head-to-head with TCU's Donnie Gibbs, the SWC leader. Bradley punted seven times for an outstanding 45.8-yard average, while Gibbs, who entered the game with a 43.4 average, punted for an average of 40.5 yards on eight attempts. Bill's longest punt was a 61-yarder following UT's first possession. The 'Horns' brilliant display of running, passing, and defending resulted in a 13–3 rout of TCU and increased the mathematical possibilities of another SWC title with one game left in the regular season.[59]

Despite his gridiron success, Bradley missed home, especially his younger brother, Duffy. They had been joined at the hip as youngsters. Where Bill went, Duffy followed. If Bill hung out with friends or played a pickup basketball game, Duffy was included. When Bill competed for Palestine High School, Duffy was in the bleachers cheering him on, regardless of the season. If anyone dared to tease Duffy about his disability, they'd have to deal with Bill, who would kick the offender's ass from one end of town to the other. "We were inseparable," recalled Bradley. "It took some getting used to when I went to college. But I'd have Duffy come out to UT to stay with me on weekends. He'd go to the football game, hang out with my teammates, and he got to know them pretty well."[60] In fact, Duffy enjoyed nearly all of the Longhorns' off-field activities except one. Bill would not allow his younger brother to go to the Chicken Ranch in LaGrange, a place the star quarterback and some of his teammates frequented after Saturday-afternoon home games.

Located midway between Austin and College Station, the Chicken Ranch was a brothel established in the early 1900s by Miss Jessie Williams. Needing a way to retain customers during the Great Depression, Miss Jessie decided to accept chickens as payment. Soon the brothel and the land surrounding it were covered in chickens, giving the establishment a convenient name. The brothel looked like a typical Texas farmhouse, with whitewashed siding and a few side buildings, which held the chickens. The unlit entrance was discreetly located at the back of the house, which featured fourteen rooms, one for each prostitute.

In 1952 the Chicken Ranch came under the direction of Miss Edna Milton, who employed sixteen prostitutes. Each girl entertained between five and twenty customers per day and charged $15 for fifteen minutes. The girls were required to give 75 percent of their earnings to Milton, who paid for their living and medical expenses. Miss Edna also classed up the joint. Only white, presentable, and sober men were admitted into the parlor, where comfortably padded chairs stood on both sides of the room. No profanity or drinking was permitted. The rooms were air conditioned, and Milton charged a quarter for the jukebox, seventy-five cents for cigarettes, and a dollar for a Coke, steep prices for the time.

Thanks to the local sheriff, a part-owner, the business flourished in the 1960s. On weekends, a line of men was often at the back door, mostly students or soldiers from nearby military bases. Coeds from UT replaced many of the older prostitutes. The going rate for their services increased to twenty dollars for fifteen minutes, and more expensive options were added, depending upon the nature and complexity of the trick requested. The Chicken Ranch became so popular that Miss Edna was earning more than $500,000 per year, with the girls keeping an additional $300 per week for themselves.[61]

Although the establishment was shut down in 1973, the Chicken Ranch inspired a Hollywood film, *The Best Little Whorehouse in Texas* (1982), starring Dolly Parton and Burt Reynolds, and the most widely known rock-and-roll song ever to emerge from Texas, ZZ Top's "La Grange."[62]

"The Chicken Ranch was a very classy place," Bill recalled. "Miss Edna only employed the most attractive coeds from UT, and they were regularly tested for venereal disease. I'm sure those girls were making good money too."

Some of the more ambitious girls made a few extra bucks by conducting business over the Christmas break. In fact, one especially forward coed gave Bill a tempting invitation. "Pretend my right leg is Christmas and my left leg is New Years," she suggested. "Then come and visit me between the holidays!"

"We weren't the only ones going to the Chicken Ranch either," insisted Bradley, referring to his Longhorns teammates. "The Aggies frequented the place too. We hated A&M so much, we used to get into fistfights in the parking lot because Miss Edna would not permit that kind of behavior inside the parlor."[63]

The hard feelings *always* carried over to the gridiron. On Thanksgiving Day the Longhorns faced their archrivals at Memorial Stadium before a near sellout crowd of 65,500. The first quarter was a dogfight. A&M coach Gene Stallings called for an onside kick to begin the game, but the Aggies failed to cover the ball, giving the 'Horns perfect field position to score. Bradley made short work of the opportunity, engineering a three-play drive that ended when he scored on a 6-yard sprint out. David Conway kicked the extra point, and Texas led, 7–0.

On the ensuing kickoff, the Aggies' Bob Long caught the ball at his 3, faked a handoff on a crisscross, and raced up to the 10-yard line, where he lateraled to running back Lloyd Currington. The tricky maneuver created just enough time for the Aggies to put up a protective wall for Currington, who streaked down the sideline until he was corralled at the Texas 23 by Mike Robuck. Wendell Housley ran for another 15 yards and a first down at the Texas 7 on two carries, and Bill Sallee nosed into the end zone on a fourth-down carry. But when Glynn Lindsey's extra-point attempt went wide, the Aggies trailed by a 7–6 margin. The score remained that way until just thirty-two seconds before the end of the first half, when Bradley threw a 61-yard bomb to split end Tom Higgins, who winged his way past two Aggies defenders for the touchdown. Conway followed with the extra point, and the Steers held a 14–6 lead at halftime.

Texas added 6 more points in the third quarter on two Conway field goals and dumped A&M quarterback Charlie Riggs for a safety at the beginning of the fourth to increase the Longhorns' lead to 22–6. The Aggies refused to go quietly, though. Midway in the fourth quarter Riggs launched an 85-yard drive, largely on three passes, capping it with a 17-yard touchdown pass to Currington with just seventy-two seconds left in the game. The Aggies pulled to within 8 points with a 2-point conversion pass from Riggs to end Tommy Buckman. But time ran out, and the 'Horns won, 22–14. The victory allowed Texas to clinch a share of second place in the SWC with Arkansas, which also finished the regular season with a 5-2 conference record.[64]

While Super Bill displayed flashes of brilliance, he was hampered most of the season by injuries to his right knee and shoulder. But he still demonstrated the mental and physical toughness to lead Texas to an overall record of 7-4. The Longhorns won six of their last seven games, including a 19–0 blowout of heavily favored Ole Miss in the Bluebonnet Bowl on December 17 in Houston. Chris Gilbert, who was named MVP of the contest, rushed for 156 yards on twenty-six carries, and Bradley scrambled for another 105.[65]

"In Bradley and Gilbert, the Longhorns have as fine a pair of backs as I have seen in a long time," Mississippi coach Johnny Vaught conceded after the game. "They complement each other perfectly and give Texas the strongest, most effective running game we have seen in quite a while."[66]

Although the 19–0 blowout of Ole Miss had Texas alumni bragging that another national title was on the horizon, Royal knew better. "I think it's all premature," he said. "We're an average football team at best."[67]

Instead, the Longhorns' coach focused on a more immediate concern—the health of his star quarterback. "Bradley's moving and not flinching as much now," he said when Dick Collins of the *Austin American-Statesman* asked him about Super Bill's earlier knee injury. "We're going to check on Bill's knee Monday and if it needs anything we will have it done during the Christmas holidays."[68]

A week later, Bradley underwent surgery to remove some loose cartilage in his right knee and have the kneecap shaved, but the leg was never the same. For the remainder of his college career and throughout his tenure in the NFL career, Bill's right knee would have to be heavily taped to support his leg. It was only the first of several injuries he would suffer.[69]

Injury was not the only concern Darrell Royal had about his star quarterback. Royal, also UT's athletic director, had made a significant investment in Bradley. He taught him how to dress with style, how to deal with the press by talking a lot but telling them nothing of real significance, and how to behave on and off the playing field. In all these ways, Royal was grooming Bill not only to be a key player in his quest for a second national title but also to represent the university's football program with the character and class he expected of all his student-athletes. Those goals proved difficult at a time when confrontation was beginning to sweep across the nation's colleges and universities.

Although UT was more conservative than other colleges, especially those on the East and West Coasts, it was certainly not isolated from the budding counterculture that emerged on the more liberal campuses. Widespread student protest over American involvement in Vietnam did not emerge until 1968, but there was increasing tension over civil rights, the new ecology movement, and administrators' determination to assert their authority.[70] The latter issue proved especially difficult for Bradley to accept. He was a freethinker who, in many ways, marched to the beat of his own drum. As a result, Bill, during the spring semester of 1967, found himself in Royal's doghouse.

The conflict between quarterback and coach began innocently enough when Royal saw Bradley walking across campus toting a baseball bat and glove.

"Where ya headed, Bill?" asked Royal.

"I'm going to baseball practice, coach," replied Bradley. "Remember, you promised me that—"

"Now, hold on a minute, Bill," interrupted the coach. "I'm going to need a quarterback who's going to give his complete attention to football. You signed a football scholarship, and I will need you at spring practice."

Bradley was stunned. He didn't know what to say. Royal had made a verbal commitment to him and his father that Bill could play baseball at UT when he signed his letter of intent. They had even shaken hands on it. But now the coach was reneging on that promise. Bradley's momentary shock was giving way to anger, as he could feel the blood coursing through his veins. Somehow, he managed to restrain himself.

"I see what you mean, coach," Bill said, biting his tongue. "I guess I'll see you at spring practice."

"Well, alright then," blurted Royal with a sly smile before he turned and walked away.[71]

When Bill returned to his dormitory, he immediately phoned his father in Palestine and told him that Royal had broken his promise. Cephas went stone-cold silent for a few moments. He simply could not believe that a man who shook hands on an agreement would break his promise, especially a man like Darrell Royal, who by all accounts had an impeccable reputation. A handshake was as good as a man's word. It had always been that way in the Bradley family for as long as he could remember.

"We'll see about that, Bill," said Cephas before he abruptly ended the conversation.

The very next day, Joe Hill Bradley drove to Austin and, without an appointment, walked into Royal's office, closed the door, and had a man-to-man discussion with the head coach. To this day, Bill does not know exactly what was said between the two men, but he remembers clearly the advice Cephas imparted the next time he spoke with his father. "From now on," he told his son, "whenever you make a deal, get it in writing."[72]

Fifty-five years later, Bill Bradley gets his dander up when he thinks about Royal's broken promise, but he tries to put himself in his coach's position. "To be fair to Coach Royal, he didn't outright lie when he said I could play baseball," Bill admitted begrudgingly. "He did let me play my freshman year. But after that he needed a quarterback, and he could not afford to let me go play baseball if I was going to be that quarterback. I needed to be at those spring practices. After all, I was on a football scholarship—not a baseball scholarship—so I had to honor his wishes. But it still pisses me off."[73]

The relationship between quarterback and coach did not improve as the spring unfolded, largely due to Bill's participation in a student protest to save the trees that lined Waller Creek located next to the practice fields. Plans to remove those the trees began in 1967, when UT's Austin campus was in the early stages of a physical transformation. Multistoried tan brick buildings to house a new humanities research center and the Lyndon Baines Johnson Presidential Library were in the offing. Other, less attractive concrete structures were being designed for new college residential halls and a seventeen-story physics-math-astronomy building, along with a sizeable addition to the football stadium. The addition was designed to house classrooms and labs for the physical education department, along with the administrative offices of intercollegiate athletics. The roof of the edifice would support an upper deck to the stadium with seating for fourteen thousand football fans.[74]

But to make room for the new building, the cedar, live oak, pecan, and maple trees that shaded the western gates of the stadium would have to be removed. San Jacinto Boulevard, which cut through the southern footprint of the structure, would also have to be rerouted about sixty-five feet to the west, which would result in the removal of additional oaks along Waller Creek, the picturesque stream that bordered the three fields where the Longhorns football team practiced. A total of thirty-nine trees—many of them well over a century old—were slated for removal, and the bed and banks of the creek were destined to be paved for erosion control.[75]

Student opposition to the project quickly developed. Some railed against the need for more seats in the stadium. Others were architecture students wanting more public input on the future development of the campus; they created substitute proposals to preserve the trees. Still others, like Bradley, were sensitive to the ecology movement and were opposed to the destruction of a place of natural beauty.[76] Bill was among the dozens of students who protested by sitting in the trees.

When Royal saw a photo of his star quarterback seated in an oak tree on the front page of the *Daily Texan*, the UT student newspaper, he was livid. Summoning Bradley to his office, the Longhorns' coach threw the newspaper down on the desk, pointed to the photo, and growled, "Bill, what do you have to say for yourself?"

"What do you mean?" asked Bradley innocently, unable to see a problem with his participation in the protest.

"I don't want my starting quarterback doing any protesting," replied Royal. "You are a football player here, not a protester!"

Still confused, Bill mustered some courage before speaking.

"Coach, you came from the Dust Bowl during the Depression," he began. "I'm sure you appreciate the shade that a tree provides, especially in 100-degree temperatures. If the school cuts down those trees, we won't have that kind of shade on this campus and wouldn't that make you mad too?"

Stunned, Royal took a moment to consider the explanation. Then he leaned over his desk and said, "Bill, let me tell you one thing: the next time you do decide to do that—"

Bradley braced himself for the explosion that was about to take place.

"You come by my office, and I'll come sit in the tree with ya!"[77]

Royal was not an unreasonable man. If he understood the rationale behind a controversial decision one of his players made, he gave him the benefit of the doubt. Bradley's explanation sounded not only logical but also relevant to the coach's own experience. Besides, the Waller Creek protest wasn't just about the trees, and Royal knew it. It was about the right of students to be heard by their university. As a result, the Longhorns' coach withdrew his objection.[78]

Royal secretly admired Bill for standing up for his beliefs, especially to those in positions of authority. Otherwise, Bradley's proclivity for speaking truth to power might have cost him his athletic scholarship. But the coach realized that his quarterback was acting on principle, and he respected that. Royal also understood that the times were changing.

"The Sixties as a composite are mixed as far as I'm concerned," said the Longhorns' coach many years later. "Some things happened that definitely changed my way of looking at things."[79]

To be sure, Royal's outlook on life was changing in the 1960s. Toward the end of the decade, he found new friends—music personalities, songwriters, and singers, some of whom were widely considered country music's outlaws. They were artists like Waylon Jennings, Buck Owens, George Jones, and Willie Nelson, who broke away from the Nashville establishment by singing about drinking, drugs, and life on the road.[80] Some of the political-minded powers connected with the University of Texas were not happy about their football coach for associating with these renegade musicians. But he didn't care. Instead, Royal invited Jennings, Owens, Jones, and Nelson to his home on a regular basis to play their outlaw brand of country music. Not only did he genuinely enjoy their music, but his association with them was his way of thumbing his nose at the Board of Regents, who constantly tried to dictate how the football program should be run.

"One reason I like to be around country-and-western entertainers," Royal once said, "is that they don't give a damn about your rank and smell."[81]

Shortly after the Waller Creek protest, Royal began inviting Bradley to his house for these private concerts. He was the only Longhorns player who received an invitation.[82] The coach and his quarterback were beginning to understand and appreciate each other on and off the gridiron.

5 Reality Check

A saying among the Texas Longhorns is that a football player can spend his time at the university three ways: He can study. He can play football. Or he can party. Even if he's an exceptional human being, a Longhorn can become an All-American in just two of these three areas.[1] It was no secret on UT's campus that Bill Bradley excelled at football and partying.

It's not that Bradley wasn't intelligent. Anyone who saw him prepare for games by watching film and studying the playbook knew that Bill could read and think critically and then apply the lessons he learned. He also loved to study history and had a knack for writing poetry. No, Bradley was intelligent all right. It's just that he placed a higher priority on having a good time with whoever was available.

One of the endearing things about Bill was that he never judged another person on anything but his or her individuality. He respected—and genuinely liked—many different people. Not all of them were football players. It's just that his role as the starting quarterback tended to limit his closest friendships to teammates, who became like a second family to him. In fact, Bill, from his freshman through senior years at UT, spent most of his time with teammates, all of whom kept the same schedule. Their fall semester was dominated by football. The spring, by practice. And the summer, by training for the upcoming season and working a "job" that was usually provided by wealthy alumni.

These alumni were known in the parlance of college football as "boosters" or "sugar daddies," and their activities were not always limited to providing high-profile athletes with part-time employment. Some were given clothing, cars, and even cash payments. Although many Division I football programs across the nation operated this way, the practices were kept quiet because the gifts violated NCAA regulations.[2] If word got out, the offending university would be given the so-called death penalty, which meant losing top recruits to another program, expunging winning seasons from the record books, and eliminating the program from postseason play.[3]

If these illicit practices occurred at UT during the 1960s, Darrell Royal certainly had nothing to do with them. The less he knew, the better. Instead, he let his assistant, Russell Coffee, deal with those alums who expressed an interest in giving their support to Longhorns football. Coffee, who recruited blue-chip high school prospects, made the connections between UT's high-profile players and wealthy alumni. As far as the NCAA was concerned, part-time employment was a legitimate exchange and often one that opened doors for a player to the Texas business industry after his college career ended. The player would spend his summer working for pay on a ranch or on an oil rig during his college tenure. The player did not necessarily have to know anything about the industry he joined. But he did have to know how to dress, how to smile, and how to court and marry an extremely beautiful and wealthy young woman from Dallas or Houston. The booster, on the other hand, would enjoy bragging rights, as well as the possibility of a future employee, son-in-law, or both.[4]

Bradley's fringe benefits, however, were limited to a football scholarship, which covered tuition, books, and room and board, and a summer job on a ranch owned by John Prothro, a wealthy oil man who lived in Tyler, Texas, on Iron Ore Lake. "Those of us who lived near Tyler got summer jobs working for Mr. Prothro," said Bill. "That included guys like me, James Street, and Tommy Asaff. None of us had a pot to piss in, so we really needed the money. It was a legitimate job too. We had to work. We lived on his ranch, slept in a bunkhouse, and hauled a shitload of hay. We also had a shitload of fun."[5]

According to Tommy Asaff, a running back on the Longhorns' 1969 national championship team, Bradley, Street, and he would often "go down to the lake house after work, sit around, and have a few beers."

"One Thursday night, we were sitting around, and James [Street] was talking about baseball," recalled Asaff. "Now, James, who played for UT's [varsity] baseball team, couldn't hit worth shit—not that I could either. But I figured I could give him some pointers. I picked up this iron poker from the fireplace to use as a [baseball] bat. When I took a big swing, the poker slipped out of my hand and went right through a beautiful stained-glass window at the other side of the room.

"I knew that whatever we broke, we'd have to pay for. But since we all went back home for the weekend, I'd have to wait until Monday to tell Mr. Prothro about it."

The following Monday, Asaff returned to the ranch early in the morning. As he pulled up in his car, he saw Bradley sitting on the hood of his Chevy.

"What are ya doing here so early?" asked Asaff.

"I was fixin' to ask you the same thing," replied Bill.

"I came in so I could tell Mr. Prothro about that stained-glass window I broke last week and ask how much I owed him for it."

"You mean that stained-glass window Mr. Prothro got as a gift from Pope Paul [VI], the one from the Vatican?" Bill asked.

At the mention of a gift from the Pope, Asaff's face went flush. "No shit! Mr. Prothro really got that window from the Pope!"

"Yep! It was one of his most prized possessions," Bradley said. "But don't you worry about that window anymore."

"Why's that, Bill?" asked Tommy as a noticeable look of relief came over him.

"'Cause over the weekend I busted up every piece of glass in that lake house when I crashed Mr. Prothro's orange Scout [jeep] into it."

"What'd you say to Mr. Prothro?"

"Well, I called him up expecting that he'd fire my ass," Bradley confessed. "But the only thing he was concerned about was if I was hurt. When I told him I was okay, he said not to worry about it, that he could replace the lake house but he couldn't replace a person if he got seriously hurt or killed."

"Well, what do you think about that?" Tommy asked rhetorically.

Before Asaff could complete the question, Bradley chirped, "I think we can tear up the whole damn ranch, and he wouldn't give a shit about it . . . as long as no one got hurt!"[6]

On another occasion, Bill was filling up Prothro's jeep at a gas pump located on a small hill overlooking the ranch. But he forgot to put the truck in park. Asaff was at the bottom of the hill when the truck began a slow downward descent. Thinking he could stop the vehicle by himself, Tommy ran up to the front bumper and braced his body against it.

Meanwhile, Bradley had gotten into his own car and was speeding down the hill when he suddenly saw Asaff in the road in front of the jeep. Desperate to avoid a collision, Bill began pounding on the horn and screaming, "Get out of the way, you dumb son of a bitch!"

At the last second, Asaff hurled himself onto the side of the road. Somehow Bradley avoided crashing into the jeep. When he finally pulled over, a grateful Asaff jogged up to the car and said, "Thanks, Bill. You saved my life!"

"Don't forget it, either, you stupid motherfucker!" Bradley snapped.[7]

Bill also became close with James Street that summer. It made no difference to him that Street was a quarterback and could possibly replace him if he didn't perform well on the gridiron. Street, who was going into his sophomore year, was quite a colorful character himself. Like Bradley, he came from a small blue-collar town in East Texas and had a magnetic personality that endeared him to teammates. He also liked to have a good time. Once, Street, in his freshman year, was partying so hard he nearly drowned in a lake, earning the nickname "Rat." However, he preferred to be called "Slick," a moniker inspired by his oily dark hair, which he combed straight back.[8] The two teammates also shared a liberal attitude on race and a love of Black music. They could often be found together at Charlie's Playhouse, a Black bar in East Austin where they would join in with the band and sing Motown. "We were the only two white guys in the place," said Bradley. "Must've looked like we took a wrong turn and got lost. But we were always welcome there."[9]

Unlike Bradley, Street was not heavily recruited. Nor was he as talented, at least on the football field. His favorite sport was baseball, which Coach Royal allowed him to play at UT because he was a third-string quarterback and didn't look as if he would go any higher than that on the depth chart. No one could've predicted that James Street would become one of the best quarterbacks in Longhorns history.

Heading into the 1967 season, Texas was ranked fourth in the national polls. UT fans dubbed it the "Year of the 'Horns," believing that the team was on the cusp of another national championship. *Sports Illustrated* even put Bradley on the cover of its September 11 college football preview edition. "Bill Bradley, who played injured last year, is more than capable of topping last season's one-legged statistics: 36 completions, 335 yards rushing and a punting average of 42.5," wrote *SI*'s Dan Jenkins, pronouncing the Texas signal caller healthy after an off-season knee operation. "Bradley is an old-fashioned triple-threat back with a flair for the dramatic. He will be the deadliest quarterback in football on the keeper play, not just because of his own style but because he can hand off to Tailback Chris Gilbert, who rushed for 1,000 yards last year." Jenkins went on to rank the Longhorns' fourth, based on the offensive tandem of Bradley and Gilbert and a "vicious defense highlighted by fast pass rushers, savage linebacking, a fleet, experienced secondary."[10] But Darrell Royal knew better. "We're an average football team at best," he insisted. "I think all the hoopla is premature."[11] Of course, Royal was correct.

Texas opened the season on September 23 in Los Angeles with a 17–13 loss against fifth-ranked Southern Cal and its sleek running back O. J. Simpson, who rushed for 158 yards. Bradley marched the Steers 85 yards in fifteen plays to score the first touchdown on the 'Horns' second possession of the game. But USC scored 17 unanswered points before Bill found the end zone on a keeper in the fourth quarter for UT's second touchdown. With 1:38 remaining, Texas elected to go for a 2-point conversion to tie the score, but Bradley was tackled behind the line of scrimmage before he could get off a pass.[12]

Another loss followed; this one was an upset in the Southwest Conference opener against eighth-ranked Texas Tech, 19–13. The highwater mark of the contest for the Longhorns came in the first quarter with a 36-yard touchdown pass from Bradley to tight end Deryl Comer, but the point-after attempt failed, limiting UT's lead to 6–0. Tech countered with a field goal before the end of the quarter. Raiders' quarterback John Scovell took control of the game in the second period, pacing Tech to two touchdowns. Texas scored again on an 80-yard run by Chris Gilbert to tie the game at halftime. After a scoreless third quarter, Tech won the contest in the final period on an improbable 54-yard field goal.[13]

The Longhorns finally posted their first victory on October 7 with a 19–0 shutout of Oklahoma State to give head coach Darrell Royal his one hundredth career win.[14] The victory was also the first of six consecutive wins for the 'Horns, including routs against Rice (28–6) and Baylor (24–0).[15] Bill's performance improved markedly with each game. "Bradley has a quick arm and he's a tremendous running threat," pointed out Taylor McNeel, Baylor's defensive secondary coach. "His passing has improved over the last several weeks. He's smart. He won't throw the ball when his men are covered. When that happens, he relies on his own running ability."[16] Bill's passing statistics during the six-game win streak show his improvement.[17]

OPPONENT	PASS COMPLETED	PASS ATT.	%	YARDS	INTERCEPTIONS
Oklahoma State	2	9	22%	27	2
Oklahoma U	6	13	46%	74	0
Arkansas	6	11	55%	89	2
Rice	14	23	61%	238	1
Southern Methodist	12	15	80%	193	0
Baylor	14	17	82%	240	0

While the numbers reinforced the "Super Bill" moniker, Bradley did everything he could to downplay the image. "I always tried to put the team first," he said in a recent interview. "Sure, a quarterback gets most of the credit when his team wins, but I realized that my teammates put me in a position to win. I never saw myself as 'Super Bill.' The press kept referring to me like that. If anything, I was 'Stupid Bill,' like my closest friends still call me."[18]

Try as he might, Bradley could not shake the "Super Bill" label, especially after *Sports Illustrated* put him on the cover of its magazine. "That was the kiss of death for me," Bradley explained. "After that cover came out, every pass rusher in the Southwest Conference wanted a piece of me. If I tried to pass from the pocket, I'd get blindsided. If I ran, I'd get punched and kicked in the pile-up after the tackle."[19] Predictably, Bill played injured most of the season. He was plagued by a hip pointer, a shoulder separation, and ongoing problems with his right knee. In fact, Bradley's right side was tapped so heavily that he lost some of his mobility and was unable to scramble as effectively as he had at the beginning of the win streak.[20]

The Longhorns dropped their last two games of the season, first to Texas Christian, 24–17, and later to A&M, 10–7.[21] In those two games, Bradley was responsible for six turnovers—four interceptions and two fumbles. When asked if his injuries were the reason for the poor performance, Bill said, "I'm not going to blame injuries. I made a few mistakes. Fumbles and pass interceptions killed us. I just didn't execute as well as I needed to win more than six games."[22] The response was classic for Bradley. He *always* assumed responsibility whenever the Longhorns played poorly, whether he was the reason for it or not. That was a heavy burden after the 1967 campaign when the 'Horns finished 6-4 overall and 4-3 in the Southwest Conference. Disgusted, Royal declined a Bowl bid.[23]

Since 1964, when Texas won the national championship, the Longhorns finished the regular season at 6-4 for three straight years. That was unacceptable to Darrell Royal. There were rumors that he had gotten soft after winning the national title, that he spent more time on the banquet circuit than he did recruiting the kinds of athletes he needed to contend for a national title on a regular basis, and that the Board of Regents wanted to replace him.[24]

Before the first spring practice in March 1968, Royal gathered his players together and told them, "We will not be 6-4 again! We may be 0-10. We may be 10-0. But we will not be a mediocre 6-4 again!"[25] He also posted a sign inside the locker room at Memorial Stadium that read,

"The Longhorn Winning Tradition Will Not Be Entrusted to the Timid or the Weak."[26]

Royal was determined to restore the winning tradition he had created at UT in the early 1960s. To do that, he intended to weed out the timid and weak players on his roster—those who were not giving their very best effort—during spring practices so he could "go to war with the toughest, meanest motherfuckers" in the program that fall.[27]

"We knew something had to change," said Bob McKay, an offensive tackle. "If it didn't change, there were some guys who were going to be gone. We worked our asses off. When you crossed [Waller] Creek [which bordered the practice fields], there was nothing else in the world that was more important."[28]

Because the NCAA only allowed twenty official workouts in the spring, Royal and his staff stretched them out from the first week of March to the middle of April, which took up half the semester. Filmed scrimmages took place every Wednesday and Saturday. Time to review the films as well as blackboard instruction were also scheduled. Three-hour practice sessions were dominated by contact drills, the least popular one being the half-line drill. "The coaches lined us up fifteen yards apart and had us run into each other," explained linebacker Corby Robertson. "We hit hard too. Helmet-to-helmet [contact] was the way we were taught. The hitting was so hard that helmets were broken in that [half-line] drill."[29]

Practices were so brutal that some players were injured. Others had to go to the hospital. Still others quit the team. Those grueling practices seemed to confirm some of the allegations that one player, Gary Shaw, would later make in his 1972 book, *Meat on the Hoof: The Hidden World of Texas Football*. Among the charges were that the drills were unnecessarily violent and that the athletic trainer denied players permission to see a team physician for what later turned out to be serious injuries. According to Shaw, "players who were low on the depth chart" were especially vulnerable, because the coaches "wanted to run them off the team so they could reallocate their scholarship money to better players."[30]

However, Shaw's allegations were discredited by other Longhorns players who insisted that "if a player was injured or had a medical issue, it was addressed by the team's trainers and doctors immediately," and that Shaw "had an axe to grind because he was not mentally or physically tough." Instead, they explained that the intensity of the spring practices enabled Royal to restore a winning tradition.[31] According to Robertson, "What we went through in those practices prepared us to become a nationally ranked team. . . . If we weren't tough, we weren't going to win. You had to earn your position on the team, and if you couldn't cut it, you didn't stay."[32]

Bradley, who was entering his senior year, bought into the program wholeheartedly. He desperately wanted to complete his college career with a national championship and realized that the spring practices were critical to building the physical and mental toughness that were necessary to achieve that goal. "That spring we'd be running grass drills and guys would be throwing up," recalled Bob McKay. "Bill was like the rest of us. He worked his ass off. What made him so special for a quarterback was that he was right there with us running those shit drills. He wasn't a prima donna."[33]

Ted Koy, a running back who played on the 1969 national championship team, explained that the grueling spring practices were "critical to [not only] building a culture based . . . on physical and mental toughness but also [instilling] confidence and comradery." "Once the 1968 season began, you could *always* count on the next guy to do his job because you knew what he had been through to earn a spot on the team."[34]

Koy was one of the players who benefitted most from the spring practices. In fact, his impressive performance convinced Royal that the Longhorns would have to go with a new offensive formation. During the spring scrimmages, Royal was still running the I formation. Chris Gilbert, who had run for 1,000 yards the previous two seasons, was slotted as the tailback. Koy, who had been the swing man between fullback and tailback the previous year, was competing for an open fullback position with Steve Worster, a blue-chipper who had played on the freshman team the previous year. The competition between the two players was fierce.

"There were two major competitions that spring," recalled Koy in a recent interview. "[Steve] Worster and I were competing for the fullback position, and we also had two players competing for the defensive end position. We ran the I formation where the fullback kicks out the defensive end and the tailback runs off him. That was the basic strategy of that offense from a running standpoint. So, in those practice drills, the defensive end had no other responsibility than to come in and smash the running back and the running back had no other responsibility than to kick out the defensive end. You can imagine how violent the contact was.

"Once, Steve hit [defensive end] Bill Atessis so hard that he broke his face mask. In the collision, Worster fractured his nose, and there was blood gushing out all over the place. The trainer came over, patched him up, and Steve went back out. He didn't miss a single rotation! That's the kind of intensity Royal wanted to see that spring."[35]

If Royal had stayed with the I formation for the 1968 season, Koy and Worster would have alternated at fullback. But Koy had exceptional speed, and Worster, exceptional power. Wanting to use those assets to his advantage, Royal decided to go with a triple-option offense to maximize the talent he had in the backfield.

During the summer, Royal got together with his backfield coach, Emory Bellard, to devise a new offensive formation that would allow the Longhorns to use Koy, Worster, and Gilbert in the running attack. Initially, the pipe-smoking, offense-devising Bellard suggested that the Longhorns adopt the Veer formation used successfully by Bill Yeoman at the University of Houston. But Royal vetoed the suggestion because the Veer, which had split backs, didn't have a lead blocker. Bellard went back to work with his yellow legal pad. Borrowing from the option-running offenses used by Franklin "Pepper" Rodgers at Kansas and Gene Stallings at Texas A&M and utilizing the principles of the Veer, Bellard devised a wholly new formation called the Wishbone because it was shaped like an inverted *Y* or a "wishbone from a turkey."[36]

The Wishbone was an effective alternative to the pass-oriented offense that had become popular in college football. It also revolutionized the college game by offering the quarterback a triple option. He could hand off to the fullback, keep the ball around the end, or pitch it at the very last second to one full-throttle halfback riding behind the other as lead blocker. The quarterback's decision would be determined by how the defensive linemen reacted. On paper, the formation was balanced and capable of running effectively in either direction. It also met Royal's criterion of incorporating a lead blocker.

Royal quickly embraced the Wishbone, which reminded him of the Split-T formation he learned as a quarterback at Oklahoma under Bud Wilkinson. The only difference was the positioning of the fullback a few steps closer to the quarterback. Royal realized that the Wishbone offered a nearly unstoppable offense for the 'Horns, who were undersized compared to the other teams in the Southwest Conference.[37] But it was not an easy transition to make.

According to Ted Koy, "The Wishbone was completely different than the I formation, which we used before. It was an extremely detailed offense that had to be run with great synchrony, with great precision. For all three running backs, the first step was so important, especially if you're going to the outside, because the lead blocker had to be parallel to the line of scrimmage for about three strides and then run down while the trailing halfback had to be on his outside hip for [the Wishbone] to work. When it works, it really screws up the opposing defense because there are so many options you can run off of it."[38]

When the Longhorns reported to preseason practice in late August, Bellard summoned the three quarterbacks—Bradley, James Street, and Eddie Phillips—and walked them through the new offense.[39] "What Bellard wanted to do was to take the wingback in a wing formation with two running backs and put him in the backfield," explained Bradley. "That gave us three running backs. I was [the quarterback] under center. One yard behind me was the fullback, who was [Steve] Worster. Then you had the two halfbacks flanking Steve about a yard and a half behind between the guard and the tackle. [Ted] Koy played the right halfback and [Chris] Gilbert was at left half. On paper, [the Wishbone] was really an ideal offense because of the strength of those three running backs. But I questioned whether it would work."[40]

Even after running the new offense throughout the preseason, the three Longhorns signal callers had serious doubts. "None of us believed that the triple option would work because it had to run perfectly," explained James Street. "There was absolutely no margin for error."[41]

Bradley, now a senior tricaptain along with Robertson and Gilbert, knew that the fifth-ranked Longhorns needed to win from the jump in 1968. He also realized that the success of the team was tied to the Wishbone and his ability to operate it effectively. But no matter how hard he tried, Bill could not make the adjustment.

Texas opened the season on September 21 with a 20–20 tie against eleventh-ranked Houston. The Wishbone was anything but successful. Bradley fumbled the ball twice and threw three interceptions while trying to execute the new offense.[42] That was unacceptable. He swore that he would be better the following week, but his performance did not improve, and the Longhorns lost to archrival Texas Tech, a 17-point underdog. The Raiders shut down UT's running attack, limiting Gilbert to just 29 yards on twelve carries. Bradley ran for 60 yards on ten carries but gained only 12 yards on the one pass he completed of four attempts. He also threw an interception.

With the 'Horns down 28–7 in the third quarter, Royal pulled James Street aside and said, "Hell, you can't do any worse. Get in there!" Street rallied the Steers, throwing for 108 yards on eight completions in seventeen attempts for two touchdowns. But it wasn't enough, and Texas lost 31–22. After the game, Royal was noncommittal about who would start at quarterback the following week against Oklahoma State.[43]

With a record of 0-1-1, the Longhorns had become a huge embarrassment to the UT administration, the alum, their fans, and themselves. Something had to be done.

On Sunday morning, September 29, Royal summoned Bradley to his office and gave him the bad news. "Bill, you are no longer my quarterback," he said matter-of-factly. "If you want to keep your scholarship, you can come out to practice today, and we'll try to find a spot for you."[44]

Bradley was blindsided by the decision. When he went to Royal's office that morning, the *last* thing he expected to hear was that he was losing his job as the starting quarterback. He thought that the head coach wanted to talk with him about making some adjustments to the offense, or at worst to bawl him out for his lackluster performance against Texas Tech. Instead, Royal, by demoting Bradley, was telling him that he failed, that he did not live up to all the hype that was expected of "Super Bill Bradley," that he could not lead the Longhorns to another national championship, that he was simply not good enough. No one had ever told him that before. It was a painful realty check.

When Bill returned to his dorm room, he broke down. Unburdening himself to his roommate and close friend, Bill Hall, Bradley struggled to comprehend the fact that he was no longer the starting quarterback. Hall, the team's equipment manager, found himself in an untenable position. Unlike the players who feared Darrell Royal, Hall had earned the head coach's trust and respect for his fierce loyalty and hard work over the last four years. Not only did he revere Royal, but he also would never do anything to disappoint him, most of all question his judgement. At the same time, Bradley was Hall's best friend, and he genuinely felt his pain.

"When Bill came back to our dorm room, he was in tears," recalled Hall. "He was very depressed and very emotional. I had known him since our junior year at Palestine High School, and I had *never* seen him that upset before. But all I could do was be a sounding board."[45]

As he sat there listening to his best friend grieve, Hall was surprised that Bill never said anything negative about his replacement, James Street. Then he realized how similar the two personalities were. Both were "extremely competitive athletes, but not from an ego perspective." "They wanted to win," said Hall, "but to win for the team. Neither was looking to get all the attention. In that way, Bill and James were carbon copies of each other. That's why they not only respected but loved each other."[46]

Hall could also sense that all the expectations and pressure that had been foisted on Bradley by the sportswriters, coaches, and fans over the last four years had come to a head. It must have been an overwhelming burden for his friend to carry. Now, as the former quarterback worked through his pain, he began to release that burden and focus on the team. After composing himself, Bradley confided, "I either quit and go home, or I gut it up and try to help the team win."[47]

If Bill gave any further thought to quitting, it ended when he phoned his father back in Palestine. "The Bradleys don't quit!" Joe Hill Bradley exploded after he learned of his son's demotion. "Your teammates voted you captain, so you go out there to practice today and show 'em what you're made of. If you quit now, you don't have a home here!"[48] Now Bill had to ante up and show his father, his head coach, his teammates, and the college football world what kind of a man he was.

News of Bradley's demotion spread like wildfire. When he got to practice on Monday afternoon, Bill saw sportswriters from every major newspaper and magazine, including *Sports Illustrated*, *Sport*, *Newsweek*, and *Time*. All of Texas—make that the nation—wanted to see how Bradley would respond to the demotion.

Although Bill was now the fourth-team wide receiver and the punter, he was still a captain, and he had to act like one. Determined to break the tension among his teammates, he approached James Street and asked him to throw a deep pass. Then he undid the strings of his sweatpants and sprinted downfield. As he dove for the ball, Bradley's pants dropped to his ankles and he landed on the turf with nothing but the sun shining on his bare ass. When he got up, *everyone* was laughing—his teammates, the sportswriters, and even Coach Royal.[49] It was a stroke of genius. That was the moment Bill Bradley became a leader.

"I give Bill a lot of credit," said Bob McKay. "He handled the demotion like you would hope any teammate would—that is, to move on and place the team ahead of himself. Bill was like everyone's brother. He was a *crazy-ass* brother, but we all loved him."[50]

After practice, Bradley gathered his teammates together inside the locker room and told them, "I want all you guys to get behind Rat [James Street] because we're going to win this damn conference and go all the way to a national title."[51]

"If he wanted to, Bill could've caused a huge split on that team," insisted Ted Koy. "He could've bad-mouthed the program or quit the team altogether, and that would have divided us. Instead, he rose above the adversity, and his example really united us as a team. I think I respected Bill even more after that."[52]

On October 5 James Street started at quarterback against Oklahoma State. Street's efforts at running the Wishbone were just as awkward as Bradley's had been until Royal allowed him to pass the ball. He hit split end Cotton Speyrer with a 60-yard aerial strike to put the Longhorns on the board late in the first quarter, and after Happy Feller kicked the extra point, the 'Horns led, 7–0. Texas increased its margin to 10–0 on a 36-yard field goal by Rob Layne in the second quarter and added a second touchdown on a 2-yard plunge by Steve Worster in the third period.

Meanwhile, the 'Horns' defense had limited the Cowpokes to a field goal, which would prove to be their only score of the game. Bradley, who punted masterfully during the contest, drove the Cowpokes back on their heels with a 67-yarder that barely rolled into the end zone with six and a half minutes to play in the game. OSU quarterback Ronnie Johnson fumbled on the next play, and end Mike Perrin recovered the ball for Texas. Five plays later, Bill entered the contest at split end and scored a touchdown on a 4-yard alley-oop pass from Street. With 4:19 remaining, the Cowpokes threatened to score, but Perrin intercepted the ball and returned it for a quick 6, icing the game for Texas, 31–3.[53]

After the game, the sportswriters searched for Bradley in the film room where they conducted their interviews. But he was nowhere to be found. "Bill asked not to come in here," Royal told the writers. "And I think that's his privilege." When asked how Bradley was taking the demotion, the Longhorns' coach said, "Bill's attitude is good. I think it would be fine if writers would leave him alone."[54]

Bradley chose to suffer in silence. He knew that anything he said to the press could be misinterpreted. Sportswriters were always looking for an angle, some tidbit of information that could be sensationalized for readers who were eager to learn anything, positive or negative, about the 'Horns. He also knew that the writers would be comparing him to Street, one of his best friends, and he did not want to detract from James's or the team's success, so he remained silent.

Of all the writers who covered the Longhorns, only one had the guts to admit that the press shared the blame for Bradley's demotion. He was Dan Cook of the *San Antonio Express-News*, one of the most insightful, humorous, and brutally honest sportswriters in Texas. In his October 8 column, Cook wrote,

> We took a high school kid, tossed a cloak on him, put him on a pedestal and called him "Super Bill." We sold him to every Longhorn booster because they were eager to buy. No matter how much was written about "Super Bill" it was never enough because football fans have enormous appetites for publicity on their favorites. So, we wrote more.
>
> In the opening hours of his collegiate career young Bill suffered a banged-up knee and a badly bruised hip. But he never whimpered or complained. He hid the pain and hobbled on, fighting to produce the gridiron miracles he'd once performed on high school fields.
>
> When the miracles failed to come, we all traced the void back to his injuries. After all, sportswriters hate to be wrong just as coaches hate to lose.
>
> Now, in his senior season and perfectly healthy for the first time, Bradley has failed to earn the cloak and title of "Super Bill." He's not even Jack Armstrong, the All-American boy. He's just a better-than-average college quarterback who passes poorly and punts brilliantly.
>
> So, everyone points the finger of guilt at either Bradley or Royal while the sportswriters assist with the directions.[55]

Cook's words, as truthful as they were, provided Bill little consolation. Bradley's time as the 'Horns' quarterback was over, regardless of the reason. What mattered more to him was the team and what they thought. On that score, Bill had nothing to fear. His teammates understood that Street's effectiveness with the Wishbone had nothing to do with Bill's leadership. Both quarterbacks were superb leaders who inspired confidence in their teammates. Bill's inability to run the Wishbone was due to a chronically injured right knee and the split-second decision-making required to run a highly synchronized offense. Those factors were beyond his control.

"After Bill tore his knee up as in '66, it continued to bother him over the next two years," explained Ted Koy. "He had to be heavily taped, and that not only limited his mobility but also his ability to run the Wishbone.

That offense had to be run with great precision. The quarterback must make a split-second decision on who's getting the ball. Because of his bad knee, Bill lacked that last-second step. Street, on the other hand, was able to make that pitch in the last nanosecond and have two blockers protect him."[56]

On October 12 Texas played Oklahoma University, and the Wishbone finally lived up to its billing. Down 20–19 and with less than three minutes to play, Texas got the ball on its own 15-yard line. Street alternated the running attack with short passes to orchestrate an 85-yard drive for a come-from-behind, 26–20 victory.[57] The following week, he quarterbacked the Longhorns to a 39–29 win against ninth-ranked Arkansas.[58] The Wishbone made both of these victories look easy, and with each successive victory Royal came to believe that he was on the cusp of another national title.

So, what had happened? Why did the Wishbone offense finally start to click for Street when it was such a dismal failure for Bradley?

"Remember, Bill only had two games to learn the Wishbone," linebacker Corby Robertson explained. "After the Texas Tech game—Bill's final game at quarterback—Willie Zapalac, our offensive-line coach, was studying the game film and noticed that [fullback] Steve Worster was getting to the point of attack before our linemen could deliver their blocks. He was also getting there without the power and momentum he needed to gain yardage. When Zapalac pointed this out to Royal and Bellard, they decided to move Worster back a few steps away from the quarterback to give him the momentum he needed to pick up yardage. All Street had to do was step back and pivot with his right foot, stick the ball out and lead Worster as he approached the line of scrimmage. I'm not taking anything away from James. He still had to read the defense and to decide on which option he should take. But the longer he ran the Wishbone the more comfortable and more effective he became as a quarterback. I just wonder how much better Bill would've run that offense if the coaches had made the adjustment to the fullback position sooner."[59]

Instead, Bradley was limited to punting duties and an occasional appearance at wide receiver. His success as a punter continued unabated by whatever regrets he still had about the demotion. Confirmation came from Leon Cross, an assistant coach at the University of Oklahoma, who wrote Bill a short letter after the Longhorns' come-from-behind victory over the Sooners on October 12. "Your play on Saturday and your punting were very important parts of [UT's] win over us," he wrote. "Only a true champion can do what you did Saturday, especially after all the criticism and unfortunate publicity you received earlier. I just wanted to tell you how much I admire your courage."[60]

Cross might have intended to offer Bradley some sympathy, but he "wasn't blowing smoke up my ass either," recalled Bill.[61]

According to Oklahoma tight end Steve Zabel, Bradley *did* play a critical role in the 'Horns' come-from-behind victory over OU. "Back in those days, if you punted the ball and it landed in the end zone but spun back out, the offense had to start on the 1-yard line, or the ball was dead wherever it stopped spinning," explained Zabel, who would become Bradley's teammate on the Philadelphia Eagles. "Billy punted left-footed, and that put a lot of spin on the ball. I'll never forget seeing those high, spirals coming down and hitting on the goal line or the 2- or 3-yard line. I'll bet he had three or four punts that went dead inside the 5-yard line. That put our offense in a terrible position. And in football, field position means everything."[62]

With Texas down, 14–6, early in the third quarter, Bradley nailed a 38-yard punt that hit five yards deep into the OU end zone, bounced back out, and died at the 1-yard line. Later, in the fourth quarter, after Texas had taken the lead, 17–14, and Oklahoma was threatening to score, Bill punted a 41-yarder that died on the opposition's 2. "Even Fred Astaire's toe doesn't have that kind of talent," observed Ed Fowler of the *Austin American-Statesman*, comparing Bradley's footwork to that of the finest dancer in American film history.[63]

Unbeknownst to him, Bill Bradley would not have to wait much longer to return to the spotlight. During the third week of October, Mike Campbell, the Longhorns' defensive coordinator, made a spur-of-the moment request that changed Bill's football career—and life—forever. The Longhorns were on their Waller Creek practice fields preparing for their upcoming game against Rice. Campbell, unhappy with the performance of his secondary, spit out a chaw of tobacco in disgust. Looking up at the tower where Darrell Royal was perched overseeing the various drills, Campbell hollered, "Hey, Darrell! You using ol' Bradley down there on offense?"

"Nope," replied Royal.

"Well, send him down here," barked Campbell.

When the head coach nodded his approval, Bill jogged down to the defense, lined up at right cornerback and found himself returning to a position he had played in high school.[64]

Defensive back Tom Campbell, one of Mike's twin sons, said that his father "recognized that Bill had quickness and speed, and that's what he wanted in the secondary. Dad also knew that it would be an easy transition for Bill because he had already played defensive back in high school and on the freshman team. Plus, Bill's experience in reading opposing defenses as a quarterback would be a major advantage, and it was. He came up with quite a few interceptions after he made the transition to defense."[65]

On Saturday, October 26, Texas played Rice in Houston, and Bradley made his first collegiate appearance on the defense at cornerback. The score was tied, 7–7, at halftime. But the Longhorns took over in the second half. Midway through the third quarter, defensive tackle Loyd Wainscott blocked an Owls' punt. Linebacker Tom Campbell recovered the ball and ran 31 yards for a touchdown to give the 'Horns the lead, and Feller made a 25-yard field goal later in the quarter to increase the UT lead to 17–7.[66]

"I really thought we could come back," said Owls quarterback Robby Shelton. "But then the interceptions by [Bill] Bradley and [Tom] Campbell killed us."[67]

Bradley's interception came off a Shelton pass intended for split end Larry Davis. It was a one-on-one situation, and Bill read the pass immediately after Shelton threw it. All Davis could do was watch helplessly as the ball fell into Bill's hands. "I thought Bradley played fairly well, especially when it was his first time back there [in the secondary]," said Davis after the game. "It's pretty hard to learn how to play the defensive backfield."[68]

Bill's interception led to another Longhorns touchdown. Tom Campbell iced the game when he returned another interception 16 yards to set up the final Texas touchdown, a 1-yard run by Bobby Callison, and Happy Feller kicked the point after for the 38–14 victory.[69]

For the remainder of the season, Bradley played in the same backfield with sophomore Freddie Joe Steinmark, a 5-foot-9, 166-pound safety who, like Bill, was smaller than most of his teammates. "But he was tough as nails," recalled Bradley, who embraced Freddie, though Steinmark was two years younger. "Freddie had talent, but he also worked his ass off. He was a great guy too—very enthusiastic, very upbeat."[70]

The next year, Steinmark starred for a Longhorns' team that captured the national title. Sadly, Freddie, near the end of the season, was diagnosed with a malignant bone tumor just above his left knee and had to have his leg amputated at the hip. Unable to play in the 1970 Cotton Bowl, Steinmark stood on the sideline with his teammates, cheering on Texas in its victory against Notre Dame, 21–17.[71]

Steinmark's heroic fight against cancer inspired Congress to pass the National Cancer Act of 1971. President Richard Nixon signed the bill into law, beginning the national "War on Cancer."[72] Freddie died on June 6, 1971. The next year he was honored by the Longhorns, who named the scoreboard at Texas Memorial Stadium after him.[73]

On November 2, 1968, Texas faced off against Southern Methodist University. The contest reunited Bradley with his Big 33 soul brother, Jerry LeVias. Unlike the previous year's game, there were no racial epithets from the Longhorns bench hurled at the powerful Black fullback, who was an ever-present danger. LeVias caught six passes for 124 yards, the first two of which set up the lone SMU touchdown. Texas tried to limit LeVias with heavy coverage on pass plays, while Bradley, who averaged 44.6 yards per punt, tried to eliminate his friend's kick-return threat by booting the ball high.[74] Aside from LeVias, Texas completely dominated the game. Street completed nine passes in fifteen attempts for 167 yards while the trio of Chris Gilbert, Steve Worster, and Ted Koy ran for a total of 380 yards to pace the Longhorns to lopsided 38–7 victory.[75]

During the next two weeks, Texas easily dispatched Baylor, 47–26, and Texas Christian, 47–21.[76] The Wishbone had transformed a Longhorns team that had averaged just 19 points in 1967 to an unstoppable offensive juggernaut that was suddenly putting up 47 points per game. Its success was due in part to powerful blocking up front by senior guard Danny Abbott and junior tackle Bob McKay, who would be a consensus All-American choice in '69. Just as important, Gilbert, Koy, and Worster also blocked when they were not carrying the ball, paving the way for Street's stealth-timed pitches and deep aerial strikes.[77]

Bradley had become comfortable in his new role as a defensive cornerback. Baylor's Bob Stephenson, a tight end who played with Bradley at Palestine High School, admitted that he was "pretty concerned about Bill's frame of mind" after he learned of his friend's demotion in early October. "This was a guy who had high expectations placed on him from a very young age," explained Stephenson. "Because he was such an amazing quarterback, Bill was also used to a lot of publicity. That demotion could've been his undoing. But when we played Texas on November 9, I saw the same old Bill Bradley—very positive, very upbeat. He refused to allow that setback destroy him as it would a lesser person. Instead, he took a bad situation and turned it into a positive."[78]

Bradley capitalized on the knowledge and experience he gained as a signal caller to excel on defense. Not only could he decoy opposing quarterbacks, setting them up for an interception, but he also learned how to frustrate a receiver at the line of scrimmage. In fact, Bill added a twist of his own to Coach Mike Campbell's philosophy of "bending, but never breaking" on defense. Realizing that he would earn the wrath of "Iron Mike" if he allowed a receiver to get behind him in coverage, Bradley, against TCU, keyed on Linzy Cole, the Superfrogs' All–Southwest Conference wide receiver. "Bill would go up to Cole at the line of scrimmage and knock the living shit out of him," said Paul Kristynik, another Longhorns cornerback. "In the first quarter, Cole didn't catch a single pass. In the second quarter their quarterback didn't even bother to throw to him."

At halftime, Coach Campbell got in Bill's face and screamed, "Bradley, what the hell are you doing out there?"

Confused, Bill had no idea he was doing anything wrong. "I don't know, coach," he said, bewildered.

"Well, I don't know either!" barked Campbell as he slapped the cornerback on his ass. "But whatever it is, keep it up!"

"What Bradley was doing was playing bump-and-run," explained Kristynik. "That is, going up to the receiver before the snap and knocking the shit out of him at the line of scrimmage. That's standard operating procedure these days. But not many people know that Bill Bradley invented it."[79]

On November 28, when Texas A&M traveled to Austin's Memorial Stadium to play the Longhorns in the last game of the regular season, Bradley was ready for revenge. The year before, Texas lost the Southwest Conference championship to the Aggies in the final game of the season. Bill had thrown four interceptions in that 10–7 defeat. He swore that he would do everything humanly possible to secure a Longhorns victory this time.

When Bradley, Gilbert, and Robertson went out to the 50-yard line for the coin toss, the referee did the introductions. "Captain Bradley, this is Captain [Billy] Hobbs [of A&M]," said the official. "Since Texas A&M is the visiting team, Captain Hobbs will call it."

Hobbs called heads, but the coin came up tails.

"Captain Bradley," the official continued, "it's tails, so you can receive the ball or choose which end of the field you want to defend."

Looking the referee straight in the eye, Wild Bill snapped, "We don't give a shit."

Startled by the answer, the official looked at Hobbs, then back at Bradley, and insisted, "Captain Bradley, you must make a choice!"

"Like I said, we really don't give a shit, but if you insist, we'll take the damn ball."

When Bradley returned to the Texas sideline, Royal walked over and asked, "Bill, what were you doing out there?"

"Don't worry about it, coach," he replied. "We're going to kick their ass."[80]

Bradley's response was prophetic. Texas trounced A&M, 35–14, with all 35 of its points coming in the first half, allowing Royal to play all of his substitutes in the second half. One of the reasons for the Longhorns' success was their defense. When the Aggies tried to run the ball, the Steers' defensive line, led by senior tackle Loyd Wainscott, shut them down, holding A&M to minus 14 yards rushing. Then, when the Aggies tried to pass, Bradley made quarterback Edd Hargett's life a living hell, intercepting him four times. That was not an easy feat either. Hargett, one of most successful passers in A&M football history, had led the Aggies to a Southwest Conference championship and a win in the Cotton Bowl against Alabama just a year before.

After the third interception, Hargett went to the sidelines and asked A&M head coach Gene Stallings, "What do I do about Bradley?"

"Don't throw anything his way!" replied Stallings disgustedly.[81]

After the game, Royal singled out Bradley for his outstanding performance. "Bill made four fantastic interceptions," said the head coach, "and he went some distance to get some of them."

Bradley's four interceptions against A&M set a Southwest Conference single-game record that still stands today. But Bill downplayed the achievement at the time. "I didn't do any flips or cartwheels when I heard about the record," he told sportswriter Jack Agnes of the *Houston Post*. "But I was glad to get it."[82]

All-American linebacker Corby Robertson, who was the captain and signal caller for UT's defense, is still in awe of Bradley's performance against A&M. "That was one of the most outstanding games I ever saw him play," insisted Robertson recently. "And Bill played a lot of outstanding games as a quarterback at UT. If he had played the whole season as a defensive back, there's no telling what he could have accomplished. Bill was such a key part of our secondary that [UT defensive coordinator] Mike Campbell adjusted the defense around him."[83]

Bradley played his final collegiate game on January 1, 1969, when third-ranked Texas faced thirteenth-ranked Tennessee at the Cotton Bowl in Dallas. It was the rubber match in the Cotton Bowl series between the two teams, with the Volunteers scoring a 20–14 upset over the Longhorns in

1951 and the 'Horns pounding Tennessee two years later, 16–0. Although the 1969 contest might have been a bowl game, Texas trounced Tennessee like it was any ordinary team, scoring 28 points in the first half while allowing none. It wasn't much better in the second half for the Volunteers. The Longhorns' offense was driven by the Wishbone trio of Chris Gilbert, Steve Worster, and Ted Koy, each of whom had a touchdown run, while wide receiver Cotton Speyrer caught two touchdown passes from James Street, the last one a 79-yarder that increased the Texas lead to 36–6.

The Longhorns' defense was just as punishing. Volunteers quarterback Bobby Scott never had a chance against the muscle of Bill Atessis, Loyd Wainscott, Lee Brooks, and Willie Zapalac Jr. during the first half. He did manage to get Tennessee on the scoreboard in the third quarter when he connected with wideout Garry Kreis for a 17-yard touchdown pass. Later, with just two minutes remaining in the game, Scott found wide receiver Mike Price in the end zone to narrow the score to 36–13, which proved to be the final tally. Aside from those two scores, the 'Horns' secondary play of Bradley, Tom Campbell, and Ronnie Ehrig shut down the Volunteers' passing game.[84]

An amusing incident occurred during the game because Bradley did not always focus on his assignment until the last second. During the first quarter, Tennessee lined up with its top two receivers—Ken DeLong and Lester McClain—on the same side of the scrimmage line. Bradley, playing defensive back, was supposed to cover DeLong, but the receiver broke loose and headed straight down the field along the hash mark while Bill sprinted in the opposite direction.

Campbell, the rover back, was assigned McClain, who darted across to the other side of the field out of his coverage. Realizing that Bill was nowhere near his assigned receiver, Campbell took off at full speed toward the end zone and saw DeLong standing alone waiting for his quarterback to throw him the ball. Hoping to break up the pass, Campbell, in a last-ditch effort, somehow managed to knock the ball out of the receiver's hand. Two seconds later, Bradley appeared in the end zone.

"Bill, what the hell are you doing?" cried Campbell, incredulous at the sight of his teammate.

"Shit, Tom," Bradley replied innocently, "I just wanted to see what you were doing over here."[85]

Texas finished the season ranked third by the Associated Press, with an overall record of 9-1-1.[86] The Longhorns also shared the Southwest Conference championship with Arkansas, both teams completing the season with a 6-1 conference record. The Wishbone had been an unqualified success with the trio of Chris Gilbert, Ted Koy, and Steve Worster rushing for a combined 3,315 yards and 37 touchdowns, while the Longhorns' offense made only 154 passing attempts.[87]

Despite the 'Horns' third ranking, halfback Chris Gilbert insisted that he and his teammates felt that "there was no team in the country that could beat us, including [first-ranked] Ohio State and [second-ranked] Penn State." "We truly believed that we were the best ream in the nation," added Gilbert. "That 1968 squad started what would eventually become the longest winning streak in Longhorn history at 30-0."[88]

Only eight of Texas's twenty-two starters were seniors in '68, so the Longhorns were poised to compete for—and win—the national championship for the next two years.[89] Unfortunately, Bradley would not be around to enjoy those two seasons, having been selected by the Philadelphia Eagles in the National Football League's 1969 draft. But his experience at the University of Texas prepared him well for the challenges he faced in professional football.

Although Bill considered his college career to be a mixed blessing, many of his Longhorns teammates believe that Darrell Royal did him a favor by demoting him from quarterback and that Mike Campbell did him an even bigger favor by making him a defensive back.[90] Not only would Bill be All-Pro at that position, but he also would become a leader for his teammates on the Eagles and one of the most popular football players in the City of Brotherly Love.[91]

6 Penthouse to Shithouse

When Bradley reported to the Philadelphia Eagles' training camp in August 1969, he didn't know what to expect. Unbeknownst to him, Herman Ball, the team's chief scout, and his assistant Jackie Graves, watched Bill play defensive back at the Hula Bowl, a college All-Star game, in January and liked what they saw so much they recommended that the Eagles sign him. But neither one contacted Bradley. Nor did Bill have any clue that he was going to be drafted until head coach Jerry Williams selected him in the third round as a "punter/player." Adding to Bradley's uncertainty was the *player* designation, indicating that his position on the field was to be determined during camp.

"Truth is, I was expecting to go to the Dallas Cowboys," recalled Bradley, a lifelong Texan who would have jumped at the opportunity to play pro ball in his native state. "Tex Schramm, the general manager of the Cowboys, and his chief scout, Gil Brandt, promised to draft me in the second round. Well, they never did. I fell to the third round, where Philadelphia picked me. Once the Cowboys broke their promise it was easy for me to hate them. I still do. As it turned out, getting drafted by the Eagles was the best thing that ever happened to me."[1]

At the time, however, the Cowboys were on the cusp of an NFL dynasty, while the Eagles were among the worst teams in the league. Even Bill had to admit that "after having all that success with the Longhorns, going to the Eagles was like going from the penthouse to the shithouse."[2] It had not always been that way, though.

The Philadelphia Eagles were established in 1933 by Bert Bell and Lud Wray, who were determined to bring a winner to the City of Brotherly

Love. To that end, Bell, the privileged son of a wealthy lawyer and an All-American quarterback at the University of Pennsylvania, and Wray, his teammate and head coach of the NFL's Boston Braves, purchased the defunct Frankford Yellow Jackets franchise for $2,500 and went to work.[3]

Inspired by the Blue Eagle of President Franklin D. Roosevelt's National Recovery Administration, Bell and Wray named the new franchise the Philadelphia Eagles. The team initially played its home games at Baker Bowl, the Phillies' ballpark, but later moved to Shibe Park, home of the Athletics. It was composed of former Penn, Temple, and Villanova players who competed on the gridiron for a few years before getting real jobs. The leatherheads played their first game on October 15, 1933, losing to the Giants, 56–0, at New York City's Polo Grounds. It was a dark omen of seasons to come. Three years later, Bell became the sole owner when he purchased the franchise for $4,500. He also became the team's coach, trainer, scout, business manager, janitor, ticket seller, and publicist. The Eagles struggled over the next decade, never winning more than four games per season.[4] Tired of operating in the red, Bell sold the franchise to Alexis Thompson, a millionaire playboy and Olympic medalist, for $165,000 in 1940.[5]

The team's first winning season came in 1943, when the Eagles merged with the Pittsburgh Steelers due to the manpower shortage created by World War II. Known as the "Steagles," the club was cocoached by Earle "Greasy" Neale and Walt Kiesling and finished 5-4-1. Never intended as a permanent arrangement, the Steagles dissolved at the end of the season.[6]

Returning to Philadelphia, the Eagles quickly became a perennial contender, thanks to Neale, who would go on to coach the team for the next nine seasons. Paced by such future Pro Football Hall of Famers as running back Steve Van Buren, end Pete Pihos, and linebackers Alex Wojciechowicz and Chuck Bednarik, the Eagles dominated the league for six seasons. They finished second in the NFL Eastern Division in 1944, 1945, and 1946; won the division title in 1947; and then scored successive shutout victories in the 1948 and 1949 championship games.[7]

Despite the on-field success, owner Lex Thompson lost $88,000 in 1948 alone. Strapped for cash, Thompson, on January 15, 1949, sold the team for

$250,000 to a syndicate of one hundred Philadelphia businessmen. The new majority owner was James P. Clark, president of Highway Express, one of the nation's largest trucking companies. Clark was a forceful, outspoken man who immediately locked horns with Neale. Their stormy relationship came to an end late in the 1950 season when Clark fired the head coach.[8] After that, the Eagles slowly regressed.

By the mid-1950s the Birds routinely finished in the bottom half of the league, dropping to last place in their division in 1958. The rebuilding process began with a new head coach, Buck Shaw, and a change in venue from Shibe Park to Franklin Field at the University of Pennsylvania. Franklin Field seated over sixty thousand, compared to Shibe Park, which had a more limited capacity of thirty-nine thousand.[9]

In just three years, Shaw brought another championship to Philadelphia. Led by quarterback Norm Van Brocklin, flanker Tommy McDonald, tight end Pete Retzlaff, and Chuck Bednarik, who played center on offense and linebacker on defense, the Eagles won the Eastern Division with a 10-2 record. On December 26, 1960, the Birds defeated Vince Lombardi's Green Bay Packers at Franklin Field, 17–13, for their third NFL championship. Fittingly, the game ended as Bednarik tackled Packers fullback Jim Taylor and refused to allow him to stand until the last seconds had ticked away.[10]

The Eagles' renaissance proved to be short-lived, as the organization experienced turmoil on and off the gridiron. Van Brocklin had come to Philadelphia from the Los Angeles Rams in 1958 with the tacit understanding that he would retire after the 1960 season and succeed Shaw as head coach. When ownership promoted assistant coach Nick Skorich instead, Van Brocklin quit the organization and left for Minnesota, where he became head coach of the expansion Vikings. Back-up quarterback Sonny Jurgensen became the Eagles' starter for the 1961 season and guided the team to a 10-4 record. Unfortunately, the Birds finished a half game behind the first-place New York Giants in the Eastern Conference standings.[11]

In 1962 the Eagles were decimated by injury and managed only three wins. Ownership was also in turmoil. Clark, who was plagued by poor health, died on April 17 at age sixty-two. Many of the other owners had sold their interest in the team, as the original group of one hundred dwindled to sixty-five.[12] The remaining partners decided to sell the team. Eagles president Frank McNamee began to entertain suitors, including the Kennedy brothers. President John F. Kennedy, an avid football fan, was considering his options after a second term in office. He would still be a relatively young man at age fifty-one, and the possibility of owning a football team appealed to him. In early October, JFK directed his youngest brother, Senator Edward Kennedy, to schedule a meeting with McNamee and the other owners to discuss a possible deal. But before the meeting could take place the president was confronted with the Cuban Missile Crisis, and he never discussed the possibility of purchasing the Eagles after that.[13]

After Kennedy's assassination, Jerry Wolman, a thirty-six-year-old millionaire real estate developer, purchased the Eagles for an unprecedented $5.5 million. In 1964 Wolman signed Joe Kuharich, a former St. Louis Cardinals and Washington Redskins coach, to a fifteen-year contract. He would serve as both the general manager and head coach.[14]

Over the next five seasons, Kuharich's teams failed to make the playoffs, as he ran the franchise into the ground. He began by trading Sonny Jurgenson, a future Hall of Fame quarterback, to Washington for Norm Snead, a much-less-talented signal caller who lacked the ability to lift the Eagles out of mediocrity. Kuharich also wasted such top-tier talent as Timmy Brown, Ollie Matson, and Ben Hawkins by failing to surround them with better players. By 1968 the fans were in full revolt. Chants of "Joe must go" echoed through the bleachers of Franklin Field. Adding insult to injury, the Eagles managed to eke out meaningless wins in two of the last three games of the season. Those two victories cost them the first pick in the NFL draft, who turned out to be running back O. J. Simpson, another future Hall of Famer. Instead, the Eagles, with the second pick, chose Leroy Keyes, who played just four years in Philadelphia.[15]

Heading into the final game of the 1968 season, the Eagles were 2-11 and scheduled to play the Minnesota Vikings after a tremendous snowfall the day before. During the game, fans vented their frustration by not only booing Santa Claus but pelting him with snowballs.[16] The ugly incident cemented the hostile reputation of Philadelphia's blue-collar fans and provided national sportswriters and broadcasters with the ammunition to damn the City of Brotherly Love in the future.

Turmoil continued in 1969, the year Bill Bradley arrived in Philadelphia. Owner Jerry Wolman had gone bankrupt and sold the Eagles to Leonard Tose, a trucking magnate, for $16,155,000, then a record for a professional sports franchise. Tose's first official act was to fire Kuharich. He then hired Jerry Williams from the Canadian Football League to coach the team and former Eagles great Pete Retzlaff to be the general manager. Because Tose had more enthusiasm than ability, Williams and Retzlaff were handed complete control of the football operation, while he wrote the checks.[17]

Tose was a self-made millionaire with a flamboyant lifestyle. He drove a Rolls-Royce, flew to Eagles home games in a helicopter, and treated sportswriters to filet mignon and shrimp cocktail in the press box. He was also, by his own admission, a compulsive gambler and an alcoholic, personal indiscretions that would eventually cost him his fortune.[18] Nevertheless, Tose was respected and genuinely liked by most of the players. Running back Tom Woodeshick said that he and his teammates considered Tose a "great guy." "He was friendly, generous, and funny," said Woodeshick. "What we respected most about Leonard was that he stayed out of the football end of things and let the coaches do the coaching. He also spent a lot of his money to bring a winner to Philly, and we all appreciated that."[19]

Bradley also respected Tose's decision "not interfere with the football operation," but he felt exploited by the owner's treatment of the players during training camp. "Tose made a ton of money on us during the preseason," Bill explained. "In those days, our contracts did not kick in until the regular season began. Instead, we had a $12.50 per diem. While we were busting our asses playing six preseason games, Tose raked in all the dough on ticket sales and concessions. You'd think he would have shared a percentage of the profits, especially since the starters played in all six of those games. It wasn't like today, when there are only three preseason games and the starters barely play a quarter."[20]

Bradley was not very happy about surrendering his lucky No. 18, which had adorned his jerseys at Palestine High School and the University of

Texas. But Eagles veteran receiver Ben Hawkins already had that number. Instead, Bill decided to adopt No. 28, in part to honor Freddie Steinmark, who wore the number at UT and was fighting a heroic battle against cancer.[21]

The Eagles opened the 1969 campaign losing four of their first five games. The only win was a 41–27 drubbing of the Pittsburgh Steelers on September 28.[22] Bradley was used strictly as a punter and performed extremely well, averaging 41.9 yards in those games. Marv Levy, the special teams coach, appreciated Bill because he punted for height, not distance. He had a 4.8 to 5.2 second hang time, which allowed his teammates to get down field quicker. Plus, he punted left footed, which created spin on the ball that made it more difficult for the returner to catch. If the returner called for a fair catch without catching the ball, the spin would make the ball roll farther toward the end zone when it hit the ground. If he tried to catch the ball, there was a good chance he would fumble it because of the spin.

For Mike Evans, a 6-foot-5, 250-pound lineman, Bradley was a godsend. "Billy punted for height—not distance—and his punts would go 40 to 45 yards," recalled Evans, who played center. "That created enough hang time for me to get down the field before the returner could catch the ball. In those days, the center could run down the field before the ball was punted, so I had a 10-yard start on the rest of the line. That really helped me out. You know, some punters could kick the ball 60 yards. I was never able to go 60 yards down field in four seconds to tackle the returner. But Bradley punted 40 to 45 yards and gave me the hang time I needed to run downfield and make a tackle in five seconds, especially when I had a 10-yard head start. I would have never been able to play on special teams if it hadn't been for Billy."[23]

Bradley had also been a punt returner for the Longhorns and hoped to continue in that role for the Eagles. He constantly emphasized that with Levy too. But the special teams coach wanted to be sure that Bill met his expectations before sending him into a game. Two weeks into the season, Levy pulled the native Texan aside and gave him a tutorial on catching the ball.

"Now, Bill," he began, "there are certain things you have to understand to be a successful returner in this league."

Bradley rolled his eyes in disbelief, but somehow managed to bite his tongue.

"First, you must position yourself about 35 to 40 yards behind the line of scrimmage," Marv continued. "Then, after the ball is kicked, you must prepare yourself by placing your elbows together for the catch."

Bill, who had been returning punts since junior high, pretended to listen carefully, occasionally nodding his head in assent.

"When the ball descends from the air, you must cradle it after the catch," instructed the special teams coach. "Only then do you begin the return."

Having completed the tutorial, Levy asked, "Are there any questions?"

"No, coach," replied Bradley. "I think I got it all down."

Then Bradley motioned to the punter on the other side of the field, who lofted a 50-yard kick. Bill got under the ball and as it was descending turned his entire body around and caught the ball behind his back.

Handing Marv the ball, Bradley exclaimed, "You mean like that, coach?"

Realizing that his student had been patronizing him, Levy just smiled and walked away.[24]

Despite his success at punting and returning, Bradley was frustrated with his limited role. Head coach Jerry Williams had still not found a field position for him. Yet Bill knew that he could contribute to the success of the team if he was able to play in the secondary. Unfortunately for Bradley, four other defensive backs were higher on the depth chart: Irv Cross and Al Nelson were cornerbacks, and Joe Scarpati and Nate Ramsey were safeties. They were also veterans with at least five years of experience in the NFL. But Bradley refused to remain silent.

On October 19 the Eagles faced the Dallas Cowboys at the Cotton Bowl. It was the first NFL game Bill played in his native Texas, and his parents and a large contingent of friends traveled from Palestine to cheer him on. With Dallas leading, 42–7, at the beginning of the third quarter, Cowboys head coach Tom Landry put in his second team. Bill, hoping to get into the game, constantly pestered defensive coordinator Jim "Gummy" Carr on the Eagles' sideline.

"Hey, Gummy!" Bradley chirped as he tugged on the coach's shirt. "Why don't you let the younger guys play?"

But Carr always brushed him off, "Yeah, yeah, we'll see."

With five minutes remaining in the game, Dallas scored another touchdown to increase its lead to 49–7. Landry substituted his starting quarterback Craig Morton for Roger Staubach, a rookie recently discharged from the navy.

Desperate to get onto the field, Bradley went back to Carr one last time.

"C'mon, coach, put me in," he pleaded. "What do you have to lose?"

Disgusted by the score and wanting the rookie punter to stop annoying him, Carr yielded: "All right, Bradley, get in there at free safety for Scarpati."

The Cowboys had a first-and-ten on their own 44-yard line. Carr called for a blitz, hoping to force a fumble. Bill knew from studying game film that the first adjustment Dallas made against a blitz was a quick slant, usually to tight end Mike Ditka.

Staubach took the snap from center and tried to throw a quick-look pass, but the blitz got to him. Scrambling, the rookie quarterback prepared to throw to the slant, where he expected Ditka to catch the ball. Meanwhile, Bradley decoyed Staubach by running downfield, only to double back to the slant. When Staubach threw the ball, Bill stepped in front of Ditka, intercepted the pass, and ran it back 56 yards down the sideline for a touchdown. It was Bradley's very first play from the line of scrimmage in the NFL and the first of five interceptions he would have against Roger Staubach over the course of his nine-year pro career.[25]

"Staubach was a telegrapher," said Bill years later, explaining his ability to anticipate the Cowboys' quarterback. "He'd telegraph where he was going to throw the ball. I knew that he'd look at the free safety as soon as the ball was snapped to see if we were in halves coverage or in man-to-man with a single safety back. I knew he'd look at me to see if I was going to go into the middle third of the field, so I'd trick him. I'd start off as if I was going into halves as he was going through his reads. Then I'd break off and sprint into the middle of the field and play the ball."[26]

After Bradley scored, Bob Hayes, a former Olympic sprinter and Cowboys receiver, hit the 5-foot-11 rookie free safety after he crossed the goal line, drawing a 15-yard penalty on the following kickoff for unnecessary roughness.[27]

"Hayes probably thought I was showing him up," chuckled Bradley. "But I was just holding the ball up high to show my parents and all the other folks from Palestine who were sitting way up in the nosebleeds [section]."[28]

Bradley continued to prepare himself for the free safety position that season. He picked Joe Scarpati's brain whenever possible and did so without reservation. Bill was brash for a rookie. But in his own mind he was simply trying to learn as much as possible to improve himself and the team. According to center Mike Evans, Scarpati was "old school." "He believed that rookies should be seen and not heard," Evans explained. "But Billy was constantly asking Scarpati questions on how to play free safety. Although Joe never volunteered any information, he would answer questions, so Billy just bled him dry for whatever he could learn. Don't think Scarpati didn't know what was happening either. He knew that Billy was out to take his job."[29]

Bradley respected Scarpati's ability, but he also knew that he could play free safety more effectively. "Joe was a smart player," he admitted. "He worked hard and got the most out of his ability. But he didn't know how to decoy like me. He'd go right to his assignment. I knew how to read offenses from the time I was in high school. I also knew how to decoy, how to fool the quarterback on his first read so I could put myself in position to intercept him."[30] Bradley eventually replaced Scarpati as the Eagles' free safety. The veteran would be traded to the New Orleans Saints at the end of the 1969 season.

"The guy who taught me the most was [veteran cornerback] Irv Cross," admitted Bill. Cross, age thirty, was in his second tour of duty with the Eagles. He had played in Philadelphia in the early 1960s, establishing himself as one of the league's top cornerbacks. Cross, a three-time Pro Bowler, was now in the twilight of his career. He was also a student of the game. Not only did he keep a file on every receiver in the NFL, noting his strengths and weaknesses, but he also took game film home every night to study it. When the Eagles reacquired Cross from the Los Angeles Rams before the '69 season, they made him a player-coach to impart his wisdom to the younger players.[31] Bradley became his star pupil.

"Irv taught me a lot about offensive play," Bill said. "We'd watch game film together, and let me tell you, it was a real education. Irv was one of the smartest men I'd ever been around. He knew the tendencies of every receiver in the league. He also knew how to break down opposing offenses. It's one of the reasons he was such a respected NFL analyst after he retired."[32]

Bradley also became a close friend of veteran Nate Ramsey. Because Ramsey played strong safety and didn't have the speed to play free safety, he didn't feel threatened by Bill like Scarpati did. Bradley respected Ramsey as a football player and loved his spirited personality. "Nate was a real good player," said Bill. "He worked hard and hit hard. He was also a yapper, always talking trash. I liked that about him. I can talk trash pretty good myself. But I think some of the other guys put up with him because he got us good deals on all kinds of merchandise."[33]

According to Bradley, Ramsey supplemented his football income by selling questionable merchandise procured at the Philadelphia shipyards along the Delaware River. Once a month, he would do business with his teammates in the Franklin Field parking lot before practice. Inside the trunk of his brand-new Buick LeSabre was every kind of product imaginable, both domestic and foreign, and for at least one-third of the wholesale price. Occasionally, Nate would run specials. One month it might be jewelry, another month men's suits or luggage. "We all did business with him," recalled Bradley. "It was like shopping at a four-wheel department store."

Linebacker Billy Hobbs made the most expensive purchase. Impressed by Ramsey's shiny, light-green Buick LeSabre, Hobbs asked Nate if he could get him a car just like it with all the same amenities, including electric windows and air-conditioning. To his surprise, Ramsey found another LeSabre like his and sold it to Hobbs for just $2,000, a whopping savings of $5,000 off the sticker price. When he bought the car, the linebacker asked, "Hey, Nate! If I'm stopped by the cops, are the serial numbers under the hood going to match those on the bill of sale?"

"Oh, yeah, definitely," replied Ramsey. "I just got such a great deal I couldn't pass it up!"[34]

The Eagles finished the 1969 season in fourth place in the Capitol Division with a 4-9-1 record.[35] Bradley played in all fourteen games as a punter, collecting 2,942 yards on seventy-four punts, with an average of 39.8 yards. He also saw time at free safety and as a punt and kick returner. He led the team in the latter categories with a total of forty-nine returns for 648 yards.[36]

The Birds did not fare as well in 1970, as they were plagued by a remarkable string of injuries. The first player to get hurt was defensive end Tim Rossovich, who tore ligaments in his ankle during the preseason but refused surgery so he could compete when the regular season began. Not only did Rossovich start all fourteen games, but he also led the team with 174 tackles. Running back Leroy Keyes was next. He tore an Achilles tendon in the second game of the season, a 20–16 loss to the Bears at Chicago's Soldier Field. Two weeks later, Tom Woodeshick, the team's leading rusher for the past three years, injured his knee and was limited to just fifty-two carries that season.[37]

Bradley tore cartilage in his left knee during the Eagles' first preseason game. He immediately had surgery to remove loose cartilage in the hope of returning as quickly as possible. Although he was out for just four weeks, Bradley was unable to play free safety when he returned. "They didn't have arthroscopic surgery back then," he said. "If you had surgery, it was an invasive procedure. That meant a lot of rehab. I really worked my ass off to get the knee healthy again too. I knew I couldn't play [free] safety because I couldn't make sharp cuts when I ran, but I could still punt. And you better believe that I was going to punt until my knee fell off. Hell, Timmy [Rossovich] was already playing injured. That's what you did back then. It was expected from your teammates. The only reason I had the surgery during the preseason was because the loose cartilage prevented me from punting."[38]

Bill returned to the team for the October 18 game against the St. Louis Cardinals and handled the punting duties admirably for the remainder of the season. But the old snap was gone, as he averaged just 36 yards on sixty-one painful punts. "Each time I lifted my leg there was a sharp ache," he said. "I didn't know what was going to happen to me. I was worried that my career might be over."[39] Despite his fierce dedication, Bradley did not make much of a difference in the team's fortunes.

The Eagles did not win their first game until November 8. It was a 24–17 upset of the Miami Dolphins, who were on the verge of making their first playoff appearance and would go on to win back-to-back Super Bowls in 1972 and 1973. Eagles quarterback Norm Snead threw two touchdown passes to All-Pro wide receiver Harold Jackson and the game winner to tight end Steve Zabel, the first-round draft pick from Oklahoma.[40] But the highlight of the season came two weeks later when the dismal Birds (1-7-1) upset the red-hot New York Giants (6-3-0) on ABC's *Monday Night Football.*

Snead ran for a pair of touchdowns and clinched the game with a 15-yard pass to Fred Hill to secure the 23–20 victory, leading their jubilant fans to tear down the goalposts.[41] But that wasn't the best of it. The November 23 game was the first time the Eagles hosted *Monday Night Football*, which was in its inaugural year. Of course, the Birds were hardly a prime-time attraction that season, and broadcaster Howard Cosell said as much to a national television audience the previous week. Apologizing for ABC's decision to feature the Eagles-Giants game, the outspoken Cosell snickered that the Eagles "couldn't even beat an all-girls' team if they tried."[42] Little did he realize that payback would come late in the second quarter of the November 23 contest.

It was 23 degrees at game time, and the weather grew even colder as a blustery wind kicked in during the first half, dropping the windchill below zero. Cosell and his television partners—Don Meredith and Keith Jackson—were seated on an open, unheated platform on the facing of the upper deck. To stay warm, Cosell, who had already indulged in a few pregame vodka martinis, continued to drink during the first half.

Minutes before halftime, the broadcaster pitched forward and vomited all over Meredith's cowboy boots. Embarrassed by the incident, executive producer Roone Arledge sent Cosell home at halftime.[43]

"When Cosell didn't return for the second half, ABC issued a statement that he came down with a sudden case of laryngitis," recalled Eagles center Mike Evans. "Of course, we all found out later that he was shit-faced drunk. Suited him right for saying we couldn't beat an all-girls' team. Between the Cosell incident and our upset over the Giants before a national TV audience, that game was my personal Super Bowl!"[44]

No wonder a poll conducted by *TV Guide* in the 1970s determined that the most-despised sportscaster in America was Howard Cosell. The same poll concluded that the most-beloved sportscaster in America was Howard Cosell.[45] *Sports Illustrated* repeated the same sentiments about the feisty—if not contemptuous—Cosell many years later.[46]

The Eagles would win only one more game that season—a 30–20 shocker against the Pittsburgh Steelers—to finish in fifth place in the NFC East with a 3-10-1 record.[47] After the season, the team said goodbye to Franklin Field, as home games shifted to brand new Veterans Stadium in South Philadelphia. Although the "Vet," as it came to be known, was not as intimate as Franklin Field, it was, in 1971, a state-of-the art facility. With a seating capacity of 65,358 for football and 56,371 for baseball, the Eagles shared the multipurpose stadium with the Phillies and played on a 126,000-square-foot Astroturf surface. The Vet was among the first of a wave of cookie-cutter stadiums, including Riverfront in Cincinnati, Three Rivers in Pittsburgh, and Busch Memorial in St. Louis. But unlike those other venues, the Vet boasted the largest, most expensive, and most sophisticated high-tech scoreboard in all of sports. It would serve as the Eagles' home field until 2003, when the team moved across the street to Lincoln Financial Field.[48]

Nineteen-seventy-one was Bradley's breakout season, the first of two straight years Bill would lead the NFL in interceptions (11 in 1971), the first of two straight years he would be named first-team All-Pro, and the first of three straight years he would play in the Pro Bowl. "Bill was an all-around player," said Harold Jackson, a wide receiver and one of Bradley's closest friends on the team. "He wasn't just a great safety or defensive back. That's what people remember because of all the interceptions he had. Bill was also a punter, returner, and kick holder. Do you know how difficult it is to do all those things in the NFL?"[49]

That was high praise coming from Jackson, who emerged as one of the top receivers in the NFL in the early 1970s. A three-time All-Pro and five-time Pro Bowler, Jackson led the league in receiving yards twice when he played in Philadelphia and once in receptions. His career statistics are among the best in the game for all wide receivers and warrant induction into the Pro Football Hall of Fame, although that honor has eluded him.[50]

Bradley and Jackson were the indisputable stars of the 1971 team. They were the only two players who were never booed by the rambunctious fans who were disappointed with the team's performance from the very start. The Eagles opened the 1971 season with a 37–14 drubbing by the Cincinnati Bengals. The Birds kept the game close during the first two quarters with a halftime score of 17–7. But Cincinnati pulled away in the second half, as the Eagles' defense embarrassed itself by surrendering 371 yards to the Bengals' offense. The sole highlight came when Bradley picked off Bengals' quarterback Virgil Carter for his first interception of the year.[51] The Eagles' home opener came the following week against Dallas, and it was not much better.

Quarterback Pete Liske threw six interceptions, and the Cowboys converted two of them into touchdowns en route to a 42–7 rout. Dallas stole another pass off rookie quarterback Rick Arrington, who entered the game in the third quarter, setting up a third touchdown. Bradley gave Arrington an opportunity to take the Eagles in for a score by intercepting his second pass of the season and returning it 30 yards to the Cowboys' 34. Arrington followed with an 11-yard pass to Lee Bouggess and another to Harold Jackson for 6 yards, giving the Birds their deepest penetration to the Dallas 18, but the drive died shortly after that.[52]

On October 3 the Eagles lost their third straight game, this one to the San Francisco 49ers, 31–3. John Brodie, the 49ers' quarterback, threw for three touchdowns. Brodie was in complete control of the game, fending off Eagles pass rushers with his quick release, the linebackers with his play-action deception, and the secondary with his strong arm. Bradley might've prevented San Francisco's final touchdown—a 30-yard pass to tight end Ted Kwalick—which came early in the fourth quarter. But he suffered a concussion in the third period and was pulled from the game.[53]

It was bad enough that Philadelphia was 0-3, but the opponents were also routing the team. In those three losses, the Eagles were outscored 110–24. Something was terribly wrong. Head coach Jerry Williams reminded the sportswriters and fans that the Eagles had "just played the three toughest teams in the NFL" and that the "toughness of the early schedule could be beneficial if we can keep morale up."[54] Owner Leonard Tose was not convinced.

Three days later, on October 6, the owner fired Williams and replaced him with defensive-line coach Ed Khayat.[55] Tose called for a press conference that afternoon with himself, the new coach, and general manager Pete Retzlaff. Surprisingly, Williams arrived before the trio and condemned Tose for not allowing him enough time to reverse the fortunes of the team. Then he accused the owner of offering him a bribe. "I was offered a sizeable sum of money to resign," he told the media. "But to accept a bribe is to lower myself to the depths of a man who is without courage and character."[56]

After Williams stormed out, Tose took control of the press conference. "I'd like to think I am a compassionate man, and what I did was a goodwill gesture to Jerry," he said, defending his decision to dismiss the head coach.[57] "I was not happy to release him at the beginning of a season, though I really view it as the end of 2½ seasons." Although the owner blamed the team's dismal 7-22-1 record during Williams's tenure on "all of us," he quickly exonerated Retzlaff of all blame and pointed out that Williams "had veto power on every trade we ever made. . . . If you want me to identify a 'last straw,' it was the way we played against Cincinnati, Dallas and San Francisco," he continued. "We were completely out of those games."[58]

Of his decision to hire Khayat, the thirty-five-year-old former Eagles defensive tackle, Tose said, "I have complete faith in Eddie Khayat, and we will give him complete backing. He was hired because of how he handles himself, how he handles the players, and his football knowledge. I think we can improve our position with him as our head coach."[59]

No sooner had the Eagles' owner completed his remarks than the team's player representative Ron Porter presented a statement drafted by the players themselves indicating that they were taking Williams's side in the controversial firing. "We as a squad feel very dismayed at the dismissal of Jerry Williams," began the statement. "It is a grave injustice that one man must bear the brunt of an entire organization's shortcomings. We as players have failed Coach Williams in our performance on the field and must take responsibility for what has happened."[60]

Bradley, who attended the press conference, stood firmly behind the players' statement. "We didn't think that ownership gave Jerry enough of a chance," he said years later, reflecting on the firing. "We were about to turn it around, and Jerry could've done it. He was a very bright man, an attorney. He had already won a Grey Cup in the Canadian Football League, which is that country's equivalent of a Super Bowl championship. What we needed was consistency, not to change head coaches."[61]

If Tose believed that Khayat was the right man to lead the team, he was sorely mistaken. The new head coach only made matters worse. Khayat, who modeled himself after World War II tank commander General George S. Patton, believed in discipline, dress codes, and short hair. Whereas Williams allowed the players to cultivate their own appearance, Khayat imposed a shave-and-a-haircut policy. He also directed the players to wear slacks, button-down shirts, jackets, and ties on road trips instead of T-shirts and bell-bottomed blue jeans.[62]

"I could only do the job one way, and that was my way," he insisted in a recent interview. "I firmly believed that good grooming instilled discipline, and discipline was conducive to good play. Back then, the players talked about doing their own thing. But when doing your own thing is more important than doing the Philadelphia Eagles' thing, then doing your own thing won't do."[63]

Khayat was out of step with the times. If he was trying to create a winning culture, he would have to start by communicating better with his players, not distancing himself from them with unreasonable policies.

Whether Khayat liked it or not, his players belonged to the postwar baby-boom generation, which embraced a more liberal outlook and lifestyle than their parents' generation. Quick to criticize the conservative establishment, these largely white, middle-class, and educated baby boomers challenged all types of authority. They protested U.S. involvement in Vietnam, the exploitative capitalism of big business, and the greed of Wall Street, while defending the civil rights of African Americans and women and championing the preservation of the environment. Their liberalism expressed itself in a hedonistic lifestyle that emphasized natural living, sexual promiscuity, drug use, and outlandish tastes in grooming, dress, and music. Males wore their hair long and favored tie-dyed shirts, colorful dashikis, and jeans. Females went braless and wore mini-skits, tight-fitting halter tops, and loose-fitting dresses.[64]

The desire for individual expression and the so-called hippie lifestyle that accompanied it had been integrated into the American mainstream by the early 1970s. Many NFL players wore more colorful clothing, grew their hair longer, donned sideburns and mustaches, and smoked marijuana.[65] On the Eagles, Bill Bradley and Tim Rossovich best exemplified the new breed of pro football players.

"There were a lot of folks who considered Timmy and me hippies because we were free-spirited, wore long hair, mustaches, and sideburns," Bill said of his relationship with Rossovich. "He was a close friend, but we were different people. I liked to have fun, and I did some pretty crazy things, but Timmy was a wild man to the point where he could be dangerous to himself and others."[66]

Rossovich, a first-round draft pick by the Eagles in 1968, was a consensus All-American defensive end and cocaptain of USC's 1967 national championship team. Known for his intense but eccentric and offbeat personality, Rossovich loved to shock others by chewing glass and lightbulbs and setting himself on fire, which he did for a September 1971 *Sports Illustrated* photo shoot and later as a guest on *The Tonight Show Starring Johnny Carson*.[67]

"It sounds insane, but it was really calculated," Rossovich said in a 1997 NFL Films interview. "It was like a magical trick. The technique was to wear two T-shirts. One T-shirt was tight against the skin. The other was the one that I'd soak in the lighter fluid. That's the one I would light. The fluid was all in the front, so the fire wasn't that close to my skin. It was pretty safe, except for a couple times when my mustache got singed. But I really did it for effect, just to get attention, when I walked into a party."[68]

Among the other stunts Rossovich pulled were biting the tops off beer bottles, diving headfirst into the whirlpool, wearing tie-dye capes and listening to Gregorian chants on the stereo, grabbing a spider off a locker room table and eating it, diving naked into a birthday cake, jumping off rooftops, and driving motorbikes off piers.[69]

"Tim was an animal on the football field, but he was also a freak of nature," recalled fullback Tom Woodeshick, one of the most conservative personalities on the team. "All those California guys were kind of strange, but Rosso was the weirdest of the bunch. I didn't have anything in common with him, so we didn't hang around together. But God, he could make me laugh!

"Once he came to a team party with just a robe on and nothing underneath. The guys dragged him into the room, dumped water on him, and then threw him a towel. Rossovich stood up and said, 'Shit! I'm at the wrong party!' Then he walked out of the place."[70]

"Timmy was crazy like that," said Bradley, who witnessed most, if not all, of his friend's pranks. "He just liked to shock the hell out of us. Sportswriters thought he was doing hard drugs. But he wasn't, at least not when he was with the Eagles. Timmy did drink and smoke some weed every now and then, but so did I, and so did a lot of guys in the NFL back then."[71]

Nevertheless, Tim Rossovich, at 6 feet 4 inches and 240 pounds, was quite an imposing physical specimen. With his wild, bushy hair and Rasputin-like gaze, he looked and acted as if he were mentally unstable. "I live my life to enjoy myself," Rossovich told *Sports Illustrated*'s John Underwood. "I can't explain the things I do much beyond that. I have more energy than I know what to do with. I can't just sit around. I get bored. A lot of what I do is silly, trying to cheer people up, trying to cheer myself up."[72] But there was more to his eccentric behavior than others knew at the time.

According to Rossovich's longtime girlfriend, Cis Rundle, an actress and one of the original Los Angeles Rams cheerleaders, "Tim was a broken soul. . . . He never knew his real father, and his stepfather didn't pay any attention to him," she explained. "That broke Tim's heart. He was desperate for attention and always tried to prove himself to others. It was as if he was trying to show his worthiness as a human being. That's what was really behind all the crazy stunts."[73]

Regardless of the reason, the Eagles' new head coach did not appreciate Rossovich's eccentric behavior. Their relationship became even more strained when the defensive-end-turned-linebacker registered his disapproval of Khayat's new grooming and dress policy. Rossovich felt his individuality was being stifled, and it "didn't make sense to [him]. . . . The length of your hair, the width of your lapels or your necktie, and whether or not you had a mustache had nothing to do with the way you played football," he explained. "Khayat said it improved discipline. I thought it was the opposite. It created a situation where guys were talking about this stuff instead of getting better as a football team." Predictably, Rossovich spoke out against the policy, and, although he eventually complied, he was the last player to do so, shaving off his mustache just five minutes before the coach's deadline.[74]

While Bradley agreed that Khayat's policy was misdirected, he complied without an argument. "Most of the players disagreed with the grooming policy," said Bill. "We all knew that the problem wasn't the long hair. The problem was Khayat's inability to bring discipline to our play. *That* is what we needed, not to cut our hair and shave our mustaches. You can't change the culture by changing appearance. You change the culture by the way you coach and by the way you play."[75] Still, Bill grew his hair longer each season he was with the Eagles. In 1971 he had a bushy perm that barely met Khayat's rule of "no hair showing outside the helmet." In later years, Bradley's perm became longer and more unruly and was accompanied by long sideburns and a full mustache.

If Khayat's new policies were supposed to translate into victories, they didn't work, at least initially. On October 10 the Eagles continued their losing ways against the Minnesota Vikings, dropping their fourth straight game, 13–0. Although the defense was, according to Tose, "superb," the offense left much to be desired.[76] It was bad enough that the Birds were defeated by their old quarterback Norm Snead, but the closest they came to scoring was on a field goal attempt by rookie kicker Jim "Happy" Feller from the 15-yard line in the second quarter that was blocked by Minnesota's Carl Eller.

Perhaps the defense was good, but the offense was awful. It was the first time the Eagles had been shut out since the ninth game of the 1962 season, a span of 120 games.[77] Eagles quarterbacks Pete Liske and Rick Arrington were woefully ineffective. Liske threw two interceptions in the first half that set up 10 of the Vikings' points. Arrington, his backup, came on in relief in the second quarter but proved to be just as ineffective.[78] "We literally stunk," noted fullback Tom Woodeshick in the most apt description of the game. "We just got the hell kicked out of us. Period."[79]

After the game, Khayat sounded just as naive as his predecessor. "When you get into a dogfight with the toughest team in the NFL and come out as well as we did, I have no complaints." The new head coach was delusional if he thought anything had changed. Linebacker Steve Zabel gave him a dose of reality when he told *Philadelphia Inquirer* sportswriter Chuck Newman, "We played like Williams was still our coach. We didn't have any different approach to this game as we had to the earlier ones." Defensive end Mel Tom agreed. "The coaching change had no effect on us," he insisted. "Everything we did today came from Jerry's training."[80]

The next week it was a different team but the same result. This time the Oakland Raiders defeated the Eagles. Arrington, who started the game at quarterback, put the Eagles in the lead, 10–0, in the first quarter. But he injured his knee in the second period, and the Birds were forced to go back to Pete Liske, who failed to put points on the board. Meanwhile, Oakland scored three touchdowns in a decisive eighty-second span in the second half to turn a close defensive game into a 34–10 rout.[81] Now the Eagles were a demoralizing 0-5 on the season. A start like that would have divided most teams, but the Eagles managed to regroup.

"All we had was each other," said center Mike Evans. "The sportswriters ripped us. The fans booed us because we weren't meeting their expectations. And Khayat was in over his head. The only thing we could count on was each other."[82] In other words, the Eagles found a way to win on their own.

Bradley and Harold Jackson worked hard to keep the team together. They were not only the two uncontested stars of the Eagles but also good friends who kept their teammates focused and united. They hosted team gatherings, constantly encouraged their teammates at practice and on game day, and made the rookies feel welcomed.[83]

"Bill was a team player in every sense of the word," said Jackson. "He was the type of guy who always tried to keep everybody up, to make everybody feel good about themselves, to keep people loose, to make 'em laugh. He always tried to help everyone. That's a very difficult thing to do on a losing team, and that's all we seemed to do at the start of that season—lose. I don't know where the Eagles would've been without him."[84]

Jackson was not as gregarious as Bradley, but he commanded the same kind of respect among his teammates, especially the younger ones. "My first year in Philadelphia was tough," said wide receiver Harold Carmichael, the Eagles' seventh-round pick out of Southern University in the 1971 NFL draft. "I was constantly being shifted between tight end and wide receiver, sometimes not finding out where I was playing until minutes before game time. There were personal challenges too. Growing up in Jacksonville, Florida, and going to an all-Black college, I'd never been around a lot of white people. Harold Jackson took me under his wing and taught me how to deal with [white] people off the field. He let me live at his apartment when I wasn't making a lot of money, and he always encouraged me on the field."

"Billy Bradley was also a big help," added Carmichael. "He would get a bunch of guys together on Monday nights, and we'd go out to a disco club. Billy called it Harold Carmichael Night. He was the first white boy I saw who could really dance. I mean he was *good*. We had some of the greatest times on those Monday nights. To this day, so many of my teammates—Black and white—are among my best friends, and Harold Jackson and Billy Bradley are at the top of the list."[85]

Carmichael's remarks are revealing. Unlike many other NFL teams, the Eagles' players—Black and white—did not self-segregate when they were off the field. While they may not have been color-blind, the teammates genuinely enjoyed each other's companionship, especially those who were single and lived downtown. Bradley, Jackson, Carmichael, defensive back Nate Ramsey, wide receivers Ben Hawkins and Billy Walik, and linebackers Billy Hobbs and Tim Rossovich were nearly inseparable. When the team was at home, they could be found mingling with fans on South Street, or at Jackson's apartment in Society Hill Towers, which became a popular place for team parties.[86] The group became so tight that Bradley, who had to stay an hour after practice to do his punting, would block the others' cars in with his Econoline janitor's van so they couldn't begin socializing without him.[87]

"Bradley was always pulling pranks like that," said Jackson. "He would get real upset if we left without him. He was a social butterfly. Everybody gravitated to him. We might not have had a real good football team, but all those guys became real close."[88]

Occasionally, Bill would invite *Philadelphia Evening Bulletin* beat writer Ray Didinger to those evening gatherings. "Billy was a great guy," said Didinger, a 1968 graduate of Temple University who took over the Eagles' beat two years later at the tender age of twenty-three. "We were roughly the same age when we met. Both of us were single. We had a lot of similar interests. We liked the same kinds of movies. We liked the same kind of music. We just hit it off."[89]

One evening Bradley and Didinger went to the Main Point, a folk music club in the suburbs. While they were waiting in line to get inside, Ray began to feel uneasy about the friendship.

"You know, Billy, this is not a healthy relationship," he said, suggesting a conflict of interest. "I'm a reporter covering a team that you play on, and we've become friends. Do you understand that if you screw up in a game, I'm going to have to write about it?"

The question took Bradley by surprise. After thinking about it for a moment, Bill chuckled, "Well, I just won't screw up! Problem solved."

When reminded of the incident, Didinger said, "I wish it had been that easy. . . . Still, I felt that I had to put it on the record, at least that one time. It still didn't faze Billy. He got along with everybody."[90]

Bradley had already played in Philadelphia for two years, long enough to familiarize himself with the city's beat writers. Bill didn't trust Gordon Forbes of the *Inquirer*, the most experienced of the group and a hard-nosed reporter. He enjoyed a wide network of connections that extended from player agents to the NFL commissioner, Pete Rozelle. But Forbes also created controversy by quoting players selectively and calling them out unnecessarily. Bill Shefski of the *Philadelphia Daily News* was much more objective in his coverage of the team. But Bradley didn't know whether he could trust him because he distanced himself from the players, never getting to know their personalities.[91] Bill not only trusted Didinger but also genuinely liked him as a person.

"I got along well with Ray and still consider him a close friend," said Bradley in a recent interview. "He was *always* fair when he interviewed me. I felt like I could be very candid with him and he understood my position. I also think Ray told the truth when he wrote about the other players. Even though our team was so terrible, he never threw a player under the bus. If he was critical, it was deserved."[92]

Khayat's first win came on October 24 against the New York Giants, 23–7. Because Pete Liske and Rick Arrington were unsuccessful in the air, the Eagles were forced to go to a ground game. Thanks to Al Davis, an obscure eleventh-round draft pick from Tennessee State, and Ronnie Bull, a ten-year veteran acquired for an eighth-round draft pick from the Chicago Bears, the Birds' offense rushed for 160 yards to put 23 points on the scoreboard. The defense held Giants quarterback Fran Tarkenton to eleven completions in twenty-six attempts and sacked him three times while forcing five fumbles. The Eagles converted three of those fumbles into Happy Feller field goals of 20, 10, and 30 yards.[93] But the victory did not prevent Rossovich from complaining about Khayat's grooming policy.

"If the situation were different and we were 5-1 instead of 1-5, I don't think we would have had to cut our hair or shave off our mustaches," the middle linebacker told Frank Dolson of the *Inquirer* after the game. "Anyway, nobody cut my tongue out. I can still speak. When I'm on the field, I have one responsibility. Play middle linebacker. When I'm off the field I still feel the same way. The length of my hair has nothing to do with how I play and nobody's going to change my mind."[94]

The Eagles won again the following week at Veterans Stadium, upsetting the Denver Broncos, 17–16. Happy Feller kicked a 27-yard field goal early in the first quarter to give the Birds an early 3–0 lead. The Eagles increased their lead to 10–0 early in the second quarter when Rick Arrington threw an 18-yard touchdown pass to wide receiver Ben Hawkins. Denver answered with a 53-yard drive resulting in a touchdown, narrowing the score to 10–7. Six minutes later, linebacker Billy Hobbs blocked a Broncos' punt on the Denver 6-yard line and ran the ball in for another touchdown just before halftime. When Feller kicked the extra point, the Eagles led, 17–7.[95]

The second half proved to be a defensive standoff, as the Philadelphia offense was unable to score. The Eagles' secondary shut down Broncos' quarterback Don Horn so effectively that Denver was limited to three field goals during the last two quarters of play. Bradley was instrumental in securing the victory. With the Birds clinging to a 17–13 lead, the free safety stopped two of the Broncos' last-period drives with timely interceptions. The first interception, Bradley's fourth of the season, came with seven minutes remaining in the game and the Broncos on the Philadelphia 10-yard line. Horn took the snap, dropped back, and lofted the ball into the end zone, hoping that one of his receivers would make the catch. Instead, Bradley raced to the ball, caught it, and ran to the edge of the bleachers where he flipped the $25 ball to a little old man in a yellow rain jacket. That action brought an automatic $100 fine from the NFL.[96]

"I don't know what they'll consider it, a forward pass or a lateral," chuckled Bill, when describing his ball flip into the stands to Bill Shefski of the *Daily News* in a postgame interview. "The fine might depend on what they rule it. I'll pay it. I just hope the guy has a couple of children and makes good use of the ball."[97]

Defensive coordinator Gummy Carr overheard Bradley's remarks and was much less amused. Interrupting the interview, Carr asked the free safety who was supposed to cover the weakside running back on the big play, suggesting that Bradley blew off his assignment on the weakside rotation defense. "Horn threw to a dead zone," replied Bill. "I am supposed to rove to the ball in that situation." Carr said that they'd "have to wait and see when they watch the game film."[98]

Three minutes after the initial interception, Bradley recorded his fifth pick of the year. With the Broncos on the Eagles' 6-yard line, Horn, on third-and-goal, threw to receiver Jack Gehrke. But Bill broke up the play, pulling the ball in with his fingertips and preventing what might have been a game-winning field goal for Denver. For those two interceptions, his teammates voted Bill the game ball.[99]

When asked why he had already collected more interceptions (5) this season than those Eagles who played free safety in earlier years, Bradley replied, "This is only my third season in Philadelphia. I don't know why there weren't interceptions before. We've always had guys around the ball. I guess we're just catching them now. It's a matter of wanting the ball and a matter of concentration."[100]

Years later, Bradley provided some additional insight into those two interceptions. "Denver's quarterback, Don Horn, would try to trick us by looking off in a certain direction after he took the snap," Bill explained in a recent interview. "That way, he'd get our defenders to zone off in that particular direction. Then the routes would convert to a directional back. It was a fake play that allowed Horn to throw to a secondary or tertiary receiver. Early in the game, Horn stayed with the fake look longer than usual. That forced us to get into our proper coverage earlier than we might otherwise have done. By the fourth quarter, I was on to him. I was able to anticipate him and pick off those two passes. That was one of my best games when you consider that just one interception can change the outcome of a game."[101]

On November 7 the Eagles traveled to Washington DC to take on the NFC Eastern Division–leading Redskins at Robert F. Kennedy Stadium. Khayat went with a two-quarterback system, this time starting Rick Arrington. Arrington completed just four passes in twelve attempts in the first half. Redskins quarterback Billy Kilmer did not do much better. On a day when a gusty wind played tricks, kicker Happy Feller missed field goals of 37, 47, 41, and 35 yards. Two of the attempts were blocked by Washington linemen, and the other two glanced off the uprights. As a result, the game remained scoreless at the half. Liske started the third quarter, and three minutes in connected with receiver Ronnie Bull in the end zone on a play-action pass. Feller's kick made it 7–0 in the Birds' favor.

The Eagles got lucky near the end of the quarter. Kilmer sailed a 45-yard cross-field pass to Boyd Dowler for what appeared to be a touchdown. Dowler caught the ball at Philadelphia's 8-yard line as Bradley closed in for the tackle. In a desperate attempt to bring down the 6-foot-5, 220-pound receiver, Bill jumped on his back. Dowler proceeded to carry Bradley—and the football—into the end zone for the score. Unfortunately for Washington, the touchdown was nullified by a holding penalty on Redskins guard Ray Schoenke.[102]

"It looked like Dowler was giving me a piggyback ride for those eight yards," laughed Bradley, recalling the play fifty years later. "It was pretty embarrassing for both of us. I gotta admit that one-on-one, my tackles slowed the receiver just long enough for our other defenders to come over and bring him down. I had to go around the knees or ankles to bring down a receiver or hit 'em when they weren't looking. I just tackled however I could and hoped my buddies would come over to help."[103]

Kilmer got revenge midway through the fourth quarter when he connected with receiver Clifton McNeil with a 32-yard scoring pass. Then Redskins kicker Curt Knight converted on the extra point to tie the score, 7–7. Kilmer threatened again with less than a minute remaining. Washington had first-and-ten with the ball on its own 25-yard line. McNeil ran a deep pattern down the right sideline, and Kilmer tried to hit him with a 53-yard bomb. Bradley, with a deftly timed leap, made his second interception of the game and took off on a 21-yard return to the Eagles' 43. Bill tried to wiggle out of bounds to stop the clock, but the Redskins would not let him. In the confusion, Khayat called the second of his team's three timeouts of the half to save thirty-five seconds on the clock.[104]

After an incompletion and a 1-yard gain, Liske called the third and final timeout with twenty-one seconds left. With the ball on the Eagles' 44, Liske, on third down, threw a Hail Mary to Harold Jackson, who was running a desperate fly pattern down the left side. The wind held the ball up in the air, forcing Jackson to come back to make the catch at the Redskins' 25, where cornerback Mike Bass smashed him to the ground. The clock was still running, but the Eagles had about eleven seconds left to attempt a game-winning field goal. As Feller ran onto the field, Redskins linebacker Jack Pardee and defensive tackle Diron Talbert loitered in the Eagles' backfield to milk the clock, and the game ended in a 7–7 tie.[105]

After the game, Bradley was given kudos by his teammates for stopping a potential game-winning field-goal drive for the second straight week. But Bill was more concerned about the sportswriters who were prowling around Feller's locker obviously waiting to ask him about his four blown field-goal attempts. Bill protected the rookie placekicker and fellow Longhorn by pulling him aside and advising him to keep quiet.[106]

Feller, nicknamed "Happy" as a child because he was always smiling, had only converted on six field goals in twenty attempts that season. "Happy and I have been together from college," Bradley told Bill Shefski of the *Daily News*. "He's been real uptight since he's been here and I don't know why. Kicking is his life. I know things aren't going so well for him now, but he'll turn it around."[107]

But Feller ran out of chances after the Redskins game. The Eagles promoted their taxi-squad kicker, Tom Dempsey. Dempsey was born with a two-fingered stub of a right hand and only half a right foot, the one he used for kicking. He had a special shoe designed with a flat face made entirely of leather. It looked like the head of a sledgehammer and often had the same effect when he struck the ball. In fact, the 6-foot-1, 260-pound Dempsey was famous for kicking a record-setting 63-yard field goal a year earlier when he was with the New Orleans Saints. Setting that record was a mixed blessing for him, though. After a demanding schedule on the off-season banquet circuit, he reported to training camp grossly overweight, and the Saints released him.[108] Disappointed with Feller's kicking performance, the Eagles claimed Dempsey midway through the 1971 season. Feller would later be traded to New Orleans, where he ended his career two years later.[109]

On November 14 the Eagles played the Dallas Cowboys at the new Texas Stadium in suburban Irving. For Bradley the game was a homecoming. He purchased thirty-two tickets for family members and friends. His parents, Mildred and Joe, were there, as were his older sister, Rosemary, and his younger brother, Duffy, and aunts and uncles from Palestine and Houston. Many of Bill's Longhorns teammates showed up, too, including tight end Kelly Baker, split end Ragan Gennusa, and his old roommate and team manager, Bill Hall.[110]

Heading into the game, Bradley led the NFL with seven interceptions, one more than Green Bay's Ken Ellis. Bill needed just two more picks to tie the Eagles' single season record of nine shared by two former safeties, Ed "Bibbles" Bawel (1955) and Don Burroughs (1960). Unlike those former Birds who played for winning teams, Bradley played for a losing team with a restrictive zone defense. Bawel and Burroughs, like Ellis, were given free rein to play the pass. But Bill made two game-saving interceptions in the 1-point win over Denver, and he made two more tie-saving picks against the Redskins while fulfilling zone assignments.[111]

"We were in a double-rotation both times against the Redskins," he explained. "My responsibility was the deep half of the weakside. It's a little easier to play the ball in the deep half when you don't have the rigid zone-man-to-man obligation."[112]

Although Bill failed to make an interception against his nemesis, Cowboys quarterback Roger Staubach, he almost scored a touchdown when he broke loose on what might have been an 80-yard punt return. Unfortunately, the play was negated when teammate Don Brumm was penalized for roughing the punter. It was just one of many mistakes the Eagles made in a sloppy 20–7 loss to Dallas. They gave up the ball twice on fumbles, twice on interceptions, once on a blocked punt, and once on Brumm's roughing-the-punter penalty.[113]

Bradley tied the Eagles single-season club record for interceptions the following week in a decisive—and rare—37–20 victory over the lowly Cardinals in St. Louis. Bill's first pick came off Cards quarterback Jim Hart in the second quarter, and he grabbed another against backup Pete Beathard on the final play of the game.[114] However, Bradley's heroics took a backseat to those of new kicker Tom Dempsey and quarterback Pete Liske. Dempsey put the Eagles ahead twice in the second half with 27-yard and 45-yard field goals. Liske came off the bench and threw a 5-yard scoring pass to Lee Bouggess to put the Birds ahead for good, 30–20, early in the fourth quarter. The victory enabled Philadelphia to escape the Eastern Division cellar, where the Cardinals found themselves after the game.[115]

On December 5 Bill set a new single-season club record for interceptions in the Eagles' 23–20 win over the Detroit Lions. He stole a Greg Landry pass in the end zone in the first half for his tenth pick of the season. When Ray Didinger of the *Evening Bulletin* suggested after the game that being the league's leading pass thief warranted an All-Pro selection, Bradley demurred.

"If you're a football player, you've got to want to be recognized as the best," he said. "But as long as our team finishes below .500, I can't be happy."[116] Nevertheless, with just two games remaining in the regular season, sportswriters were eager to see if Bradley could break the NFL single-season record of fourteen interceptions set by Dick "Night Train" Lane of the Los Angeles Rams in 1952.[117]

On December 12 Bradley snagged his eleventh and final interception of the season against the St. Louis Cardinals at the Vet. It came in the first quarter amid an offensive barrage. After Tom Dempsey put the Birds ahead, 3–0, with a 27-yard field goal, Bill made an easy steal off Cardinals quarterback Jim Hart. His 28-yard return set up another Dempsey field goal, this one from 22 yards out. Minutes later, Pete Liske connected with Harold Jackson on a 69-yard touchdown pass, increasing the score to 13–0. St. Louis never recovered, losing the game, 19–7.[118]

After the game, Bradley gave all the credit for his eleven league-leading interceptions to his teammates on the defense, especially the linemen for creating those opportunities with their pass rushing. "We have some kind of defense here," he told Ray Didinger of the *Evening Bulletin*. "I'm just glad to be part of it. All I ever wanted was a chance to play in the NFL and now I've got it. I couldn't be happier."[119] Later that month the Associated Press selected Bill as the lone Eagle on its All-Pro team.[120]

Philadelphia completed the 1971 season the next week with a 41–28 victory over the New York Giants at Yankee Stadium. Owner Leonard Tose was so ecstatic about his team's third-place finish in the NFC East with a 6-7-1 record that he announced his decision to give both head coach Ed Khayat and general manager Pete Retzlaff two-year contracts.[121] Not all the players were happy about it, though.

"[Khayat] just has to change some of his ideas on what a football player should look like and be like," said linebacker Tim Rossovich. "We're going in the right direction and I'm not going to do anything to mess that up. I want to be here when this team goes to the Super Bowl. But there's a distance between us. We could've had the same results with mustaches. He has our respect. Okay. Now he must stop treating us like children."

Although Bradley was not as affected by the grooming policy, he did say that Khayat had "taken us as far as we can go on discipline. . . . From here on, he has to do it with football." At the same time, Bill also fired a warning shot at Retzlaff. "I know Pete bases his personal [salary] negotiations on performance," he added. "So he's gonna have to do some big talking to me."[122]

Bradley intended to make the head coach and general manager pay for his All-Pro caliber services in the near future.

7 Billy Bo Bitch

Bradley spent the summer of 1972 motoring across the country in his 1967 Volkswagen Bus with the words "Cottonmouth Blues Wagon" painted across the sides. The flashy name was a nod to his native Texas, where *cottonmouth* means "thirsty" and *blues* refers to his favorite style of music. Put the words together, add a six pack of beer and a mouth harp, and you've got two of the free-spirited safety's favorite pastimes and the place where he loved to practice them.

Bill took exception to those who disparaged his VW van as an "old beat-up piece of junk," as did the local sportswriters and some of his teammates. "There's nothing 'beat-up' about it," he insisted. "As a matter of fact, I put a lot of work into that wagon. Just removed all the bumps, put in carpeting and a bed and dyed the curtains."[1] As it turned out, those renovations were completed at an opportune time. Bradley would be doing a lot more traveling in that van after the Eagles opened their training camp in mid-July.

After weeks of negotiating a new contract with general manager Pete Retzlaff ended in a stalemate, Bradley decided to hold out of preseason training camp. Bill was seeking a hefty raise from the incredibly low salary of $21,000 the Eagles were paying him to $42,000 for the '72 season.[2] "I didn't think that asking them to double my salary after the year I had was unreasonable," he recalled in a recent interview. "When I signed in 1971 for $17,500, I had a few clauses in my contract stipulating that if I led the league in interceptions, I'd get a $10,000 bonus. If I led the Eagles in interceptions, I'd get $5,000. If I made All-Pro, I'd get $5,000. If I averaged 40 yards a punt, I'd get $2,000.

"After the season ended, I led the NFL and the Eagles with eleven interceptions, and I made All-Pro, so I was entitled to a $20,000 bonus, which was to be automatically added to the base salary for the following year. I didn't expect to get the $2,000, even though I averaged 39.9 yards a punt, which was close enough to the 40-yard average we agreed on. But Retzlaff only gave me [an additional] $3,500, which increased my total earnings for [the] '71 season to $21,000. He didn't offer me a raise for 1972 because the Eagles didn't have a winning season."[3]

Bradley pointed out that all the bonus clauses in his previous contract were for *individual* achievements—not team achievements—and that the general manager signed off on those bonuses. Bill also felt that he should be paid as much as Paul Krause of the Minnesota Vikings, the top defensive back in the league, who was then earning $60,000 per season.[4] But Retzlaff's final offer was $23,625, which amounted to a 35 percent increase. Bradley balked, leaving him no other choice but to hold out.[5] He hired Mark S. Stewart, president of Sports International, to represent him.

Like the other agents who began recruiting NFL clients in the 1970s, Stewart was sleek, elegantly dressed, and impeccably groomed. Insisting that he would "take no percentage of [Bradley's] contract with the Eagles for his services," the agent intended to make his money by managing Bill's future endorsements.[6]

Retzlaff did not trust Stewart from the start. He believed in the old-fashioned way of negotiating contracts, which was strictly between the player and the general manager. Agents got in the way because their objective was to make as much money for themselves as for their clients. They also enlisted the media to sell their client's side of a dispute to the public.[7] Retzlaff knew how to play that game too.

Conveniently ignoring the bonus clauses he agreed to in Bradley's 1971 contract, the Eagles' general manager insisted that Bill had a legal obligation to report to training camp. "According to the standard NFL player contract, Bill Bradley is already signed for the 1972 season," explained Retzlaff to Gordon Forbes of the *Philadelphia Inquirer*. "He is legally obligated to play for the Philadelphia Eagles this season due to the renewal of the reserve clause which binds a player to his team unless he is released or traded."[8]

Salary disputes were not uncommon in the 1970s, but player holdouts were rare. Few athletes had the courage to challenge the NFL's pay structure or the owners and general managers who controlled it. Player salaries had always been meager. When the league was established in 1920, players were paid on a per-game basis at less than $100 per contest. They had to work another job to make ends meet.[9] Things changed in 1926, when star halfback Red Grange signed a nineteen-game deal with the Chicago Bears that earned him roughly $100,000.[10] It was the first large NFL contract. After that, salaries were based on the star quality of the player and the wealth of the team's owner. By the late 1950s the average player salary was about $6,000 per season. Not until the NFL Players Association won recognition in 1970 did the owners agree to a $12,500 minimum salary for rookies and $13,000 minimum for veterans.[11] Player salaries gradually increased in the 1970s due to the threat posed by the new World Football League, which began outbidding the NFL for star players.[12]

It was difficult to blame Bradley for his decision to hold out. He never had a lot of money. Having grown up poor, Bill scrimped and saved whatever he earned on part-time jobs. Now, at age twenty-five, he was in the prime of his football career. If Bradley was going to make serious money, now was the time to collect. He had a good case for a significant raise in salary too.

Not only did Bill lead the NFL in interceptions as the Eagles' free safety, but he was also the team's punter, served as an emergency quarterback, held for the kicker, and returned punts. He rightfully wanted his salary to reflect his value to the Eagles and his status as one of the top defensive backs in the game. After all, he didn't know how much longer he would be able to play in the NFL. Pro football is a violent sport. It subjects the player to career-ending, sometimes life-threatening injuries. Each time Bradley stepped on to the gridiron, he momentarily realized that he was putting his life on the line. For Bill, that sobering reality raised the question of whether he was being justly compensated for his sacrifice.

In the summer of 1972, the answer to that question in his mind was a resounding "No!"

Unfortunately, Bradley did not improve his relationship with Retzlaff when training camp opened on July 17 at Albright College in Reading, Pennsylvania. Refusing to report to the team, Bill antagonized the Eagles' general manager instead by parking his Cottonmouth Blues Wagon on the street next to the practice field and selling home-made bologna sandwiches and sodas to fans watching the team train. "You know, I made $175 a day selling those sandwiches and Cokes," he recalled years later. "That was a hell of a lot more money than the $12.50 per diem the players were getting paid during training camp. Remember, our salaries didn't kick in until the regular season started."[13]

Anticipating that Retzlaff would challenge him, Bradley purchased a vendor's license, allowing him to conduct business at that spot. Just as he predicted, the general manager walked over to the VW van when he saw Bill doing business with the fans. Believing he would win the confrontation, Retzlaff, with a smug grin on his face, demanded to see the license. To his surprise, Bradley handed over the document. Retzlaff examined the license carefully and, after seeing that it was official, stormed off.

Some of Bill's teammates watched the scene unfold from the practice field and were amused by it. They knew exactly what he was doing. Bradley had sought the approval of his teammates beforehand by explaining that his holdout "wasn't just about me but about all of us who were getting stiffed on bonus money by management."[14]

Most Eagles players appreciated Bill's position and supported it. "If I had any money, I'd do the same thing Billy B is doing," said tackle Ernie Calloway. "But I'm broke because I sign everything the Eagles put in front of me. Billy's too smart for that. More power to him."

Safety Nate Ramsey agreed. "I'd like to see Billy in camp, but he has his grievances. It's his prerogative to stay away until he gets the money he's owed."

Others were put off by Bradley's decision to boycott the training camp. "Regardless of what his reasons are, I think [holding out] was done in poor taste," said linebacker Ron Porter. "He had an obligation to tell management and the coaches that he was planning to do that.

"Losing your all-star defensive back is a blow," Porter added. "But we just have to get the best 11 men [on defense] and go from there."[15]

Defensive coordinator Jim "Gummy" Carr echoed Porter's discontent. "Bill Bradley had a great year in 1971, but this is 1972," Carr told Ray Didinger of the *Evening Bulletin*. "Last year was actually Bill's first year playing regularly at free safety. He still has an awful lot to learn.

"This is an important training camp for him. But he's not here. What am I supposed to do? Cry about it? We just have to do the best we can with the people we've got available."[16]

Still others had mixed feelings. "Look, I wouldn't have done what Bradley did and not report to training camp," said halfback Tom Woodeshick in a recent interview. "But I sure understood why he did it. We all wanted to make the most money we could when we were playing because a pro football career is so short. I also felt bad for Pete Retzlaff, though. He was one of my favorite teammates and one of the best tight ends in the NFL. Pete was also a student of the game. To be honest, he should've been a head coach, not a general manager. I don't think Pete had the stomach to deal with all the politics that came with a front office job."[17]

Bradley's position became more problematic when middle linebacker Tim Rossovich asked to join him after the first week of his holdout. Rossovich, a four-year veteran, was earning $35,000 and wanted $50,000 for the 1972 season.[18] But he didn't have as much leverage to negotiate as Bradley. Rosso, a Pro Bowler as a defensive lineman in 1969, asked to shift to middle linebacker, a higher profile position, a year later. But he did not have the skills to play linebacker, which requires greater agility and speed than he possessed. Had the Eagles been a winning team, Tim probably would not have been allowed to make the change. In other words, Rossovich was expendable. That he did not get along with head coach Ed Khayat did not help his case either.

"Billy might've weakened his bargaining power by holding out with Tim," said Steve Zabel in a 2023 interview. "Billy held out first, and he really deserved to get a big raise. He was All-Pro and had led the league in interceptions. I'm not so sure that Tim had a right to hold out. He wasn't anywhere near the player Billy was, and he missed six weeks of the season in 1971 with a leg injury.

"Don't get me wrong. Tim and I were good friends, and he was a *very* tough player. But he was a little 'off-the-bubble.' He loved to do things to get a rise out of other people. Khayat really didn't care for that. Nor did he like Rosso's California, hippie lifestyle. Tim knew it too. He used to provoke Eddie by wearing tie-dyed robes in the locker room and hanging homoerotic pictures on his locker because he knew it bothered Khayat. When Timmy held out, he gave the Eagles a very good reason to get rid of him."[19]

Rossovich knew he did not enjoy the same bargaining power as Bradley. That's *exactly* why he asked to join his friend in holding out. After Retzlaff spent a total of two hours during the offseason discussing the linebacker's contract with his agent, Len Schaeffer, it was clear to Tim that the Eagles had no intention of raising his salary. But Schaeffer believed that if his client joined Bradley—the best player on the team—Retzlaff would have to reach an agreement with his client in order to get both players into training camp. "Teams typically wait until the last moment to negotiate with players," explained Schaeffer. "They'd rather do it at training camp because they know the player is anxious. He either hopes to make the team, or to retain his position, so he'll sign for whatever management offers him. We thought we had a better chance of getting paid what Tim wanted by not reporting to camp and forming a negotiating team with Bill Bradley and his agent, Mark Stewart. It's kind of like a package deal where the Eagles couldn't sign one without the other."[20]

On Stewart's advice, Bill stopped provoking Eagles management by selling sodas and sandwiches to hungry fans outside the Reading training camp facility. Instead, Bradley and Rossovich spent the next fifteen days down at the South Jersey shore, where they worked on conditioning and enjoyed the nightlife. They started in Atlantic City, but when the sportswriters tracked them down, they escaped to Margate.[21] "Timmy and I drove the press crazy during that holdout," recalled Bill. "They wanted to talk to us, but they couldn't find us because we kept moving. First, we went down to Atlantic City and got a place. When they got wind of where we were, we snuck out the back door and checked into another place in Margate. When they found us again, we snuck out and went to Somers Point. Timmy and I tried to stay one step ahead of the press so they'd leave us alone.

"We had a workout schedule each day, and we stuck to it. We'd start with a three-mile run. Then run sprints. After that we'd toss the ball around. At night we hung out at a few different places, like Maloney's and The Gables in Margate and Bay Shore's in Somers Point."[22]

The holdout ended on August 1, the day after Retzlaff traded Rossovich to the San Diego Chargers for a first-round draft pick. The deal put an abrupt end to speculation that the general manager would negotiate a two-in-one package deal.[23] When asked by John Flynn of the *Philadelphia Inquirer* if he regretted the holdout, Rosso replied, "There's nothing to regret. I enjoyed fifteen beautiful days with my best friend. We worked out hard in the day and harder at night.

"Maybe we compounded problems by not being in camp, but we certainly didn't create the problems that already exist on the team. The owner, the general manager, and the head coach destroyed the chemistry we built in 1971. But I still think the Eagles can win despite management if they just play for each other."[24]

The next day, Bradley met privately with Pete Retzlaff. Bill's agent, Mark Stewart, was not permitted to attend the hour-long meeting.[25] As it turned out, Stewart's advice was not needed. Bradley and Retzlaff agreed on a three-year contract worth more than $125,000.[26]

"What was most important to me about that contract was the incentive clause," said Bill. "The clause stipulated that all bonuses achieved would automatically be added to my base salary, which meant that I'd receive all of the bonus money I earned whether the Eagles won or not."[27]

While Bradley was elated over his new contract, he was also sad to see Rossovich go. "I'll miss him," he admitted. "A lot of people see Tim as an awesome-looking person who does some crazy things. But they don't look beneath the surface. He is a very sincere person, very warm-hearted. I know he will be missed by a lot of his teammates here."[28]

Bradley did not go unpunished for his holdout. When he reported to camp on August 2, he was demoted to third string safety behind Steve Preece and Pat Gibbs. It took him nearly three weeks to regain his starting role. But his first appearance in an exhibition game demonstrated his resolve. It came on August 13 against the New England Patriots. Bill entered the game in the second half and fired up the defense with his aggressive play. On the final play of the game Bradley made a pick to seal the 29–20 victory. "It was like starting the climb all over again," said Bill when asked about his demotion. "You get less work in practice when you're not on the first team. But I'm back now and that's all that really matters."[29]

Unfortunately, the Eagles posted a 1-5 record in the preseason. The last exhibition game was a humiliating 34–17 defeat by the Buffalo Bills. "The team is totally demoralized right now," Tom Woodeshick told the *Philadelphia Daily News* after the game. "Khayat told us all that if anybody said anything detrimental about the club to the media, he'd have us suspended from the league. Everybody's sick and tired of his mandates. I want to see him run out of town."[30]

Those were harsh but accurate words coming from a ten-year veteran who had given his heart and soul to the Eagles. Khayat, after learning of Woodeshick's remarks, cut him from the team. It was yet another example of the head coach's intolerance for dissent.

Ironically, Ed Khayat was hired by owner Leonard Tose not because of his football knowledge, which was average, but because of his supposed ability to communicate with the players.[31] However, his military-type discipline did not go over well with most of the Eagles' younger players who chafed at his grooming policy, and now he had angered the veterans with his threat to suspend any player who spoke candidly to the press.

"Eddie was ridiculously tough," recalled Steve Zabel, who became the team's middle linebacker after Rossovich was traded. "We had two-a-day practices for nine solid weeks of training camp. A lot of players got hurt. Morning practices were taken up with the nutcracker drill, where the offense went up against the defense with no holds barred.

"I'll never forget playing the Redskins in Washington in an exhibition game that ended at 9:00 p.m. Then we got on the bus and drove all the way back to Reading. We didn't get back until 1:00 a.m., and we were on the field by 9:00 a.m. the next morning. Khayat had us go full-speed, goal-line scrimmage. It was crazy."[32]

While Bradley considered the head coach's disciplinary measures absurd, he was in no position to criticize him, not after receiving a significant pay raise. Instead, Bill was diplomatic when asked about Khayat and his military-like player's code. "You've got to respect the man," he told Gordon Forbes of the *Philadelphia Inquirer*. "He's an honest man. He's consistent. You've got to respect him for that, even if you don't always agree with him."[33]

Bill was a natural leader, though. He saw that team morale was at an all-time low. Having resolved the contract issue, he turned his complete attention to football and encouraging his teammates. "Let me tell you, Billy was a phenomenal athlete, probably the greatest one I've ever seen," gushed rookie linebacker John Bunting, who was selected by the Eagles in the tenth round of the 1972 draft from the University of North Carolina. "I'm not saying he was the strongest or the fastest, but I'd never seen anyone else do the things that he did on the field. When he arrived in camp, the energy on the team reached another level.

"Billy was very intense and had the ability to focus in on practice," Bunting explained. "He had an even keener mindset on game day. He knew exactly what was happening on the field—what alignment the running backs were in, the splits of the wide receivers, the quarterback reads. Billy had all that knowledge, plus an uncanny sense of where the ball was going after it was snapped. That's why he was so great.

"To be honest, I was in awe of Bill Bradley after I saw what he could do on the field. As a rookie, you're supposed to be seen and not heard, so it took me a little while to approach him."[34]

Super Bill carried that same high energy into the regular season. The Birds opened in Dallas on September 17. The Philadelphia defense dominated the first half, highlighted by Bradley's first interception of the season and a fumble recovery. Still, the Super Bowl champion Cowboys managed a razor-thin 7–6 halftime lead.[35] In the second half, the Birds were done in by a combination of poor conditioning and temperatures that exceeded 100 degrees at field level. Dallas opened the half by picking off two John Reaves passes and running them back for touchdowns. It could have been worse.[36]

Having identified a vulnerability in the Eagles' secondary, the Cowboys put a wide receiver in motion to clear the cornerback, leaving Bill, the weakside safety, to cover the middle field by himself. The first time Dallas ran the play, quarterback Craig Morton showed play action to bring Bradley up, which left the middle open for speedy receiver Bob Hayes. Morton hit him perfectly in the hands for what should have been an 81-yard touchdown play. But Bill startled Hayes at the last second by screaming at him and forcing a dropped ball. After that, Bradley won the cat-and-mouse game with Morton by zoning in on the intended receiver. Regardless, the Eagles were humiliated by the 28–6 stomping, which was Dallas's tenth straight victory over Philadelphia.[37]

The next week, the Birds opened at home against the Cleveland Browns. Unfortunately, Bradley had a schizophrenic performance, and his second-half heroics could not make up for the blunders he made in the first half.

With the score tied 3–3 in the first quarter, Browns quarterback Mike Phipps floated a swing pass to Leroy Kelley in the left flat. Bill came up fast and dove for Kelley's legs but could not hold on for the tackle. Kelly dashed 22 yards to set up the Browns' second field goal of the game. Five minutes later, after Cleveland increased its lead, 13–3, Bill leaped over Browns receiver Frank Pitts, attempting to intercept a goal-line pass and missed. Pitts caught the ball and ran it into the end zone, making the score 20–3 in Cleveland's favor.

On Philadelphia's next possession, quarterback Pete Liske managed to get the Birds' offense into Browns territory. With thirteen seconds remaining in the half and a fourth-and-long, Khayat sent in kicker Tom Dempsey. But the field goal attempt went wide to the right, and the Browns held a 20–3 halftime lead.[38]

Cleveland scored another touchdown early in the third quarter, to make the score 27–3. At that point, Khayat pulled Liske and put in second-string quarterback John Reaves, a first-round draft pick from the University of Miami. Reaves proceeded to direct an 80-yard drive for the Eagles' first touchdown of the season. On Cleveland's next possession, Bradley transformed into "Super Bill" and made a juggling interception of a sideline pass intended for Kelly.[39] "It was a hot play," he remembered. "I didn't grab the ball cleanly, so I tried to control it by juggling it back and forth until I could pull it in. I certainly didn't do it for show! If I had caught that ball cleanly, I could've gotten more yards on the return than the 15 I picked up."[40]

Bradley's interception set up the second Philadelphia touchdown of the afternoon and narrowed the score to 27–17. Cleveland punted on its next possession, and Bill returned the ball 60 yards down sideline to the Browns' 20. "They over-pursued to the right, and under-pursued to the left," Super Bill explained after the game. "So I ran up the middle, then hit the sideline. But I waited too long to make my cut behind the blockers. Otherwise, I would have scored a touchdown."[41]

Instead, the Eagles, after three failed plays from scrimmage, called on kicker Tom Dempsey to try a 26-yard field goal to put the Birds within a single score of tying the game. But Dempsey's attempt went wide to the right.

Unfortunately, Bradley was involved in both field goal failures. Bill was Dempsey's holder during the 1971 season, but when he did not report to training camp, Khayat reassigned the duty to Steve Preece. Bradley resumed the holding role when Preece was cut after the first regular season game.[42] True to his nature, Bill tried to take the rap for both blown field goals. "There are no excuses," he told the sportswriters. "My holds have got to be better."[43] But Dempsey refused to let his teammate shoulder the blame.

"Each holder is different," he explained, giving the media a brief tutorial. "Each one holds the ball and sets himself differently. Steve held the ball with his left hand and placed his right knee on the ground and his left leg behind him. Billy uses the conventional style where he holds the ball with his right hand and has the left knee on the ground and the right leg extended. I have to adjust to Billy, and we just haven't worked together that much this season. I'm confident that we'll figure it out. Remember, I led the league in percentage a year ago when Billy was holding for me."[44]

On October 2 the Eagles played the rival New York Giants on *Monday Night Football*. Despite the sellout crowd of 65,720 passionate fans who packed Veteran Stadium, the Birds turned in another forgettable performance, losing 27–12.[45] Even ABC broadcaster Howard Cosell had to admit that the "Eagles defense was as flat as a pancake," allowing the Giants' offense to "go through them as though they were tissue paper." Minutes before halftime, with the Giants leading, 14–3, Cosell pronounced the Eagles "dead" and the game "just too painful to watch."[46]

The following week, the Eagles traveled to Washington to take on the Redskins at RFK Stadium. Bradley had two picks. The first one came in the second quarter, killing a Redskins seven-minute, 75-yard drive. Washington had third-and-three at the Eagles' 3-yard line. Quarterback Sonny Jurgensen took the snap from center, dropped back, and saw wide receiver Charley Taylor wide open in the end zone before launching an underthrown pass. Super Bill stole the ball and returned it 15 yards for his fourth interception of the season.

Interception number 5 came in the third quarter after Jurgensen engineered a 69-yard drive that began at the Redskins' 29. With third-and-goal at the Eagles' 2, Bradley stole a touchdown with a one-handed interception in the end zone on a play-action pass intended for tight end Jerry Smith.[47] "Bradley was tough to beat," said Jurgenson after the game. "He's also the best free safety in the league. I have to do a better job keeping the ball away from him."[48]

Bill's heroics could not stop Jurgensen, though. The Redskins' future Hall of Famer threw for two touchdowns in the third quarter to seal the 14–0 win for Washington. The second tally was the most frustrating for Bill, who was beaten in coverage by Charley Taylor. Taylor then raised his two arms in the end zone in a self-congratulatory act. Irked by the gesture, Bradley walked over to the receiver and slammed the football out of his hands.[49]

After the game, Taylor dismissed any bad blood between the two players. "Me and Billy are just two country boys from Texas," he said when asked about the altercation. "No place for hard feelings between us. The man's a real competitor and I enjoy playing against him."[50]

Bradley felt differently. On the next Redskins possession, teammates had to intervene to prevent a brawl between the two players. The memory still stings Bill fifty years later. "Taylor was one of the very first showboaters in the NFL," he recalled. "Those were the days before guys started doing end zone celebrations. I thought it was bullshit. But I got him back later in that game.

"He was running across the middle [of the field], and I clotheslined him. Nailed him so hard that he didn't get up for a good long while. The refs didn't catch it either. I didn't want to put him in the hospital, but I wanted to teach him a little humility."[51]

The Eagles got a huge dose of humility themselves on October 15 at the Vet when they dropped their fifth straight game, this one to the Los Angeles Rams, 34–3. It was their most pathetic showing of the season. Rookie quarterback John Reaves, starting his third game, threw two costly interceptions and committed three fumbles before being yanked with 10:48 left to play. The defense was just as bad, giving up 166 yards on the ground to Rams rushers and 147 yards in the air to sore-armed quarterback Roman Gabriel.[52]

Despite the lowlights, an amazingly patient sellout crowd of 65,720 hometown fans watched silently while their team unraveled. Midway through the fourth quarter, they finally had had enough and erupted in a deafening serenade of "Good-Bye, Eddie!" Khayat later insisted the jeering went for naught because he suffered from a "chronic hearing problem."[53]

Bradley felt the fans' pain, though. Enraged by the poor performance, Bill, with minutes left to play, stormed off the field, threw his helmet down on the ground, and kicked over the trainer's table. Unbeknownst to him, Don Boyne, an assistant trainer, was kneeling behind the table preparing an icepack. The table collapsed, hitting Boyne in the head and momentarily knocking him out. "I remember that outburst," said Ray Didinger, who was covering the game for the *Evening Bulletin*. "Boyne was a really nice fellow. I felt bad for him. So did Billy after he saw what happened. Those were frustrating times for Bill. He was leading the league in interceptions and going to the Pro Bowl, but he was still angry because the team was losing. He *always* put the team first."[54]

It was no secret that all the losing bothered Bradley. He was an intense competitor who failed to find any satisfaction in personal success when it wasn't translating into victories for the team. "Look, I'm proud of what I did in my pro career, and I still am," insisted Bill recently. "But my time in the NFL was bittersweet because I never enjoyed a winning season and I worked so hard to become the best at my position and to become a good teammate. You'd like to reap the rewards for all that hard work, but it never came."[55]

The Eagles finally won their first game on October 22 at Kansas City with a 21–20 upset of the Chiefs. Pete Liske, starting at quarterback for the first time since September 24, threw two touchdown passes of 36 and 41 yards to Harold Jackson and a third score of 67 yards to Ben Hawkins to steal the victory.[56] But the joy was short-lived.

When the Birds traveled to New Orleans the next week to play the winless Saints, they were embarrassed again, losing 21–3. Kicker Tom Dempsey was responsible for the Eagles' only score with a 17-yard field goal that came in the second quarter.[57] It proved to be the first of nine consecutive field goals for Dempsey over a three-game span in which he was responsible for all of Philadelphia's scoring. He booted two field goals against St. Louis the following week in the Eagles' 6–6 tie with the Cardinals. Fortunately, Jim Bakken, the St. Louis kicker, blew a 27-yard attempt with seventeen seconds left to play that would have given the Cards the victory.[58] Dempsey was perfect again on November 12 at Houston's Astrodome, converting on all six attempts ranging from 12 to 52 yards. Singlehandedly the kicker lifted the Birds to their second and final victory of the season, an 18–17 snoozer against the Oilers.[59]

Meanwhile, Bradley stole two more picks in the November 5 game against the Cardinals to increase his NFL-leading seven interceptions on the season. The second pick was the more impressive of the two. It came in the third quarter on a Tim Van Galder pass to Fred Hyatt, a 6-foot-3, 200-pound wide receiver. Bradley jumped four feet off the ground to catch that ball. "I was able to make that interception because of my experience as a high jumper and broad jumper in high school," he explained. "That taught me how to power step for a jump and then gather the ball. I guess

I was fortunate to be born with all kinds of coordination that transferred across all the sports I played."[60]

Many years later, Bill explained the art of playing free safety and why he was able to be so successful as a ball hawk. "To play the position effectively, you have to have good hands, speed, quickness, [and] the ability to change direction and do it quickly," he said. "You also have to be a good actor before the ball is snapped. For example, when the quarterback gets the snap from center and as he's dropping back, he's immediately trying to identify the defensive coverage. Is there a safety in the middle with man-to-man on the edges, or cover man free? If there are two half safeties in the middle, the coverage is either half zone or half man. If there are two safeties, the coverage is either man-to-man or zone coverage underneath. At that point, when the quarterback is trying to identify the coverage, you've gotta decoy him with a false read.

"Because I was a quarterback in high school and college, I knew that when a quarterback dropped back to pass, he'd immediately look to see if the defense was in half safeties (man open) or three-deep safeties (man closed). I knew how to trick quarterbacks by making them misread our defense by disguising our coverages."[61]

But reading and decoying the quarterback was only part of Bradley's success. Whenever he gave a fake look, he also had to act in concert with the rest of the defense, especially the linebackers and the secondary. "We all had to work on the fakes in practice where we gave the offense a single high free safety, but you show two half safeties. We'd start out like we're staying in half safeties, but then we'd immediately go to a system where one safety is going back and the other is going to the middle."[62]

Finally, whatever success Bill enjoyed as a ball hawk was due just as much to the defensive line as it was to his own abilities as a free safety. "If the Eagles didn't have a damn good pass rush, I wouldn't have been nearly as successful as I was those two years I led the league in interceptions. Garry Pettigrew, Tim Rossovich, and Mel Tom were excellent on the line, and Billy Hobbs, Ron Porter, and Steve Zabel were every bit as talented at linebacker. Those guys created the opportunity for me to pick off so many passes, especially when they went into a five-man blitz with zone coverage behind it. They gave the quarterback so much pressure, he was forced to release the ball earlier than he wanted to."[63]

If the Eagles thought they had turned their season around with their razor thin 18–17 win over Houston, they were sorely mistaken. Not only did they lose their remaining five games, but they were blown out in three of them. On November 19 the Birds were throttled by the Cowboys at the Vet and in front of a national television audience, 28–7. Bradley also had his ninth and final interception of the season.[64] At least Philadelphia scored a touchdown in the game, the first since October 22, when they defeated the Chiefs in Kansas City. The Eagles dropped a similar game to the Redskins on December 3, when they lost at Washington, 23–7.[65] Between those two losses however came the most crushing defeat of the entire season, if not in franchise history, when the Giants humiliated the Birds, 62–10, at New York's Yankee Stadium on November 26.[66]

"What can I say? I'm embarrassed," Bradley told Ray Didinger of the *Evening Bulletin* after the blowout. "We're all embarrassed. We've been apart all season. We've forgotten how to win.

"Maybe I'm responsible for some of it by holding out," he added. "One thing is obvious to me, though. We miss Timmy [Rossovich]."[67]

Philadelphia lost its last home game of the 1972 season on December 10 against the Chicago Bears, 21–12. For Eagles fans, the greatest excitement came in the fourth quarter. With the Bears clinging to a 14–12 advantage, quarterback Bobby Douglass engineered a 68-yard drive to extend Chicago's lead by 6 points. When kicker Mac Percival came in to attempt the point after, Douglass, the holder, fumbled the snap. But he managed to recover and connected with linebacker Dick Butkus in the end zone for the extra point. Butkus, gloating over the catch, shoved the ball in front of Bradley's face. Disgusted by the showboating, Bill slammed the ball away.[68] But he was not quite finished.

As Butkus was receiving a congratulatory hug from tackle Randy Jackson, Bradley shouted, "Kiss my butt, Butkus! You fat fuck!"

No doubt, the Bears' legendary linebacker had heard the kiss-my-butt crack before. What infuriated him was being called a fat fuck. Butkus, sensitive about his weight, turned and chased Bradley 30 yards down the sideline until Bill found refuge on the Eagles' bench next to a gaggle of his own linebackers.

"I'll get you for this, you little shit," swore Butkus, before returning to the Chicago bench.[69]

The Eagles completed their frustrating season on December 17 in St. Louis. Losing to the Cardinals, 24–23, the woeful Birds clinched last place in the Eastern Division with a 2-11-1 record.[70] Bradley, who played the entire game with the flu, nearly had a tenth interception but came up short. "Other teams weren't throwing much the last four games," Bill noted when asked why his last pick came nearly a month ago. "When they did throw the ball, they didn't throw to the deep middle, which is my [coverage] zone. I wound up playing the run like a middle linebacker."[71]

Still, Bradley's nine interceptions that season were good enough to lead the NFL for the second straight year, making him the first player in the league's history to have back-to-back years leading that category. He also earned an invitation to another Pro Bowl and a spot on the All-Pro first team.[72]

On December 18 owner Leonard Tose fired head coach Ed Khayat and his entire staff, and general manager Pete Retzlaff resigned. It was a disappointing end to what had promised to be a good season after a strong finish the year before.[73]

Bradley looked forward to the offseason. While he dedicated himself fully to football for six months of the year, he savored the other six when he could do as he pleased. It gave him time to dabble in various business interests, which often led to other, more appealing opportunities. For example, Bill established a business back home in Palestine that made travel bags and then partnered with Macy's and Nieman Marcus to sell them. That venture resulted in a brief career as a runway model at both department stores.

In fact, Bradley, who had impeccable taste for men's clothing, became a fashion plate during his years in Philadelphia. The modeling allowed him to date some of the most attractive women in the fashion business too.

"Hell, I was young and single and free to do whatever I wanted to do," he recalled in a 2022 interview. "I met a lot of gorgeous women. The ones who most attracted me were tall and thin but also wholesome looking."

For as outgoing as Bill was with people, he was very bashful in the company of beautiful young women. Desperate to date one of the most stunning models by the name of Olive, Bradley pretended to be gay, hoping to appear less threatening than other men who were on the prowl. Then he mustered the courage to approach her. Speaking in an affected manner, Bill walked up to the model's make-up table and struck up a conversation by remarking, "Oh, honey, that outfit looks so wonderful on you!" Eventually, Olive revealed her name and her various interests, which included dancing. Then, after they completed their runway modeling, Bradley suggested that they go to a disco.

Once out on the dance floor, Bill blew his cover. Known at the most popular Philadelphia-area nightclubs as the "Dance Hall Doctor from Texas," several people came up to him to say hello. If that didn't raise suspicion, Olive knew for sure that Bradley was straight when she saw his macho style on the dance floor.

"Oh, Bill, you're not gay!" she chuckled.

"Can you blame me, though?" he replied. "I just wanted to go out with you so badly. I didn't want to scare you off either, so it was the only way I knew to get a date."

Impressed by his candor, Olive admitted that the ploy was "sheer genius" and agreed to go out with him again.[74]

Bradley loved to spend his summers traveling across the country in his Cottonmouth Blues Wagon, visiting friends, taking in a few bluegrass festivals, and camping in national parks. During the summer of 1973, however, Bill traded in his VW van for air-conditioned Cadillac limousine and spent a month traveling across country with his old pal, Tim Rossovich. They began in South Philadelphia and headed south en route to Rosso's home in Manhattan Beach, California. Needless to say, two longhaired football players cruising through the Deep South in a Cadillac limousine attracted some attention.

"We pulled into a Burger Chef in Mississippi, and the folks inside stopped everything when Timmy walked in," recalled Bradley. When he returned to the car a woman approached the two hippies and asked if they were with a rock band.

"Yeah, we're with a band," replied Bill tongue-in-cheek, "but we couldn't fit the other ten members in the car."

A week later, the two friends were stopped at a red light in Houston, and the driver next to them could not stop staring at Rossovich, who was sitting in the back. "You know how unreal Timmy looks," explained Bill. "Not only is he huge, but he's got all that bushy long hair." Still staring at Rossovich when the light turned green, the motorist hit the gas pedal and slammed into the car in front of him. "We just pulled away laughing," Bradley chuckled.[75]

When he wasn't traveling, Bill remained in South Philadelphia, where he rented a rowhouse about 200 yards from the Vet. The house was decorated with memorabilia from his high school and college athletic careers. But in one corner of the living room there was a wooden oak coffin with a four-inch mattress resting on the lid. Built by his old high school friends Curtis Fitzgerald and Hal Sumrall, Bradley was so touched by the gift that he slept on top of it at night and planned to be buried in it after he died.[76]

Bill was a fixture in the neighborhood, where he routinely played pickup basketball and Wiffle ball games in the streets with local youngsters and dated many of their older sisters, but only the most attractive ones. On late summer afternoons he could be found at the Vet taking batting and fielding practice with the Phillies. According to Eagles center Mike Evans, Super Bill was "so good at the sport he could've easily played Major League Baseball." One September afternoon before practice, the Eagles held a home run derby at the Vet, and Bradley won the event, slugging six of eight pitches over the fence. Even Phillies players who were watching were impressed by his hitting prowess.[77] But as much as Bradley loved baseball, he focused his complete attention on football when the Eagles went to training camp in July 1973.

There was a new head coach in town. Owner Leonard Tose hired Mike McCormack, an assistant with the NFC champion Washington Redskins, to reverse the fortunes of his struggling franchise. McCormack knew that success would have to be immediate. Tose was impatient. He had fired two head coaches in as many years. The fans were tired of losing. The

Eagles had posted one winning season out of the past eleven. Nobody in Philadelphia wanted to hear about a five-year rebuilding process. Fans wanted to win now.

If there was any coach who could achieve that goal, McCormack appeared to be the one. He came from a winning pedigree. McCormack, a 6-foot-4, 250-pound offensive lineman with the Cleveland Browns in the 1950s, played for the legendary Paul Brown and later coached for Vince Lombardi and George Allen, two other Hall of Fame coaches. He saw firsthand how Allen reversed the fortunes of the hapless Redskins in a single year by trading draft picks for veterans who could play right away. He planned to use the same formula with the Eagles.[78]

McCormack began with an excellent draft, selecting tackle Jerry Sisemore from Texas, tight end Charles Young from USC, center Guy Morriss from TCU, safety Randy Logan from Michigan, and cornerback Joe Lavender from San Diego State. Then he acquired quarterback Roman Gabriel, a three-time Pro Bowler, from the Los Angeles Rams for Harold Jackson and two first-round picks, and fullback Norm Bulaich, another Pro Bowler, from the Baltimore Colts for two more draft picks.[79]

"I'm anxious to get started this season," Bradley chirped on the first day of training camp, which had relocated to Widener College in Chester, Pennsylvania. "McCormack is a competitor, and I like that. He had a great draft. He brought in Roman Gabriel, who's a much better, much more established quarterback than we've had in years. He also got [Norm] Bulaich who'll immediately improve the run game. We finally have an offense that will put up a lot of points."[80]

Harold Carmichael, who was named cocaptain by McCormack before the regular season began, would have a breakout year. "Offensively, we were better than we had ever been," said Carmichael in a 2022 interview. "Bulaich and [Tom] 'Silky' Sullivan added depth to our running game. Young was a deep threat, and I could pull down a high pass. Gabriel was the perfect veteran quarterback for us too. He was smart and had a great arm. We really lit it up that year."[81]

Despite all the optimism coming out of training camp, Philadelphia opened the 1973 season by losing to St. Louis (24–23), Washington (28–7), and Buffalo (27–26) and tying the New York Giants (23–23).[82] Bradley, who went the first two games without an interception, finally broke his dry spell against Sonny Jurgensen in the loss against Washington. "Bradley's like a ghost," said Jurgensen. "He's there, but you don't see him until it's too late."

"I enjoy playing against Sonny," Bill admitted. "He's a competitor and we needle each other. He'll look across the line at me to check where I am and I'll just smile at him. I must get to him sometimes because he smiles back."[83]

Unfortunately, Bradley's interception total slipped to just four in 1973 because he was no longer able to roam as freely as he had in previous seasons. McCormack's defensive coverages did not allow him to play the ball as easily forcing him into a more disciplined role. Bill was also asked to mentor the two rookies playing alongside him, Randy Logan and Joe Lavender, which also limited his ability to freelance. To lighten Bradley's workload, McCormack reassigned punting duties to Tom McNeill, who had been acquired from the Minnesota Vikings.[84]

"I'm not worried about the interceptions," Bill insisted. "I'll get my chances. Besides, if I had a choice between leading the league in picks and playing for a winner, I'd take being on a winner every time."[85]

The Eagles won their first game on October 14, defeating the Cardinals in St. Louis. Trailing 24–13 with less than two minutes remaining, Roman Gabriel connected with Harold Carmichael on a 27-yard pass. Then, before the clock ran out, Gabe hit rookie Don Zimmerman with a 23-yard pass. The wide receiver carried three Cardinals defenders into the end zone, putting the Birds ahead, 27–24, and sealing the Philadelphia victory.[86]

After losing to the Minnesota Vikings, 28–21, the next week, the Birds upset the Dallas Cowboys, 30–16, at the Vet on October 28. Gabriel and Carmichael led the offensive attack, connecting twice on touchdown passes. But the defense monopolized the big plays, stealing passes, prying loose fumbles, and gang-tackling at the point of attack.[87] Although the rookie safety Randy Logan and linebacker Steve Zabel came away with the interceptions, Bradley was instrumental in leading the defense. "Billy wasn't only a captain of the defense but also the heart and soul of it," recalled linebacker John Bunting, who played with such ferocity against Dallas that he broke his left arm tackling running back Calvin Hill. "Billy just had this insatiable desire to win. He was so jacked to play the Cowboys that he was actually crying in the locker room before the game. That's how much he hated Dallas. It rubbed off on me too. When you see a teammate with that kind of passion, you don't want to let him down."[88]

The Eagles won their third game the following week against the New England Patriots. Trailing 17–0 in the third quarter, Gabriel threw a pair of touchdown passes to tight end Charles Young. Rookie defensive end Will Wynn then recovered a fumbled punt snap and ran 24 yards for a third touchdown in less than six minutes. Although New England rallied to take the lead, 23–21, in the last quarter, Gabriel would not be denied the victory. Marching the offense down field on a drive that started at the Eagles' 20, Gabe put the Birds on the Patriots' 12 before Tom Dempsey kicked a three-pointer to put them ahead, 24–23. Linebacker Steve Zabel saved the win by blocking Jeff White's 47-yard field-goal attempt on the final play of the game.[89]

On November 18 the Eagles traveled to Dallas for a rematch against the hated Cowboys. Although the Birds lost, 31–10, Bradley did everything possible to help his teammates. Not only did he record an interception, but he also returned three kicks for gains of 26, 28, and 32 yards and resumed his former role as the Birds' punter in the second half. McNeill, the regular punter, had his second horrific performance in a row, averaging just 37.2 yards on four punts and had three of them run back by the Cowboys for scores.[90]

Bradley punted four times in the second half, averaging 47.7 yards a kick and getting one off at 52 yards. More impressive, the Cowboys did not gain a single yard in returns against him.[91]

"Bill might've gone in earlier, except that he's had a broken hand," McCormack told the press after the game. "The cast just came off last week. But we knew eventually he'd be punting."

Bradley insisted that he was "not trying to lead the league in punting, just wanting to hang the ball up there.

"A good consistent 38- to 42-yard average is fine if you can get from 4½ to 5 seconds of 'hang time' on your punts," he explained.[92] But Bill was so amped up against the Cowboys that he far exceeded that average. One of his punts traveled 48 yards with a remarkable 5.1 hang time and nearly hit the roof of Texas Stadium.[93]

When Roman Gabriel suffered an elbow injury at the end of the second quarter, Bill was an injury away from returning to quarterback. If backup John Reaves got hurt, Bradley would have had to take the snaps because Rick Arrington, the taxi-squad quarterback, did not dress for the game. It would have been interesting to see what Bill could have done as a play-caller, especially back home in Texas where he once starred at that position for the Longhorns. But Bradley made no secret of his preference.

"I'd rather be the hitter than the hittee," Bill confessed.[94] Nor did he make any secret of his disdain for an old nemesis, Mike Ditka, who was in his first year as a special teams coach with the Cowboys. "Billy just hated Ditka when they played against each other," recalled linebacker and special teams captain Kevin Reilly in a recent interview. "Billy would always trash-talk him, and Ditka would go after him. It didn't matter that Ditka was a coach now. Billy was going to go after him again.

"Bill came into the game to punt in the third quarter and kicked the ball towards the Dallas sideline," explained Reilly. "I was following the ball because it was buzzing down my side. Ditka, watching the punt like everyone else on the Cowboys' bench, was literally standing on the playing field and screaming at one of his players. Suddenly Bradley came bolting down the Dallas sideline, blew past me, and bore in on Ditka, who didn't see him at all. Billy blindsided him with a forearm to the head and decked him. Nobody saw it but the Eagles players who were running down that sideline.

"Ditka just flipped out! You could see the veins in his neck he was so pissed off. He threw down his clipboard and started calling Billy every name in the book.

"As we were running off the field, all the Eagles were chanting, 'Billy Bo Bitch! Billy Bo Bitch!'"[95]

When asked how he acquired the colorful nickname, Bradley attributed it to his fierce competitiveness. "I hated losing, and that's all we did in Philly," he explained. "I'd get so mad that I'd bitch at our linebackers who wouldn't block. If they didn't, I'd have a 275-pound lineman on me annihilating my 180-pound ass. Because of all my bitchin' the linebackers started calling me 'Billy Bo Bitch.'"[96]

However, linebacker John Bunting, who gave Bradley the moniker, tells a slightly different story. "One of the reasons I gave him the name 'Billy Bo Bitch' was because he bitched a lot on the field. We had a porous defense without a very strong line back then. That meant Billy was in play on every snap. He worked his ass off, and if he didn't think you were giving your fullest effort, he'd start bitching at you.

"The other reason I gave him that nickname was because he was a bitch of a player. Billy was not the prototypical free or strong safety. At barely 6 feet and 180 pounds, he wasn't a monster. Not many opponents feared him. I think that's why he was such a trash-talker. But he never backed off anyone either.

"I'd see Billy hit a 6-foot-4, 235-pound tight end like Jackie Smith of the Cardinals and bounce right off him. Billy had to play with every bit of strength and energy he had in his body. But he was a tough bitch of a player. We were just lucky he was our bitch!"[97]

On November 25 the Birds picked up their fourth victory, this one against the New York Giants, 20–16. Running back Tom Sullivan rushed for 156 yards, and Tom Dempsey kicked a 51-yard field goal to seal the win. A 38–28 loss to the San Francisco 49ers followed, but the Eagles rebounded on December 9 to defeat the New York Jets, 24–23. The Birds rallied from a 17-point deficit on a 45-yard interception return by John Outlaw and a 40-yard field goal by Dempsey.[98]

Philadelphia closed out its season on December 16 against the Redskins at RFK Stadium in Washington DC. The Eagles jumped out to a 10–0 lead in the first quarter on a 34-yard touchdown pass from Gabriel to tight end Charles Young and a 44-yard field goal by Dempsey. But the Redskins stormed back with a 24-point second quarter thanks to three

Billy Kilmer touchdown passes and a field goal. Kilmer threw two more touchdowns in the second half to secure the 38–20 Redskins victory, but not before Bradley intercepted him on a pass intended for his nemesis, wide receiver Charley Taylor.[99]

"I could trick Billy Kilmer even better than [Sonny] Jurgensen," said Bradley many years later. "He wasn't very elusive in the pocket, and we had a good pass rush. When Kilmer got pressured, he was forced to get rid of the ball because he couldn't extend the play by scrambling. I knew I could break on some of his first looks and get a jump on the ball."[100]

After Bradley retired, he became good friends with Kilmer. Once, at an NFL alumni event, the former Eagle walked up to the one-time Redskins quarterback and said, "Billy, I just want to thank you and Sonny [Jurgensen]."

"What for?" asked Kilmer.

"For putting me in the Pro Bowl in 1971 and 1972," replied Bradley. "'Cause I intercepted you guys more than any other quarterbacks those two years I lead the league in picks."[101]

Bill also relished the fact that his final interception of the season came off the hands of Redskins All-Pro wide receiver Charley Taylor. Bradly remembered the dig Taylor gave him after their altercation the previous year, when he told the *Philadelphia Inquirer* that the free safety could be a "great leader on defense for the Eagles, if he changed the 'hot dog' he has in him. . . . If he doesn't, it'll be tough for the other guys to respect him."

Taylor accused Bill of being a hot dog because he was always involved in sideline disputes or temperamental displays. But Bradley defended his behavior as the "only way I can survive in the league."

"A lot of guys have big physiques," explained Bill, who was only 5 feet 11 inches and weighed 180 pounds at most. "I just don't have their size. I either bring them down to my size physically—which ain't ever going to happen—or reduce them to my size with my mouth. Besides, who's to say that I'm not a leader? Leadership comes in many different ways."[102]

The Eagles completed the 1973 season third in the NFC East with a record of 5-8-1. It was a three-win improvement over the previous year. Other hopeful signs raised fan expectations for 1974. Quarterback Roman

Gabriel was voted the NFL's Comeback Player of the Year, leading the league with 3,219 passing yards and twenty-three touchdowns. Wide receiver Harold Carmichael led the league with sixty-seven receptions for 1,116 yards, while Charles Young led all tight ends with fifty-five catches. Tom Sullivan emerged as one of the best running backs in the league, rushing for 968 yards. Gabriel, Carmichael, and Young were also named to the Pro Bowl, along with Bradley, who made his third appearance, this time as a punt returner.[103] Bill was also the best ambassador the Eagles had off the playing field.

During his eight years in Philadelphia, Bradley was involved in many community-service projects. In the off-season, he played on a basketball team established by Eagles trainer Otho Davis to help players stay in shape and to raise funds for local charities. The team traveled across southeastern and central Pennsylvania and southern New Jersey, playing games against college and high school teachers and occasionally a semipro team. Bradley was one of the star players. "In the winter of 1973–74, we must've played sixty basketball games," recalled linebacker John Bunting. "That's when I really came to appreciate Billy's athletic ability. He could do anything. He could dunk a basketball, hit a hook shot, you name it."[104]

In a game against a semipro team from Allentown, for example, Bradley grabbed a rebound with his back to the basket, then flipped the ball backward and over his head to score on a shot that hit nothing but net.[105]

One of Bill's finest performances came against the faculty of Kutztown State College in central Pennsylvania. Prior to the charity event, a lovely Italian girl he had been dating for several months had broken up with him. Bill showed up at the game wearing black socks up to his knees because he was, as he put it, "in mourning over the breakup."

If that was true, it certainly didn't take Bradley long to forget about her. Not only did he score 30 points and record twelve assists that night, but also after the game he went into the bleachers and began sweet-talking some of the coeds.

While his teammates were loading up the bus to return to Veterans Stadium by 11:00 p.m., Kevin Reilly spotted Bradley with two pretty college girls, one on each knee.

"Billy, it's time to go," Reilly beckoned. "We're loading up the Winnebago."

"Tell 'em to go ahead without us, Kev," replied Bradley.

"How we gonna get home?"

"Well, these girls said we can stay the night in their dorm rooms," Bill said dismissively. "We'll find a way to get back to Philly tomorrow."

"How we gonna do that?" persisted Reilly.

Bradley, wanting to focus his energies on the two girls, was beginning to get annoyed with his teammate. "Look, Reilly," he snapped, "trains made this country! There's gotta be a train station around here somewhere. We'll find it and take a train home tomorrow. If you don't want to do that, get on the damn bus and go!"

Once assured that he could spend the night in the dorms, Reilly agreed to stay. The next morning, Bill, after a night of servicing the girls, located a station for himself and his teammate and hitched a ride in time to catch the next train to Philadelphia.[106]

Although Bradley certainly enjoyed playing basketball for charity, as well as the fringe benefits that came with it, his favorite community involvements were with youngsters. Bill was one of the first Eagles to jump on board to raise money for a home to accommodate families with children who were being treated at Children's Hospital of Philadelphia. "I did a lot of fundraising appearances for that project," Bradley recalled. "Once I went to a strip mall in Northeast Philly where they put me in the crow's nest of huge truck with a lift on the back. They gave me a few dozen mini plastic footballs with the Eagles logo on them. I'd signed each one and then chucked 'em down to the crowd below. I had a blast. I loved doing that kind of thing. Just to see the faces of the kids light up made it all worthwhile."[107]

The Birds eventually partnered with McDonald's to raise some $42,000 to build what would become known as the Ronald McDonald House at 4032 Spruce Street. Opened on October 15, 1974, Philadelphia's Ronald McDonald House was the very first of 365 similar houses that exist today in sixty-three countries on six continents.[108]

Bradley was also recruited by Mayor Frank Rizzo to become involved with the Philadelphia Murals Project to eradicate graffiti on inner-city buildings. Rizzo knew the impact a successful professional athlete could have on the gangs who were doing the graffiti, so he enlisted Bill to go out into the neighborhoods and talk with them.

"The police would identify the kids who were doing the graffiti, and then I would go out into the community and talk to them to understand why they were doing it," Bradley explained. "What I found out is that many of them were good kids who genuinely liked to do art. I tried to encourage them to use their artistic talent in a constructive way. Those who agreed would be sent to art classes to learn how to paint murals.

"I am very proud of that program," Bill added. "It laid the foundations for literally dozens of beautiful neighborhood murals you see in the city today. In fact, Philadelphia gained national recognition for those murals."[109]

Bradley credits his love for kids to his younger brother, Duffy, and other youngsters with special needs. "I was protective of my younger brother," he admits. "Special-needs kids are the most genuine people I know. They're innocent and very trusting. But that's why they need someone to advocate for them.

"When I left home to play in the NFL, I made sure to see Duffy as much as possible. In the off-season, I'd go back to Palestine and saw that he and his special-needs classmates were being schooled in two trailers that had no air-conditioning. I put up the money to have those trailers renovated so they were more comfortable for the students. It was the beginning of a long association with Anderson County's [Texas] Special Education unit."[110]

Bradley's teammate Kevin Reilly, who also became a good friend of Duffy, insists that "any family that has a special-needs child often has other children who are sensitive to people's needs and feelings.

"They know how difficult life can be," he explains. "This is what I saw in Billy. He would do anything for anybody in need. I think that came from his relationship with Duffy. He was 'Billy Bo Bitch' on the playing field but one of the most compassionate individuals I know off it."[111]

8 Bamboozled

By 1974 Bill Bradley was at the top of his game. Not only had the Eagles' free safety led the NFL in interceptions two years in a row, becoming the first player to achieve that distinction in the history of the league, but he also was a two-time All-Pro first teamer and had appeared in three Pro Bowls. Nevertheless, Bill did not get much attention across the league in those three years because the Eagles were a losing team, posting a record of 13-26-3.[1] Billy Bo Bitch was still just twenty-seven years old, though, and his future looked bright.

Under head coach Mike McCormack, the Eagles were starting to win again, and the team appeared to have the necessary ingredients to compete for a Super Bowl in the near future. Roman Gabriel, an experienced quarterback with playoff experience, enjoyed a talented young core of receivers led by wide receiver Harold Carmichael and tight end Charles Young. Tom "Silky" Sullivan was developing into one of the league's most dangerous running backs. The defense, which already enjoyed a strong secondary with the duo of Bradley and sophomore cornerback Joe Lavender, was strengthened in the off-season with the acquisition of All-Pro middle linebacker Bill Bergey.[2]

McCormack, who firmly believed that the Eagles could contend in 1974, gave up two first-round picks and a second rounder to acquire Bergey from the Cincinnati Bengals. There was nothing calculated about the risk. McCormack saw Bergey as the key to his defense. At 6 feet 3 inches and 245 pounds, the former Bengal had size combined with remarkable quickness and agility. But what really set him apart from other linebackers was his fire. Bergey hit opposing ball carriers with a vengeance that could not be taught. He was born to play middle linebacker.[3]

Bergey admitted in a recent interview that he "really didn't want to go to Philly," but the Eagles' brass "pulled out all stops to sign me."[4] Not only did they offer the All-Pro linebacker a five-year, $1 million contract, which would make him the highest paid defensive player in the NFL, but they also were willing to part with their three top draft picks to secure his services.[5] "When I visited, [owner] Leonard Tose put me up at the Ritz," Bergey remembered. "We dined at Bookbinders, and I toured the city in his limousine. [General manager] Jim Murray was just as desperate to sign me. Those two sold me a bill of goods you wouldn't believe, and I bought it hook, line, and sinker. In the end, I was grateful to them for bringing me to the Eagles."[6]

Bradley was excited about the acquisition. "Bergey was some kind of football player," he said. "I could see how athletic he was when he came over. Bill hit harder than [Dick] Butkus and had much more mobility. He could go sideline to sideline more quickly than any other linebacker I'd ever seen. Bill was *exactly* what we needed to anchor the middle of the defense. I really thought that we would be a contender after we got Bergey."[7]

Linebacker John Bunting echoed Bradley's enthusiasm. "We were all excited when the team got Bergey," he recalled. "He was built like a freakin' bear and still had tremendous agility. He was also an unbelievable tackler. Bill had remarkable instincts for the game. He was the best player on our defense for many years. I really believed that the Eagles had turned the corner after we got him, like we were going all out to win and to win immediately."[8]

Whatever optimism Bradley and Bunting had and the high hopes the team entertained for the upcoming season were put on hold at midnight on June 30, when the NFL Players Association went on strike. The walkout was triggered by a stalemate in contract negotiations with the owners. The biggest point of contention was the players' demand for an end to the Rozelle Rule limiting free agency.[9] Named after then NFL commissioner

Pete Rozelle, the Rozelle Rule stated that if a team signed a free agent, it must compensate his former team. If the two teams could not agree on compensation, the commissioner could unilaterally name any compensation he saw fit. The rule appeared to allow for more labor freedom but actually restricted free agency.

The origins of the Rozelle Rule can be traced to the *reserve clause* established by the NFL in 1921. According to the clause, whatever team initially signed a player owned the rights to him, even after the contract expired. The only way a player could change teams was to be released or traded. If traded, the new team owned the player. Once a player's contract expired, the team had one year to re-sign him. If it failed to do so, he was free to sign anywhere he chose. But there was an important catch: if the club and player did not reach agreement on a contract, the team could force a one-year extension with a 10 percent pay reduction. Teams could do this year after year. If a player did not negotiate a favorable contract, he was forced to remain with the same team, playing for less money each year.

The reserve clause was modified in 1947 by the creation of the *option clause*, which enabled the team to automatically keep a player for only one year after his contract expired. The first player to challenge the option clause was Raleigh Owens, who in 1963, after playing out his option year with the San Francisco 49ers, signed as a free agent with the Baltimore Colts. Shortly after, the NFL owners instituted the Rozelle Rule to prevent free agency and safeguard their bargaining power. In so doing, the owners insured that they would not lose a good player without compensation or lose the upper hand in negotiations that they had always enjoyed.[10]

"The owners controlled us," fumed Bradley, recalling the Rozelle Rule. "The players weren't free to go anywhere else because the team owned our rights. If the general manager decided to cut your pay by ten or twenty percent, you couldn't do anything about it. You'd have to play at 80 percent of your salary. We had no choice but to go on strike."[11]

The strike was a gutsy move for a players' union that had been certified by the National Labor Relations Board and recognized by the owners just four years earlier. Players demanded the right to switch teams once their contracts expired and to veto possible trades—the two stumbling blocks that led to a breakdown of negotiations the week before. Ed Garvey, executive director of the players' union, predicted a long strike and stated his confidence "that we can hold out until a new collective bargaining agreement is signed."[12] Speaking for the owners, John Thompson sounded just as confident that all the teams would "proceed with their plans to open their training camps and play exhibition games, even with rookies and free agents if necessary."[13]

Determined to secure free agency, the players, on July 3, went on strike. Carrying placards and wearing T-shirts bearing the slogan "No Freedom, No Football," they threatened the opening of preseason training camps by picketing outside NFL stadiums. In Philadelphia, Eagles veterans and their wives stood outside the team's practice facility at Widener College in nearby Chester, Pennsylvania, and admired Bradley's hand-painted sign. The artwork featured a brown football as a landscape and rising above it was an orange sun partially obscured by three white fleecy clouds. The sign bore the words "Set Yourself Free." When Stan Hochman of the *Philadelphia Daily News* asked Bill for an interpretation, Bradley replied, "Pretty soon the clouds will clear and there will be nothing but football and sunshine."[14] Unfortunately, the free safety's optimism was not shared by many.

Both the players and the owners competed for the allegiance of the rookies and free agents who did not become eligible for union membership until the regular season began. "We won't find out where the newcomers stand until they cross the picket lines," said Tom Dempsey, the Eagles' player representative. "We're not going to apply any threats or get involved in any violence. We're just going to talk to them and explain that what we're doing will also be for their benefit."[15]

At the outset, it appeared as if the players held the upper hand in negotiations. Sixty NFL players had already jumped to the fledgling World Football League (WFL) a month before the strike began.[16] Others were threatening to do the same if the owners did not agree to free agency. If nothing else, the WFL signings threatened to raise stagnant salaries in the NFL, which were among the lowest in the four major North American sports. But as the strike lingered into mid-July, players began to cross the picket line to join their teams. Only a few Eagles veterans broke ranks with their striking teammates. The two biggest defectors were quarterback Roman Gabriel and recently acquired middle linebacker Bill Bergey.

Gabriel crossed on July 25, when he joined the coaching staff, free agents, and rookies at Widener in defiance of a union order. When asked about his decision, the $125,000-a-year signal caller said that he "owed it to [owner] Mr. Tose, who brought me to Philadelphia when other people said I couldn't compete anymore."[17] Bergey crossed two days later, reporting to camp on July 27. "I feel badly [*sic*] that I'm letting down the Players' Association," he said. "But I also felt like I was letting down my teammates and the coaching staff."[18]

Most of the other Eagles veterans remained loyal to the Players Association. Under player rep Tom Dempsey's leadership, they picketed in shifts outside of the Widener training camp. Bradley helped organize workout sessions at a local high school field to keep himself and his teammates fit. "Billy was a lifesaver for me," said offensive lineman Jerry Sisemore, who was just in his second year in the NFL. "Coming from rural Texas, I was in culture shock going to a big East Coast city like Philadelphia. Billy knew that, and he took me under his wing. When the strike came, I had no money and had a family to support. Billy let me stay at his apartment on Rittenhouse Square and helped me find a job at a lumber mill stacking two-by-fours. He was the most loyal friend I had."[19]

The tide turned in favor of the owners when the strike reached its fortieth day. Players across the NFL broke ranks by the hundreds. They had believed that the strike would be short-lived, but now they were running out of money and buckled under the pressure of ownership, who threatened to release them if they didn't report. Finally, on August 11 the Players Association agreed to suspend its holdout. Asking members to report without a new contract bargaining agreement, the union decided to pursue free agency through a lawsuit filed three years before.[20] The following day, Bradley and the remaining strikers reported to Widener.[21] But the damage was done. The fallout would have an adverse effect on the Eagles' team chemistry.

After posting a 4-1 record to start the 1974 season, including a 13–10 upset over the Dallas Cowboys in the home opener, the Eagles lost six straight.[22] The strong bond that existed the previous year when the younger players rallied around Gabriel's leadership was gone. The team's offensive linemen were especially mad, harboring ill feelings toward the quarterback for crossing the picket line. "They were all union guys," explained an Eagle who asked to remain anonymous. "Linemen are the tightest group in pro football because they have the hardest job. They get the shit kicked out of them every game, and there's no personal glory in it for them. The quarterbacks and the halfbacks get all the glory. So, when a lineman gets his back up about something, you had better watch your ass. They didn't fight as hard to protect Gabe as they had the year before. It was a subtle way of letting him know that they didn't appreciate what he did when he crossed that picket line."[23]

McCormack refused to believe that his team's poor performance was the result of the strike. Instead, he complained about the "worst pass blocking [he'd] ever seen." But then he benched Gabriel in favor of rookie Mike Boryla for the final three games. Boryla won all three of his starts, and the Birds completed the season with a 7-7 record.

The 1975 season was worse. McCormack opened the campaign with Gabriel at quarterback, but by early November the team was floundering with a 2-7 record. Gabe was benched again in favor of Boryla, who won two of the last five games. The Eagles finished the season with a disappointing 4-10 record.[24] McCormack was fired on December 22, a day after the final game.[25]

"Gabriel's decision to cross the picket line was only one reason for the loss of our team's chemistry," insists Bradley. "There were other reasons too. Mike McCormack tried to break our union. He met with the striking players and threatened us, saying that he couldn't guarantee any of us jobs if we didn't report. [Owner Leonard] Tose and [general manager] Jim Murray were no better. They offered some of the star players $20,000 to cross the line, but we refused to do it. Others accepted the money, and we lost total respect for them. After the strike, it was hard to trust those guys. That's what destroyed our team."[26]

Other Eagles agreed with Bradley's assessment. "I think the strike killed us as a team," said fullback Norm Bulaich. "McCormack put a lot of pressure on the players by threatening us. If anything, that threat just solidified our decision to strike. Then Gabe and Bill Bergey crossed the line. We really didn't need our two biggest stars to do that. It killed the chemistry we were developing as a team."[27] Linebacker John Bunting did not appreciate McCormack's attempt to intimidate the players, but he placed greater blame on Gabriel for crossing the line. "We all admired Roman because he was a very good team leader," explained Bunting. "Then he becomes the first Eagle to cross the line! We all thought that Roman got paid to do it too. It was shocking for us to see that."[28]

For Bradley, the players' strike also resulted in a personal setback. One of his best friends, kicker Tom Dempsey, was traded to the Los Angeles Rams. Whereas the Eagles and Dempsey claimed that the deal had nothing to do with his role as a player rep during the strike, it was difficult to deny that hard feelings on both sides existed.[29] "Demps and I were very close because I was Tom's holder," said Bill. "We used to go out drinking at the Philadium in South Philly all the time. We had a lot of heart-to-hearts in that bar. Demps had a great sense of humor too. I'd always kid him about how overweight he was. But he took it like a man. I even made up a song titled 'Big Fat Demps,' sung to the tune of Jimmy Dean's 'Big Bad John.'" Tom really loved the song. There were a lot of verses, but the only clean ones were:

Big Fat Demps came into town as big as a boulder
And we all knew some day he'd kick his holder
Big Fat Demps.

We went up to Buffalo for that important game
And O.J. ran all in vain
Dempsey came on for that important point
He missed it by a mile, he was smokin' a joint
Big Fat Demps.[30]

Kidding aside, Bill was so upset about the Dempsey trade that days later he phoned two of his teammates and the trio went to the Philadium to toast the place kicker in absentia. The beer flowed all evening until the watering hole closed at 2:30 a.m. Shamelessly drunk, the three Eagles ambled over to Veterans Stadium determined to preserve Dempsey's memory for future generations of fans.

Once they arrived, Bradley pointed to a huge bronze statue of a running back standing outside the entrance of the stadium and remarked how much it resembled Tom. When his teammates agreed, they decided to alter the figure so it would look *exactly* like Dempsey with half a right foot. Eager to begin the operation, Bradley phoned a welder he knew, who joined the three drunken teammates at the Vet.

With torch in hand, the welder began to remove half of the statue's right foot. Suddenly, a Philadelphia policeman pulled up in his patrol car, got out, and walked up to the culprits. Twirling his night stick with one hand and pointing a flashlight at the group with the other, the cop asked, "What do you guys think you're doing?"

Doing a double take, the officer immediately realized that he had just caught three Philadelphia Eagles and a welder defacing public property.

"Hey! What the hell are *you* guys doing out here so late at night?" he asked in disbelief.

Bradley, always ready and willing to offer an explanation, replied, "We want to make this statue resemble our old teammate Tom Dempsey. We think that he should be remembered in this city long after his playing days are over!"

Bill knew he was pushing the envelope. No one in their right mind would jerk around with a Philly cop, not when the entire police force had gained an infamous reputation across the country for their routinely brutish behavior.

"This doesn't look good," grumbled the policeman. "You know you shouldn't be defacing a public statue, and you know I'm going to have to do something about it."

Suddenly the prank did not seem very funny to the three drunken football players. "What are you going to do, officer?" asked Bradley, doing his best to act innocent.

"Tell you what," said the cop. "You have that welder put the foot back on that statue so it doesn't come off, and I won't say a word about it to anyone. Then all four of you get the hell out of here!"

Bradley and his teammates did as they were told, satisfied that they had done their best to honor their dear friend, "Big Fat Demps."[31]

Although Bill might have lost one friend, he was reunited with another, Tim Rossovich. The free-spirited linebacker had been exiled to San Diego two years earlier. But the Chargers quickly tired of his outlandish behavior and released him. He returned to the City of Brotherly Love in 1974 to play for the new World Football League's Philadelphia Bell.[32] According to his longtime girlfriend, Cis Rundle, Tim "remained a troubled soul" who was "struggling with drug and alcohol addictions" and "desperate to find peace of mind."[33] Bradley, who remained close with both Rossovich and Rundle, was excited about the reunion. "It couldn't have happened at a better time for me," confessed the free safety. "I was hurting after Dempsey was traded. I really missed him. But Timmy kinda filled the void."[34]

Since the WFL season began in mid-July and ended in mid-November, Bradley and Rossovich spent most of their off-field time together. Bill kept a close watch on his former teammate. If Tim drank too much, Bradley was his designated driver. If Tim walked into a party and set himself on fire, Bill was nearby to douse the flames. Rundle, who was living out on the West Coast, always knew she could count on Bradley to protect Tim from himself. "Billy was my rock," said Cis, who was then a double for Farrah Fawcett on the TV series *Charlie's Angels*. "Farrah, who met and became good friends with Bill in college, always reminded me that he was one of the most loyal people she knew, that Bill would do everything he could to keep Tim safe. And she was right."[35]

Rossovich was at the tail end of his pro football career. He would play for the Philadelphia Bell for just two seasons before ending his career with the Houston Oilers in 1976.[36] Unbeknownst to Bradley, his NFL career was also winding down. The beginning of the end came in 1976, when the Eagles hired Dick Vermeil as their new head coach.

Vermeil began his coaching career as an assistant at Del Mar (California) High School in 1959. Personable but also intense, the young coach demanded excellence and accountability, pushing himself as hard as he did his players. During the next ten years, Vermeil worked his way up through the college ranks before the Los Angeles Rams hired him as a special teams coach in 1969, later promoting him to quarterbacks coach. In 1974 Vermeil was hired as the head coach at UCLA. He compiled a 15-5-3 record in two seasons, leading the Bruins to their first conference championship in a decade. After coaching UCLA to a 23–10 upset victory over first-ranked Ohio State in the 1976 Rose Bowl, Vermeil was offered the reins of the Eagles by owner Leonard Tose. Not wanting to relocate his family, Vermeil, who was content as a college coach, initially rejected the offer. Then, after considerable soul-searching, he changed his mind.[37]

On February 8, 1976, the thirty-nine-year-old Vermeil signed a five-year contract to coach the Eagles. He took over a wretched 4-10 team that had not won in nearly a decade. Even worse, the McCormack regime had mortgaged the team's future by trading the top three draft choices for the next two years and the top two picks the year after that. Unable to rebuild with high draft picks, Vermeil would have to reverse the fortunes of the woeful franchise through plain, old-fashioned hard work, sacrifice, and character-building.[38]

"When I went to Philadelphia, I had to place my players in an environment which, if they bought in, would eventually make them better individual performers and, collectively, a better football team," recalled Vermeil in a recent interview. "But it wasn't going to happen overnight. We had to handle adversity properly. We had to handle losing properly. We had to take losing as an experience to get better and not as an excuse to feel sorry for ourselves. We had to develop the mental toughness to accept the criticism in the evaluation process that goes on in the NFL and to keep believing in ourselves."[39]

Vermeil's "evaluation process" began on July 3, when the Eagles reported to the NFL's earliest training camp. Players were ordered to keep their helmets on and chin straps buckled during the stifling heat of two-a-day practices. The drills were endless, and there were no water breaks unless Vermeil permitted them. Then there were wind sprints. *Everything* was filmed at a time when few if any NFL coaches taped their practices. After the first ten days of the grueling camp, ten of the younger players packed up and left.[40] Vermeil didn't care. He was determined to find and keep the best players. Those who didn't buy in were cut. He had more patience with veteran starters, but when cornerback Joe Lavender refused to report to camp after two weeks because he was still negotiating his contract, the head coach cut ties.[41] Lavender immediately ended his holdout, but it was too late. Vermeil remained firm and had him traded to Washington for defensive tackle Manny Sistrunk and three draft picks.[42] The new head coach was making a statement. Now all the players—rookies, veterans, and free agents—clearly understood who was in charge. Either they sucked it up and bought into his program or they were gone.

Bradley was one of the very few veterans who understood what Vermeil was trying to do and immediately bought in. Since arriving in Philadelphia in 1969, Bill had played for four different head coaches and three defensive backfield specialists. Each time a coaching change was made, the Texan willingly gave his total allegiance to the newcomer. While all those coaches taught Bradley how to become a better, smarter player, none gave him "as good a feeling" as Vermeil. After training camp ended, Bill told Phil Jasner of the *Philadelphia Daily News* about his admiration for the Eagles' new head coach and how similar he was to Darrell Royal, his coach at Texas: "Coach Vermeil is trying to change the culture of a losing team. That requires a lot of hard work and sacrifice. He's just like Darrell Royal, my coach at Texas. 'Character' meant everything to him. Same thing here. The only way to build character is to work your ass off. Coach Vermeil's philosophy is to 'work practice to death.' His training camp was extremely physical, very demanding, even brutal. But I can honestly say that I was in the best football shape I'd ever been in by the time the season began."[43]

Others were less willing to conform to Vermeil's hardline approach. "I thought Vermeil was a 'Harry High School' because he refused to lighten up on us in training camp," admitted Bill Bergey, who would become captain of the defense and one of the head coach's staunchest allies. "We weren't allowed to take a knee. We had to keep our chin strap buckled. We could only take a drink when he said so. He filmed everything too.

You couldn't let up, or he'd catch you on film and call you into his office. Hell! I was All-Pro! I had been All-Pro for the last two seasons, and this guy tells me that I can't even take a drink of water when I want to! Sure, I knew he was trying to instill the discipline that was obviously lacking on our team. But he was going overboard."[44]

If Bergey thought his All-Pro status made him exceptional, he was sorely mistaken. One morning, the linebacker tested Vermeil. Noticing that there were no cameras near the practice field, Bill figured he could catch a break and wouldn't be caught. During a seven-on-seven drill, Bergey simply went through the motions, allowing a rookie guard to block him on every down. He did not realize that Vermeil had an assistant filming the drill from the top of a dormitory. After lunch, the head coach summoned the linebacker to his office.

"Bill," Vermeil began, "you know that seven-on-seven drill this morning?"

"Yes," Bergey replied innocently.

"Well, I just got through looking at the film."

"You were taking film?" Bergey exclaimed in disbelief. Now he knew he had been caught loafing.

"Bill," continued the head coach, "there was a rookie lineman that blocked your ass all over the place, and he is going to be cut next week. Now how do you think I'm going to feel when he says, 'But coach, I blocked an All-Pro's ass all over the place in that seven-on-seven drill!'"

Humiliated by the question, Bergey could only mumble, "Not very good."

"I want you to do me a favor," Vermeil said. "I want you to watch the film tonight, and after you watch it, I want you to burn the damn thing!"

From that moment on, Bill Bergey busted his ass for Dick Vermeil, both in games and in practice.[45]

Harold Carmichael was another convert. "We didn't know what we were getting when Coach Vermeil came in," recalled the Hall of Fame receiver. "He was a young guy from UCLA. We felt he was cocky at first and that he didn't know what he was doing in the NFL. At training camp, we were doing grass drills plus two-and-a-half to three-hour sessions on the field twice a day. We thought he was crazy. But after the first two weeks, we all understood what he was trying to do. He was commanding respect. He let us know that he was the boss. After that training camp, I had so much respect for coach because he taught me to do a job better than anyone else. He inspired me by challenging me and by surrounding me with good people, people who held me responsible for the way I played."[46]

The Eagles lost their first game of the 1976 season to the Cowboys in Dallas, 27–7. But the Birds rebounded the next week, giving Vermeil his first victory as an NFL head coach in the home opener against the New York Giants, 20–7. Roman Gabriel was still recovering from off-season knee surgery. In Gabe's absence, back-up Mike Boryla coordinated a successful rushing game. Fullback Mike Hogan, a rookie, gained 93 of the team's 211 rushing yards on nineteen carries. With the Eagles clinging to a 13–7 lead in the fourth quarter, Vince Papale, a thirty-year-old rookie from a gritty Delaware County, Pennsylvania, semipro league, set up the Birds' final touchdown by recovering a fumbled Giants punt on New York's 3-yard line. A heartbreaking defeat came in week number 3, when the Eagles lost at home to the Washington Redskins, 20–17. Again, the Birds rebounded to defeat the Falcons, 14–13, in Atlanta the following week.[47]

Win or lose, Vermeil never let up. He worked his players hard, made them accountable to him and to each other, and constantly preached about the importance of sacrifice and character. His approach appeared to be working. Philadelphia was playing inspired football. The players felt as if they had a chance to win every game, regardless of their opponent's talent. The fans were beginning to have faith in their team and the new head coach. Then the Eagles hit a wall. Beginning on October 10 with 33–14 drubbing by the St. Louis Cardinals, the Birds lost eight of their next nine games, with the offense scoring just two touchdowns in four weeks. The only win came on October 31 against the lowly New York Giants, a 10–0 whitewash, the first shutout the Eagles enjoyed since 1968. Philadelphia would win just one more game—a 27–10 victory over the Seattle Seahawks in the season finale—and finish fourth in the NFC East with a 4-10 record.[48]

Despite the setback, Vermeil had earned the trust of his players in part because he pushed himself just as hard as, if not harder than, they did. He also worked longer and harder than any other NFL coach. He was a stickler for detail and responsible to a fault. He spent many nights on a cot in his Veterans Stadium office so he could watch game film. When he did go home, his mind remained on his team. The players also knew that Vermeil genuinely cared about them. During pregame warm-ups, he circulated among them, embraced them, and wished them luck. When he addressed the team before games, his eyes often filled with tears. He dreaded the final cut of the preseason because it was almost always a player with heart, one who gave his very best but fell just short of the ability to make his squad. Vermeil took those cuts very personally, probably because he could relate more to those players than others with greater talent.[49]

"I didn't coach football players, I coached people to play football," the head coach explained recently. "To me, the person came first. If he was a good person with some ability, then it was just a matter of giving him the opportunity to succeed. That was the best part of coaching."[50]

Vermeil was a *teacher*-coach. Football was very personal for him. Bradley admired that kind of dedication. It was another quality that reminded him of Darrell Royal, his head coach at Texas. Because both men genuinely cared about their players, they never sugarcoated the hard decisions that came with the job either. "Dick was a straight shooter," said Bill forty years later. "He never came at you from left field. He was always direct, always honest with his players. There just weren't many coaches like that in the NFL back then, or today for that matter."[51] One of those hard decisions was telling Bill Bradley that his time in Philadelphia had come to an end.

On Wednesday, June 1, 1977, Vermeil met with the thirty-year-old free safety in his Veterans Stadium office for a heart-to-heart talk. Training camp was just six weeks away, and he was committed to rebuilding with younger players. There was no room for an aging veteran like Bradley no matter how popular he was or how much football he had left in the tank.

"Bill, I know you work hard, and you've been here a while," began Vermeil. "But you're getting up in age."

Bradley could feel a lump in his throat. He knew what was coming next.

"I've got younger guys who can play free safety," the head coach continued. "Artimus Parker has started there before. We drafted Martin Mitchell from Tulane, and he's a guy many people feel was an excellent college safety. Plus, we just signed Herman Edwards as a free agent from San Diego State, and we're really high on him."

Stunned by Vermeil's words, Bill lapsed into a daze.

"Look, Bill, we just can't use you anymore."

The execution was abrupt, final.

There was stone-cold silence in the room. Myriad thoughts raced through Bradley's mind as feelings of shock yielded to consternation and anger.

I'm still capable of playing well, he thought. *I have at least two, maybe three more good years left. How can this be happening to me, an All-Pro? I've given this organization and this head coach everything I had. I was loyal when few, if any, players stood by them. And this is the thanks I get?*

Somehow, Bill managed to pull himself together. "Coach, I don't want to be where I'm not wanted," he murmured as tears welled in his eyes, the only indication of the sadness, frustration, and rage that percolated inside of him. "All I ask is that if you are going to trade me, I'd appreciate it if you'd send me to a team that is above .500 or, even better, to a team that has a chance to make the playoffs."

"I'll do what I can, Bill," replied Dick, ending the meeting with a firm handshake.[52]

Vermeil proved good to his word. During the next three weeks, he negotiated with the Los Angeles Rams (winners of four straight NFC West Division titles), the Miami Dolphins (which had won back-to-back Super Bowls in 1972 and 1973 and would return to the playoffs every year between 1978 and 1985), and the Minnesota Vikings (which had been NFC Central champions for the previous four seasons). Dick also kept Bradley informed in keeping with his policy of "open communications, especially when the trade involves a person of high character like Bill."[53]

On June 20 the Eagles traded Bradley for an undisclosed draft pick to the Vikings. He and his agent, Mark Stewart, immediately agreed to a new, two-year contract worth $70,000. Bill was not only "honored that Minnesota wanted him" but also "elated that he was going to a winning team with a lot of veteran players, mostly guys in their thirties.

"I just didn't want to start all over again with a young team," he added.[54] But that still didn't eliminate the hurt of leaving Philadelphia, a place he had grown to love during the past eight years. It was the only NFL city Bradley had ever called home. "I wanted to finish my career in Philly," Bradley admitted in a recent interview. "Sure, I wanted to be on a winning team. I would have given anything to play for Vermeil on that 1980 NFC championship team, to finally go to a Super Bowl after all those years of losing. I would've wanted that just as much for all the Philly fans as for myself. But even that doesn't take away from my experience. Even though our teams lost, we were close, like brothers. So, leaving Philly was very painful for me."[55]

The day after the trade, Bill took out a full-page advertisement in the *Philadelphia Daily News* to express his gratitude to the fans. "I've always felt that when the day came that I had to leave Philadelphia, it would be one of the saddest days of my life," began the open letter. Admitting that "it's been hard to hold back tears," Bradley wrote that from "the first day I put on the green and white [uniform], I always tried to do the very best for the team, the fans and myself." While those teams didn't always win, "I was able to achieve a lot in my career" because of "my preparation and the help of my teammates and you, the fans. . . . For that, I love you. I am grateful. And you will always have a place in my heart."[56]

The open letter was accompanied by a poem, also written by Bill, titled "Game Face Forever":

> All I ask of you now
> Is to lay me huddled in your hearts
> Like a favorite coat kept in the closet
> To wear on a cold night . . .
> When there are no players playing,
> No passes caught or punt spiraling
> To keep us company

No cheers to keep our bellies warm
When we wonder if morning will rise again,
When the lights are dim in our bright lit world—
When the autumn cold crashes our warmth–
Wrap me around yourself snugly
Don't store me away in some attic
Just hang me somewhere where I can be of use occasionally
Hang me softly in the front of the closet of your mind
And remember I'm there.[57]

To be sure, Bradley was not Walt Whitman. But the poem, with its football metaphors and southern charm, came from the heart. Anyone who read the verses and knew Bill realized just how painful the trade was for him.

Linebacker John Bunting, one of his closest friends, knew how devastated Bill was by the trade. Together with several teammates, Bunting organized an impromptu farewell at the Phillies–St. Louis Cardinals game at Veterans Stadium on Thursday night, July 14. "We know that Billy gave the fans a lot of thrills in his years here," explained the Birds' linebacker. "I also know there are lots of people out there who'd like to say good-bye to Billy, maybe shake hands. So, we're going to have him up in the center-field bleachers at the Vet before the Phillies' game. It'll give the fans an opportunity to say good-bye, express their gratitude and wish him good luck."[58]

Bradley could not have asked for a better send-off. Not only was baseball his favorite sport, but also the Cardinals were his favorite baseball team as a youngster. Bill could not have imagined the outpouring of love and affection he received that evening. So many fans flocked to the center-field bleachers to wish him well that the Philadelphia police were called in to disperse the crowd. Overwhelmed by the reception, Bill broke down and cried. "I guess I made a heck of a lot of friends here," he murmured through a veil of tears. "I sure am going to miss Philly."[59] Philly was going to miss him too.

Aside from the passion and fierce competitiveness Bradley brought to the gridiron, he left a very impressive football legacy in the City of Brotherly Love, including:

Making thirty-four career interceptions, which remains a franchise record.[60]

Returning 111 punts, another franchise record at the time of his trade.[61]

Becoming the first NFL player to win consecutive interception titles, with eleven in 1971 and nine in 1972—and still the only Eagle to achieve that distinction.[62]

Accounting for 1,904 yards in kick returns and interceptions, despite never playing for a winning team.[63]

Nearly fifty years after Bill's playing career ended, some sportswriters consider him to be among the top twenty Eagles of all-time, placing him in the same rarified company as Hall of Famers Chuck Bednarik, Harold Carmichael, Brian Dawkins, Steve Van Buren, and Reggie White.[64]

Unfortunately, all the individual achievements could not erase the fact that Bill's eight years in Philadelphia were plagued by the incompetence of the Eagles' organization. There was no consistency in the front office's decision-making, no consistent coaching staff, no consistent roster. It seemed like every year was a rebuild, just like the one Vermeil was orchestrating.

Considering the delicate situation, the head coach did his best to portray the Bradley trade as a win-win for both parties. He told Ray Didinger of *Philadelphia Evening Bulletin* that if Bill had remained with the team, "the young guys like Artimus Parker, Martin Mitchell and Herm Edwards weren't going to get the chance to play and develop." On the other hand, "Bill's going to an experienced, successful team in which he won't be forced to do a lot of head-on tackling."[65] The head coach was even more optimistic with Gordon Forbes of the *Philadelphia Inquirer*. Envisioning Bradley as "Minnesota's starting free safety," Vermeil predicted that such a status would "mean higher compensation [for the Eagles], probably a second-round pick. . . . Bill will be better off, too. The Vikings let their free safety play that deep, roaming centerfield, so he won't have to take those 240-pound backs head on the way he did here."[66]

In the end, few of those predictions came to fruition. When Bradley went to Minnesota, he competed for starting free safety against thirty-five-year-old veteran Paul Krause. "Krause was near the end of his career and was in a contract dispute with the Vikings," recalled Bill. "I thought I had made the team coming out of training camp. But three or four days after the final cut, [Vikings head coach] Bud Grant released me. My guess is that I was brought in as a threat to force Krause to resolve the salary issue, and it seems to have worked."[67]

While the Vikings may have used Bradley as a ruse to scare their All-Pro safety into settling his salary dispute, their decision to release him was still strange. Bill went to Minnesota with a two-year guaranteed contract, which meant that he was going to receive a weekly check whether he played or sat on the bench.[68] Apparently, the Vikings' front office either felt that Bradley's $70,000 price tag was worth their effort to sign Krause, who would go on to become the NFL's all-time interception leader, or perhaps Krause himself insisted on Bill's departure before settling his own contract dispute. Regardless, Bradley's tenure with the Vikings was short-lived. Things did not work out much better for the Eagles.

Artimus Parker, considered the favorite to be Bradley's successor at free safety, was cut by Vermeil near the end of training camp.[69] Martin Mitchell, the Birds' sixth-round draft pick out of Tulane, lasted one year in the NFL before switching to the Canadian Football League.[70] Although Herm Edwards, the cornerback the Eagles signed as a free agent out of San Diego State, became a fixture on Vermeil's defense for the next nine years, he was used strictly as a cornerback and never competed for Bradley's safety position.[71]

Bradley's departure hurt the Eagles more than it helped them, at least in the short term. Bill was not only the team's starting free safety but also its most versatile player, one who could punt, return, and, if necessary, quarterback. Predictably, Vermeil, in 1978, signed John Sciarra, his former UCLA quarterback, to fill some of those roles. Sciarra played for the Eagles for the next six years as defensive back and punt returner. He was named Most Valuable Player for Special Teams in 1979 and in 1980, when the Eagles went to the Super Bowl.[72]

Still, Bradley harbored no ill feelings toward his old team. "Of course, I was sad that I didn't go to the Super Bowl with them," he chuckled in a 2023 interview. "But I felt great for the guys I knew like [Harold] Carmichael, [John] Bunting, [Jerry] Sisemore, and [Guy] Morriss. That NFC title was the highlight of their careers after all those years of losing."[73]

After the Vikings released Bradley, he returned to his hometown of Palestine, Texas, where he intended to begin a new life away from football on his eighty-six-acre hay farm. Then other NFL teams started contacting him. Head coach Bum Phillips of the Houston Oilers called in August to ask about Bill's health and availability. Phillips promised to sign him if anyone on the secondary or special teams became injured.[74] "I would've loved playing for Houston because I grew up a die-hard Oilers fan," Bradley gushed. "But nothing happened."[75]

Al Davis, principal owner of the Oakland Raiders, called in late September. Davis was one of the most controversial owners in the NFL. He served as his own general manager, having more authority over day-to-day operations than any other owner in the league. Bradley did not know if he could trust him. With his slicked-back hair, dark sunglasses, tracksuits, and Brooklyn-tinged speech, Davis hardly looked like a football magnate. But he was also extremely successful. Between 1967 and 1985, the Raiders won thirteen division championships, one AFL championship (1967), and three Super Bowls (XI, XV, and XVIII).[76]

In January 1977 Oakland won the first of those three Super Bowl titles. Davis, whose motto was "Just win, baby," was shameless in his efforts to repeat.[77] He might have considered Bradley as insurance to return to the Super Bowl. Although Jack Tatum, the Raiders' starting free safety, was a vicious tackler and was two years younger than Bill, he had never had more than four interceptions in a season. He was also hobbled by a shoulder injury. Bradley, on the other hand, was a healthy—and natural—ball hawk. Before the Eagles' Mike McCormack saddled him with assigned coverages in 1974, Bill averaged 6.3 picks a season.[78] If he was allowed to play a deep, roaming center field, there's no telling how many interceptions he would make.

Bradley flew to Oakland on September 20 and was given a room at the airport hotel. Davis called to welcome him and promised Bill the opportunity to work out at the Coliseum the next day. But the following morning the owner called to postpone. After three days passed and Bill still had not seen the practice field, he caught on to Davis's scheme. The Raiders' owner planned to keep Bradley away from other NFL suitors until he determined Oakland's needs in the secondary. Angered by the deceitfulness, Bill was determined to get even.

"I figured, 'What the hell!'" recalled Bradley years later. "Davis was paying for everything. I got the phone book, found a masseuse, and called her up. She came to the hotel and gave me a full body massage with a happy ending. One of the best I'd ever had! Of course, Davis paid for it. I thought about staying another day and inviting her back, but I decided to let him off easy. So, I got on a plane and went back home."[79]

Bradley did not hear from another NFL team until mid-November when Chuck Noll, the head coach of the Pittsburgh Steelers, phoned. He needed a punter and a safety. Bill flew to Pittsburgh on the morning of November 13 and joined the Steelers for practice at Three Rivers Stadium the following afternoon.[80] Noll was running his players through a series of brutal blocking drills, including the bull in the ring, where one player gets in the middle of a circle of other players, who take turns hitting the man in the middle; the Oklahoma drill, where a running back, offensive lineman, and defensive lineman hit each other like gladiators in a confined space; and the triple butt, where a tackler buries his head in the numbers of an advancing runner from 10 yards away as they circle around pylons to repeat the contact twice more. Noll stood on the side berating his players and chiding them, "Do it again! Do it again!"

Bradley, a free safety, saw no sense in participating in blocking drills intended for linemen and fullbacks. But he joined the scrum of cornerbacks in the vicious workout anyway. Going against linemen twice his size, Bill was knocked around a half dozen times until he became disgusted and left the field. He showered, dressed, and called a cab to return to his hotel. When Noll caught Bill leaving the stadium, he confronted him.

"Bradley," he yelled, "Where are ya going? I haven't seen you punt!"

"Coach, you're not going to see me punt either," he replied, trying to control his temper. "I saw absolutely no sense in doing those blocking drills. I am a free safety, not a lineman! I was All-Pro, and a three-time Pro Bowler. You knew exactly what you were going to get from me without having to see me block. I don't need this shit. I'm leaving!" Having made his point, Bill got into the cab, closed the door, and drove off.[81]

Returning to Palestine, Bradley convinced himself that his playing days were over and that he would not humiliate himself again if another NFL team contacted him. It was time to move on, to go forward with his life. He had already laid the groundwork for his future by purchasing an old Victorian mansion in his hometown and opened a restaurant called Colonel Barton's.[82] Between the restaurant and his farm, Bill insured himself not only a steady income but a busy schedule as well.

Then, with just four weeks remaining in the NFL season, Larry Wilson, the general manager of the St. Louis Cardinals, called. Mike Sensibaugh, the Cards' starting safety, had been injured and was out for the season. So was their punter, Duane Carrell. Wilson asked if Bradley would be willing to help them out. Had it been any other football executive, Bill would not have considered the offer. But Wilson, an outstanding free safety in his playing days, was his idol as a youngster. Still, Bradley had reservations.

"Larry, I really appreciate the offer, but I'm trying to start a new life back here in Texas," he told the Pro Football Hall of Famer.

"Look, Bill, we're 7-3 right now," said Wilson, refusing to take no for an answer. "All we have to do is win one of our last four games to get into the playoffs. I think you can put us over the top. I really need you here in St. Louis."

"You have back-ups, don't you?" replied Bradley, still not sold on the idea.

"They're injured too."

"Both of 'em, the safety *and* the punter?" Bill asked in disbelief.

"Yep!" said Wilson. "I really need you!"

"Okay, Larry, you swear on a stack of Bibles that if I come out there, I'm going to be starting?" Bill was softening. Deep down, he wanted to suit up just one more time.

"Absolutely," promised the Cards' general manager.[83]

Bradley arrived in St. Louis on November 22 and went immediately to Busch Memorial Stadium. Entering the Cardinals' locker room just an hour before practice, he was shocked to find no one there but the equipment manager. No sooner did Bill locate his locker and begin unpacking his gear when a group of hulking linemen came running out of the showers and dogpiled him. The culprits were Jackie Smith, Conrad Dobler, Dan Dierdorf, and James Victor "J. V." Cain—all his sworn enemies when he was with the Eagles. "They were smiling this time, though," chuckled Bradley. "We had our moments against each other in the past, but we decided it was now a common cause. We'll beat up on someone else."[84] Bill's words were prophetic.

Bradley's first game as a St. Louis Cardinal was on Thursday, November 24, against the Miami Dolphins at Busch Stadium. Better known as the Thanksgiving Day Massacre, the Cards were humiliated before the hometown fans in a 55–14 blowout.[85] To save face, Conrad Dobler, an offensive lineman regarded by *Sports Illustrated* as the "dirtiest player" in the NFL, instigated a brawl near the end of the game.[86] Billy Bo Bitch, always known as a battler or a dirty player—depending upon the color of the jersey—took a couple of good swings against the Dolphins. "It made me feel pretty good to take up battle with my [Cardinals] teammates," he admitted after the game.[87]

"What a turn of events that [brawl] was," Bill chuckled recalling the incident. "Just a year earlier, those same Cardinals considered me the dirtiest motherfucker in the NFL. But after that game, we were like brothers."[88]

St. Louis failed to make the playoffs in 1977, losing the remaining three games of the season to finish 7-7.[89] For Bradley, the .500 record was the best finish he had experienced since 1974, when the Eagles under Mike McCormack posted the same record.[90] Sadly, Bill never experienced a winning season in his nine seasons of NFL play. He completed his career playing for two teams that compiled a collective record of 35-76-5.[91]

Although Bradley is proud of his accomplishments as an NFL player and grateful for the friends he made during the decade he spent in Philadelphia, he does have two regrets. "I would have liked to play for a winner, just once," he admitted. "Of course, winning a Super Bowl would've been nice too. I also believe that players of my era deserve a better pension than what we received from the league today."[92] It's difficult to find fault with either of those claims.

Had Bradley played for a consistent winner, his achievements would have garnered national attention. He might also have more career interceptions, fewer injuries, and a longer career, all of which would have increased his chances of being considered for the Pro Football Hall of Fame. But the NFL's poor pension plan for veterans of his era is truly unconscionable.

During the 1970s, a player was not fully vested until he played ten years in the league. He also had to be on an NFL roster for at least a total of four games in each of those years to achieve that status, and he had to be vested for four years and two games to be eligible for the retirement package. That all changed in 1993, when the owners and the Players Association agreed to a new collective bargaining agreement. The new agreement lowered the eligibility for an NFL pension to five years and included more than $1 billion for a severance package, a 401(k) retirement account, annuities, and a better health-care plan. But some four thousand players who had already retired, like Bradley, were not eligible for those benefits. In addition, their pensions are about a third the size of those of current players, which are upward of $200,000 a year.[93]

"Those of us who played in the NFL before 1993 built the league," Bradley noted. "We made it the multi-billion-dollar business it is today, and yet our retirement benefits pale in comparison to today's players who won't have to work another day in their lives. The NFL and the Players Association have an obligation to those of us who played before 1993 and who are now struggling physically and mentally from the concussions we sustained during the years we spent in the league."[94]

Despite the reservations, Bradley left his mark not only on the Philadelphia Eagles but also on the league itself. In an NFL film highlighting

Bill's pro career, the legendary sports broadcaster John Facenda said that Bradley's "abundant talent [was] laced with a strong dose of temper and competitive fire" and that the free safety was not only the "Eagles' leader" but also "a gamebreaker who turn[ed] defense into instant offense for Philadelphia" as well as a "genuine triple-threat" who punted, returned, and played free safety. "But Bradley's true worth [was] not his statistics but his infectious spirit," according to Facenda, "a spirit that lifts a team through bad times and good. In short, Bill Bradley [was] a winner in every sense of the word."[95]

1. Mildred "Millie" (Rainey) Bradley.
Courtesy of the Bradley family.

2. Joe Hill "Cephas" Bradley.
Courtesy of the Bradley family.

3. Rose May Bradley, Bill's older sister. Courtesy of the Bradley family.

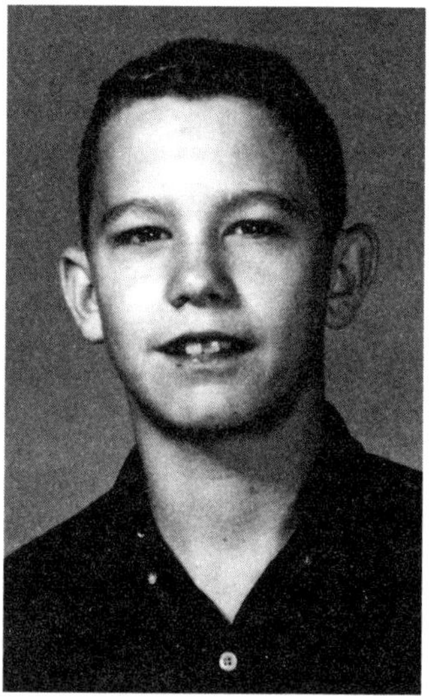

4. Bill, age thirteen. Courtesy of the Bradley family.

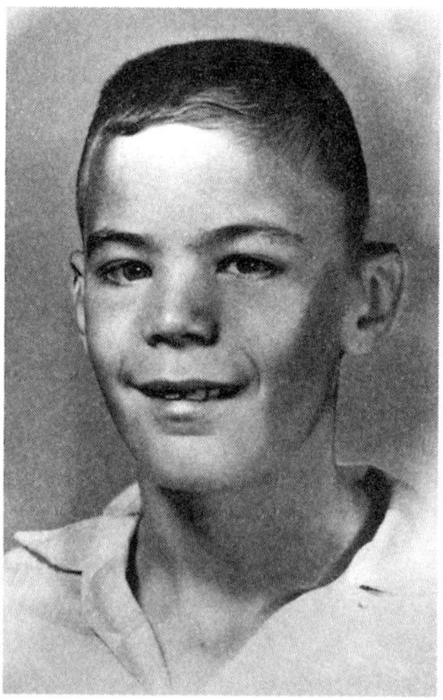

5. Ralph "Duffy" Bradley, Bill's younger brother. Courtesy of the Bradley family.

6. Palestine Junior High School's Athletic Leadership Award winners (*left to right*): Curtis Fitzgerald, Jimmy Groh, Harold Sumrall, Bill Bradley. Courtesy of the Bradley family.

7. Palestine Wildcats, 1964 Texas high school football champions (Class AAA). Courtesy of the Bradley family.

8. (*Left to right*) Bradley poses with Curtis Fitzgerald and head coach Luke Thornton, December 12, 1964, after Palestine upset Wichita Falls–Hirschi, 28–23, in the Texas state semifinal game. Courtesy of the Bradley family.

9. Bradley quarterbacked the Texas All-Stars to a 26–10 victory over the Pennsylvania All-Stars at the 1965 Big 33 game at Hershey, Pennsylvania. Courtesy of the Bradley family.

10. Jerry LeVias, shown here as a fullback with Southern Methodist University, nicknamed Bill his "blue-eyed soul brother." Heritage Hall records, box 6, SMU 2007.0406. DeGolyer Library, SMU.

11. Bradley was the Longhorns' starting quarterback in 1966, his sophomore year. University of Texas at Austin.

12. Longhorns coach Darrell Royal poses with the 1968 team captains (*left to right*): Bradley, Corby Robertson, and Chris Gilbert. University of Texas at Austin.

13. Bradley grew his kinky locks so long between 1971 and 1974 that he was hardly recognizable from his days as the close-cropped quarterback of the Texas Longhorns. Courtesy of the Bradley family.

14. When the free-spirited lineman Tim Rossovich held out for a higher salary with Bradley in the summer of 1972, the Eagles traded him to San Diego. Courtesy of the Bradley family.

15. Bradley's Cottonmouth Blues Wagon was his preferred mode of transportation in the offseason. Courtesy of the Bradley family.

16. Bill, pictured in front of Veterans Stadium, enjoyed a part-time career as a male fashion model in the 1970s. Courtesy of the Bradley family.

17. Bradley the multifaceted star: punter, returner, and ball hawk who led the NFL in interceptions in 1971 and 1972 with eleven and nine picks, respectively. Courtesy of the Bradley family.

18. Eagles Hall of Famer Harold Carmichael was mentored by Bradley during his early years in the NFL. Courtesy of the Bradley family.

19. Matthew Wright, Bill's stepson, as a high school quarterback. Courtesy of the Bradley family.

20. The Bradley family (*left to right*): Carissa, Susan, Matthew, and Bill. Courtesy of the Bradley family.

21. Bill with his favorite Philadelphia sportswriter, Ray Didinger. Courtesy of the author.

9 Teacher-Coach

After his playing career ended, Bradley became involved in several ventures. With his laid-back approach and affable personality, Bill was a natural businessman with an uncanny ability to sell anything to anyone. For three years, he remained in Philadelphia where he invested in a sports management company and made public appearances. But in 1980 Bradley sold his share of the company and moved back home to Palestine, where he already owned an eighty-six-acre hay farm, and purchased an old feed store that he converted into a gas station and convenience store. He stayed in shape by baling hay and selling it to local farmers. When he was not doing that, Bill, who lived in a small room in the rear of his store, pumped gas, checked oil, and spun yarns for customers about his days in the NFL. He also engaged in some good-old fashioned bootlegging.[1]

"I got these cases of Coors Beer, but at that time I couldn't sell them in my store," explained the former Eagle. "Instead, I displayed the cases in the front window with a sign that read, 'The beer is free, but if you want to tip me for it, feel free.'"[2]

Whenever Bill needed a break from baling hay, checking tire pressure, or selling beer, he served as a host for the Norwegian Cruise Line, which partnered with the NFL Players Association to have former footballers entertain their guests. In return, Bill, an eligible bachelor, received free room and board as well as the opportunity to "peruse and cruise" some of the most attractive female passengers on the seven-day excursions. That was only part of his enjoyment, though.

"I introduced some pretty funny events on the ship," recalled Bradley. "I came up with this shuttle race where you had to tape your hands, place a volleyball between your legs and hop for thirty feet. I even got the captain of the cruise ship to come down for a medal ceremony. I had a blast!"

Bill enjoyed the gig so much that between 1982 and 1990 he went on a total of thirty-three all-expenses-paid cruises. In fact, there was once a five-week period when his "feet didn't once touch American soil."[3]

In 1984 Bradley's career path took an unexpected turn when he joined the United States Football League, a new professional circuit that played a spring and summer schedule. He began as a personal assistant with the Houston Gamblers. The next year, Billy Schott, a former Longhorns kicker and good friend, persuaded Bill to try his hand at coaching with the San Antonio Gunslingers of the same league.

The Gunslingers were owned by Clinton Manges, a real estate and oil titan. Since the San Antonio City Council did not trust the oil tycoon due to his controversial business dealings, Manges hired Bradley and Schott to comb the local malls to secure a few thousand names on a petition to establish the franchise. The petition worked, and San Antonio had itself a professional football team. Because of his tremendous wealth, the USFL did not require Manges to make an initial capital investment. Instead, the real estate magnate paid for team expenses out-of-pocket as they arose, though he'd been in financial trouble since 1980.[4] As a result, the Gunslingers were a cash-strapped team. The fans would go to the concession booth to buy hot dogs and sit down at the same table being used by the trainer to tape players' ankles before the game.[5] "You could eat a hot dog, get wrapped, and sign autographs all at the same time," chuckled Bradley.[6]

The team's situation became dire in June 1985, when Manges's oil fortune collapsed and he stopped paying the bills altogether. After a game in Jacksonville, Florida, the chartered plane sat on the runway because Manges had not paid for the flight home. The players were left to wonder if they would have to hitchhike back to San Antonio. Of greater concern was whether they would even get paid. Every two weeks, they would race each other to the bank to cash their paychecks because they knew that half of those checks were likely to bounce.[7] "It looked like the Daytona 500," said Schott, who was assistant general manager, special teams coach, and equipment manager. "Even Hollywood couldn't make this stuff up!"[8]

"Probably the most fun day we ever had came with just four games left in the season," said Bradley, who served as the team's defensive-backs coach. "All the coaches were out there on the field waiting for the players, thinking, *Well, they may or may not show up today for kickoff since this is a pay period*. We didn't know what they were going to do. Suddenly, they came jogging out of the dressing room as a group. It was just unbelievable. They came out there onto the field shouting, 'Check! Check! Check the defense! Check bounce! Check bounce!' and the whole place just broke up laughing!"[9]

While the USFL signed NFL stars like Jim Kelly, Steve Young, and Herschel Walker to multi-million-dollar contracts, the typical Gunslinger made just $25,000 a season.[10] Manges owed $34 million to 150 creditors, including his football team.[11] Predictably, the Gunslingers played out the 1985 season before being disbanded. By that time, Bradley was an assistant to Pepper Rodgers on another USFL team, the Memphis Showboats. Rodgers, who quarterbacked Georgia Tech to an undefeated season in 1952, returned to his alma mater as head coach in the mid-to-late 1970s before going to the USFL.[12]

"Rodgers was a stand-up-comedian football coach," recalled Bradley. "I met him in a bar one night at a coach's convention in Mobile, Alabama, and listened to him telling jokes. He was funny as hell. I laughed my ass off."[13]

Frustrated with the cash-strapped Gunslingers, Bill asked Rodgers if he had a job opening with the Memphis Showboats. "Bradley, I liked the way you laughed at my jokes," replied the Showboats' head coach. "Hell, you can come work for me anytime!"[14]

Bill approached his position as a defensive-backs coach with the passion of a camp revival preacher. But he credits Rodgers with giving him his first lesson in coaching. Once, when he first went to Memphis, Bradley saw a player across the field make a mistake and yelled, "Hey man! What are ya doing?" Then he continued to correct the player by screaming at him.

After Bill finished his ear-wrenching instruction, Rodgers beckoned him with his index finger. "Bradley, I like you," he began in a calm but stern voice. "But I can get any bum off the street to come yell at the players.

If you see something that you don't like in the future, I want you to jog over to the player and correct him in a normal tone of voice."[15]

Rodgers reminded Bradley that just because he starred in the NFL did not mean that he had the talent to coach at the pro level. Bill appreciated the advice. He was only thirty-two years old, which was young for an assistant at the time. He needed to learn how to make the transition from player to coach.[16]

Unfortunately for Bradley, his time with Rodgers in Memphis lasted just one season because the USFL folded. The reason generally cited is Donald Trump's desire for a fall schedule. Trump, then a real estate mogul, was the owner of the New Jersey Generals. In the summer of 1985, he began pressuring the other owners to reschedule the USFL's games to the fall to compete for fans—and dollars—with the National Football League. However, many of the renegade league's teams were having financial trouble, and the USFL did not have the fall TV contracts that supported the older, more established league. Instead, the owners took on the NFL in the courts by filing an antitrust lawsuit, hoping to either merge with the NFL or win a sizeable financial settlement. Neither happened, and the USFL soon folded.[17]

Whereas Bradley cut his teeth as a coach in the USFL, the Canadian Football League (CFL) is where he perfected his ability as a teacher-coach. The CFL, founded in 1956 as the Canadian Football Council, evolved from earlier amateur rugby leagues that adopted a style of football. Two years later, the circuit changed its name to the Canadian Football League and established two divisions. The British Columbia Lions, Calgary Stampeders, Edmonton Elks, Saskatchewan Roughriders, and Winnipeg Blue Bombers compete in the Western Division, while the Hamilton Tiger-Cats, Ottawa Redblacks, Montreal Alouettes, and Toronto Argonauts play in the Eastern Division.

The CFL's rugby origins are still reflected by the Grey Cup, first awarded in 1909, when Governor General the Earl Grey donated the trophy to the team winning the Senior Amateur Rugby Championship of Canada. Since 1954, the Grey Cup has been awarded annually to the winner of the CFL's championship.[18]

Bradley began his CFL coaching career in 1988, when Lary Kuharich, head coach of the Calgary Stampeders, hired him as his defensive-backs coach. The two men had known each other since Bradley's days with the Philadelphia Eagles. Lary's father, Joe, drafted Bill in 1969, when he was head coach of the Eagles. Later, in the early 1980s, Lary and Bill worked together with the Gunslingers, where Lary was the offensive coordinator. Kuharich believed that Bradley's free-spirited style would complement that of his more straitlaced defensive coordinator, Wally Buono.[19]

"When I went to the CFL, I really learned how to coach," admitted Bradley. "Unlike in the NFL where you have four downs, eleven men on the field, and a 50-yard line, the CFL only gives you three downs to get a first. You have twelve men on the field, a 55-yard line, a 20-yard end zone, and everyone can be in motion at the same time. That means the defenders can come out of the backfield running full speed when they hit the line of scrimmage when the ball is snapped. It's also a longer field. The CFL was a passing league. Going there was the best thing that ever happened to me as a football coach. You learn a lot. You also learn how to be creative. When I finally got to the NFL, coaching was easy because of what I learned in the CFL."[20]

Regardless of the league, a defensive-backfield coach at the pro level has an extraordinary amount of responsibility. In addition to planning and conducting daily practice sessions, game film must be studied to prepare for the next week's opponent. Scouting reports must also be completed and reviewed with the players. "It's a hell of a lot of work," admitted Bradley, who never aspired to be a head coach. "I worked my ass off when I went into coaching. Coaching is teaching, and it's demanding. I just couldn't go in front of the players and say, 'I made All-Pro three years, y'all better listen to me.' I had to gain their respect by showing them that I could teach the finer points of the game."[21]

Bradley helped coach Calgary to a division championship in 1990 before moving on to the San Antonio Riders, which played in the World League of America. Two years later, Bill returned to the Canadian Football League, where he spent the next five seasons as a defensive coordinator with the San Antonio Texans (1993–94), one of the first U.S. expansion teams;

Sacramento Gold Miners (1994–95); and Toronto Argonauts (1996–97). His tenure with Toronto was the most successful, as he helped the Argonauts capture two Grey Cups, the equivalent of Canada's Super Bowl.[22] But Bradley's most enduring experience occurred in 1994 while he was with the Sacramento Gold Miners. That's when he met Susan Wright, a divorcee and mother of two young children.

Wright, a native of northern California, lived in the same neighborhood as Bradley. Mutual friends introduced them by scheduling a blind date, which began at the Final Four of the NCAA Basketball Tournament in Sacramento and ended at the symphony. Having enjoyed each other's company, the couple began dating on a regular basis.

"I could see immediately that Bill was a very genuine person," recalled Susan, who had sworn off marriage at the time. "He doesn't really care about material things. He's pure and honest. He's a real person, no pretense whatsoever, which is very rare. Those were the most important things that attracted me to Bill."[23]

Bill cited the same qualities in Susan, plus her "good looks, charming disposition, intelligence, and goal-oriented approach to life." Wright operated a preschool and day-care center, as well as a catering business that prepared convenient breakfast foods and coffee for clients who lived in her neighborhood. The arrangement allowed her to be with her own children around the clock, while also learning the skill set of an entrepreneur. "Susan is a doer," said Bill. "There's no grass growing under her feet. When she says she's going to do something, she does it and does it well. That shows commitment and perseverance. All of those qualities attracted me to her."[24]

Bradley and Wright dated for almost six years before they were married on June 26, 1999. Her son, Matthew, was twelve years old, and daughter Carissa was nine at the time. "I worried about them," Susan confessed. "Bill's career as a football coach meant that we would have to relocate, and kids need stability. I also thought that it wouldn't be fair to Jay, their [biological] father, to take them out of Northern California, where he lived. But Bill was just so great with my kids, my family, and me. I finally allowed myself to be happy, and we were married."[25]

Susan's happiness was not achieved without sacrifice, though. Bill had left the Canadian Football League in 1998 for the NFL, where he was a defensive-backs coach with the Buffalo Bills. That meant she had to not only relocate her family but also do so across the country to upstate New York. The life of an NFL wife is not an easy one. Like the players, coaches are absent from home for long periods, including preseason training camp and, during the season, frequent trips to other cities for road games. During those absences, a mother becomes a single parent, shouldering duties usually shared by both spouses. In Susan's case, she would carry out that role in a different and unfamiliar part of the country. In addition to caring for her own children, Susan also assumed responsibilities as a homemaker and spouse for Bill, with the emotional support that those roles entailed. Bill realized that. He appreciated the sacrifices Susan was making for him and made sure to be fully present for his soulmate and the children whenever he was at home. In fact, Susan admitted that Bill "*always* made time for Matthew, Carissa, and me" and that there were times when "he was more present with the kids because I was always running around doing things."[26]

Matthew and Carissa did not share their mother's reservations about relocating to the East. "We had a really great childhood because of Bill's coaching career," recalled Carissa in a recent interview. "We had a lot of unique experiences that other kids don't have, by living in different places just about every three years. It was an exciting childhood."[27] Susan was pleasantly surprised by her children's ability to not only adapt but also thrive. "The kids considered it an adventure," she admitted. "They adapted much better than I ever would have imagined."[28]

Of course, Bill made *everything* an adventure for them too. He assumed his new role as a father figure with the same contagious enthusiasm he displayed on the gridiron, quickly endearing himself to both children. Matthew accepted and looked up to Bill. They bonded through sports. Regardless of the season—football, basketball, or baseball—Bill found the time to practice with Matt and to attend his games. "When Matthew was competing, Bill could hardly watch," Susan recalled. "He could not sit down. He was always pacing back and forth. I think he was more nervous for my son than Matthew was himself."[29] Carissa also accepted Bill immediately.[30] "In fact, Bill treated Carissa as if she were his own little girl," said Susan. "He was very involved in her activities too. When, for example, Carissa had a synchronized swimming event, Bill was there wearing his 'Synch Dad' cap and cheering her on."[31]

Bradley even made sure to encourage Jay Wright, the children's biological father, to stay in their lives. Other men might have discouraged an ongoing relationship between a divorced father and his children, viewing it as competition. But Bill thought it was important that Matt and Carissa knew Jay not only for his sake but also for theirs. "I couldn't imagine not seeing my kids if I were divorced," he explained. "Jay was still their father, and nobody could take his place, so I made sure that he was always welcome in our home."[32] That kind of compassion endeared Bill to Susan and her children even more.

Between 1998 and 2000, Bradley served as defensive-backs coach for the Buffalo Bills. Buffalo had become a perennial Super Bowl contender in the 1990s under Marv Levy, once Bradley's special teams coach with the Eagles. Wade Phillips, a defensive coordinator under Levy, took over as the Bills' new head coach. He was the ideal candidate for the position. Phillips, the son of the legendary Houston Oilers coach Bum Phillips, began his professional career as a linebackers coach in the mid-1970s with his father's Oilers. Wade remained on Bum's staff as the pair headed for New Orleans. He became the interim head coach of the Saints when his father stepped down in 1985. The next year, Wade went to the Philadelphia Eagles as defensive coordinator before taking the same position with the Denver Broncos in 1989. Promoted to head coach in 1993, Phillips was fired the next year after Denver had a mediocre season but was quickly hired by Buffalo's Marv Levy as a defensive coordinator.[33]

"Wade had a great football mind," remembered Bradley, who considers himself part of the Bum Phillips–Wade Phillips coaching tree. "He also knew how to manage his personnel. He was very loyal to them. He treated everyone the same way. That's why he was able to keep the Bills competitive after he took over from Marv."[34]

To be sure, there were high expectations for Wade Phillips after succeeding Levy, who had taken Buffalo to the Super Bowl four straight years. Unlike his predecessor, however, Phillips did not have All-Pro quarterback Jim Kelly, a future Hall of Famer, who had retired. Instead, he inherited Rob Johnson, a fourth-round pick out of the University of Southern California, and acquired Doug Flutie, who had quarterbacked the CFL's Toronto Argonauts to two Grey Cup titles. Other stars from the AFC championship years had also left.[35] But Phillips still possessed the core of a winning team that included three playmakers: wide receivers Andre Reed and Steve Tasker and running back Thurman Thomas. All three players were All-Pro and former Pro Bowlers. Reed and Thomas would later be inducted into the Pro Football Hall of Fame. "What it all came down to was having good players and having them do what they do well," explained Phillips.[36] Of course, "having them do what they do well" also depended on good coaching.

Phillips promoted linebackers coach Ted Cottrell as his replacement at defensive coordinator. Cottrell, a seventh-round pick of the Atlanta Falcons in the 1969 draft, began his coaching career at the collegiate level with Rutgers in 1973 as a defensive-line coach and, later, defensive coordinator. In 1981 he moved on to the NFL as a linebackers coach with the Kansas City Chiefs and, later, as a defensive-line coach with the Arizona Cardinals and Bills. Widely considered an innovator of the 3-4 defense, Cottrell, in 1999, transformed the Bills into the NFL's first-ranked defense.[37] Bradley played an instrumental part in the success too.

"Bill was a fantastic coach because he played the defensive backfield at a high level," explained Cottrell in a recent interview. "He was also very meticulous in his scouting reports and practice plans. He had good communication skills too. He prepared the most detailed diagrams so the defensive backs could understand their coverage assignments."[38]

Once, during a practice session, the secondary was running through its coverages, and a recently acquired cornerback blew his assignment. Bill and Ted sat him down between themselves, and Bill pulled out his diagram. When Bradley asked the confused player to point to his assignment, the cornerback eyed the sketch and said, "I have no idea."

Bill, who took great pride in his artwork, was so upset that he stayed up all night redrafting the diagram. When he was finished, the drawing had morphed into a three-by-five-foot poster and was even more elaborate than the previous one, featuring different colored routes and directional arrows.

When Bill arrived at practice the next day with his new diagram, the cornerback saw the drawing and blurted, "Wow! That's a real neat poster!"

"Yeah, it is, isn't it?" Bradley exclaimed. "So now you'll understand where the hell you're supposed to be when I ask you!"[39]

Phillips also credited Bradley for his excellent communication skills. "The secondary was a big part of why we were the No. 1 defense in 1999," he insisted. "That's not a coincidence. Bill is such a great coach because of his ability to communicate with the players. He got the most out of them, and they really wanted to play for him."[40]

One of those players was free safety Kurt Schulz, who credited Bradley with having a huge impact on his career. "Bill had such a different coaching philosophy than the previous defensive-backs coach," recalled Schulz. "When Bill arrived in training camp in 1998, he told me that my play was like that of a robot. It was a perfect analogy. I was too rigid, too structured. Nor did I take many risks. Bill changed that. He taught me how to play more by instinct, how to improvise, and how to take calculated risks."[41] Schulz learned well. During the next three seasons, the Bills' free safety had 16 interceptions, an average of 5.3 a year. Those three seasons were the best of Schulz's NFL career and enabled him to sign a hefty contract as a free agent with the Detroit Lions.[42] "I think Bill was a phenomenal coach because he played free safety so well in the NFL, but that was only part of his success," explained Schulz. "Many naturally gifted athletes can't coach because they can't understand why others can't do what came so naturally to them. Bill wasn't only a naturally gifted athlete, but he also had a high football IQ and excellent communication skills, which allowed him to teach the game."[43]

The Bills made the playoffs twice during Bradley's three-year tenure in Buffalo. In 1998 the team went 10-6 and finished third in the AFC East, losing to the Miami Dolphins in the Wild Card Game, 24–17.[44] The 1999 season was bittersweet, though. The Bills finished second in the division with an 11-5 record, and the defense only gave up 229 points, or 14 points a game. While that was the second fewest in the NFL that year, Buffalo had the first-ranked defense overall with outstanding starters. Playing a 3-4 defense in front, the Bills featured Ted Washington, a four-time Pro Bowler at nose tackle; Bruce Smith, a defensive end and future Hall of Famer; and Phil Hansen at the other defensive end. The outside linebackers were Sam Rogers and Gabe Northern, and the interior linebackers were John Holecek and Sam Cowart, who was All-Pro. While the linemen and linebackers stifled the opponent's rushing game, the secondary cut down the opposition's passing attack, with Henry Jones, a Pro Bowler, at strong safety; Schulz at free safety; and corners Thomas Smith and Ken Irvin.[45] "But at the end of day," Schulz insisted, "our success was due to Ted [Cottrell] and Bill [Bradley], who made things as simple as possible for us and just let us play. They also gave us ownership by asking us our opinions, which also made us accountable. After all, if you have a say in game planning, you're going to make damn sure that you carry it out."[46]

Unfortunately, the Bills' season ended quickly in the playoffs against the Tennessee Titans in a Wild Card Game called the Music City Miracle, at the Adelphia Coliseum in Nashville, Tennessee.

The so-called miracle happened at the end of the game. Buffalo had taken a 16–15 lead on a field goal with just sixteen seconds left on the clock. On the following kickoff return, Titans tight end Frank Wycheck threw a lateral pass across the field to Kevin Dyson, who then ran 75 yards to score the final touchdown, Tennessee winning, 22–16.[47]

The defeat haunted Wade Phillips for the remainder of his time in Buffalo. Had he started Doug Flutie at quarterback instead of Rob Johnson, according to the prognosticators, the Bills would have scored more than 16 points and won the contest with a comfortable margin. But before the game Phillips made the controversial decision to start Johnson despite the fact that Flutie, the NFL's Comeback Player of the Year, had been the starter for all but three games during the season. It was Flutie—not Johnson—who led the Bills to the playoffs with his precision passing and ability to run. Phillips later insisted that he was ordered by Bills' owner Ralph Wilson to play Johnson.[48] Regardless of who made the decision, playing Johnson instead of Flute led to a stinging defeat that marked the end of Buffalo's six-year playoff run.

Although the Bills ranked first in past defense in the NFL in 2000, a testimony to Bradley's coaching, Buffalo finished with an 8-8 record.[49] "A couple things happened that season," recalled Ted Cottrell, the defensive coordinator. "We had salary-cap issues, and many of the guys we had trained on defense, including the backups, were let go. We couldn't keep the veterans together, and that really hurt us. In fact, it's one of the problems I have with the NFL today. Free agency and the salary cap have made it impossible for many teams to compete. You can be in the Super Bowl one year and have a losing record the next if you can't retain your star players."[50] Perhaps owner Ralph Wilson did not appreciate that fact because he fired Wade Phillips along with Cottrell and Bradley after the season. The Bills would not return to the playoffs until 2017.

Bradley and Cottrell were reunited when Herm Edwards, the new head coach of the New York Jets, hired them in 2001. The team improved on its 9-7 record from the previous year, finishing 10-6. New York also qualified for the final wild-card position in the AFC but lost to the Oakland Raiders, 38–24, in that round.[51] After opening the 2002 season with a 37–31 victory over Buffalo, the Jets were trounced by New England (44–7), Miami (30–3), and Jacksonville (28–3) and lost a 29–25 heartbreaker to Kansas City.[52] Frustrated with the 1-4 start, Edwards gathered all of the coaches together and told them to "start looking for a job." Cottrell, infuriated by the suggestion that the poor record reflected his coaching, stormed out of the room, swearing that his defense would reverse the fortunes of the team.[53]

Joining forces with Bradley, Cottrell revised the 3-4 scheme they had used in Buffalo, incorporating elements of the 4-3 defense that would improve the pass defense and the blitz. "Ted trusted me with the secondary," said Bradley. "He allowed me to take charge of it while he concerned himself with the linebackers and the D-line. It's not that we didn't have our differences, but we always worked them out."[54] Cottrell echoed Bradley's assessment of their relationship.

"Bill is one of my closest friends," said the former defensive coordinator. "He has a high football IQ, and he's as honest as the day is long. He's also very opinionated. We would argue all night about an issue, but we always made sure that we worked it out. There aren't many people like that. I knew I could always trust Bill because we have a mutual respect for each other."[55]

After Cottrell and Bradley changed the defense, the Jets won eight of the next eleven games to finish the regular season 9-7. New York white-washed the Indianapolis Colts, 41–0, in the Wild Card Game but then lost to Oakland in the Divisional Playoffs, 30–10.[56]

The Jets failed to defend their AFC East title in 2003, finishing the season with a 6-10 record, the first losing record since their 1-15 campaign in 1996. It was also the first time the team missed the playoffs since 2000.[57] Although Edwards managed to keep his job, Cottrell and Bradley were fired.

"Herm was an honest, religious guy, but I didn't enjoy coaching for him," admitted Bradley. "He overstepped his boundaries by trying to run the defense. Then he blamed us for the team's 1-4 start. While I always liked Herman as a person, I disliked what he tried to do to us in New York."[58]

In addition to coaching in the NFL, Bill was adjusting to life as a father at home. Matthew, now a teenager, was presenting a formidable challenge. "The high school years were tough for Matthew, as they are for most teens," remembered his mother, Susan. Sometimes Bill became the target of Matthew's frustration, and the two of them butted heads. Sensitive over the fact that he was not Matt's father, Bill, according to Susan, "didn't feel it was his place to discipline him." "I think Bill's reluctance was due in part to his fear that as a former NFL player he would let his temper get the best of him," she explained. "If that happened, he might not be able to control himself. The tension between them was difficult for me because Matthew needed a male figure in his life, and Bill possessed many of the same qualities I wanted Matthew to have."[59]

High school was a mixed blessing for Matthew. When Bill was coaching with the Jets, the family lived on Long Island, and Matt attended St.

Anthony's High School, a Franciscan Roman Catholic college-preparatory school with an extremely successful athletic tradition. Matt quickly distinguished himself as a star quarterback on the varsity football team and the ace pitcher of the varsity baseball team. "My brother was smart, athletic, charismatic, and very popular," said Carissa, his younger sister. "It was always easy for him to make friends. Matthew would get to a new school, and he would immediately be the big man on campus. But he also took risks. Not all of them were healthy either. Matt loved to experiment, especially if fun was involved.

"I was different. I didn't play sports. I wasn't outgoing. I had one or two close friends, but that was it. I was also a good kid. I didn't take risks. I was very responsible. I followed the rules. I was very black-and-white that way. Matthew knew that, too, so he was very protective of me. He shielded me from the way he lived his life. I hated that. Here I had a brother who was the most popular kid in the school, and I would've loved to hang out with him and his friends, who were also popular. But Matthew wouldn't allow that.

"I don't mean to suggest that Matthew and I weren't close. We were. We had a lot to bond over. Our parents were divorced. Our relationship with our father wasn't very easy when we were growing up. And we were both adjusting to a new father figure with Bill."[60]

At the same time, Bill made it clear to both Matthew and Carissa that as much as he loved them, he could never replace their father. "I know it was easy for Bill to fall in love with my mother, maybe not as easy to fall in love with Matthew and me," Carissa admitted. "Still, Bill came into our lives and loved us for who we were. He accepted us as a family and even accepted my biological father."[61]

Once, when Carissa was a youngster, she asked Bill if she could call him "Dad."

"You already have a dad," replied Bill. "Jay is an amazing dad."

"Then what should I call you?"

"You can call me whatever you want. But you need to remember that you already have an amazing father and that no one can replace him."

That simple and honest exchange "spoke volumes" to Carissa about Bill as a person and the "respect he had for [her] family as a whole. . . . That and the fact that Bill was always 100 percent present in my life and unjudgmental meant so much to me," she said. "It is the truest form of love that anyone can give."[62]

In 2007 Bradley was reunited with Ted Cottrell once more, this time with the San Diego Chargers. That season, San Diego finished the first in the AFC's Western Division with an 11-5 record. The Chargers' defense also led the NFL in takeaways (48), interceptions (30), and passing rating defense (70.0) It was the first time a Chargers team ever led the league in any of those categories. San Diego defeated Tennessee in the Wild Card Game (17–6) and the Indianapolis Colts in the Divisional Playoff (28–24) but lost in the AFC Championship Game to the New England Patriots (21–12), which were just beginning a dynasty.[63] The next year, San Diego slid to 8-8 but still clinched the AFC Western Division. The Chargers defeated the Colts in the Wild Card Round (23–17) but lost to the Pittsburgh Steelers in the Divisional Round (35–24).[64]

Cottrell, the defensive coordinator, was made the scapegoat in October when he was fired by head coach Norv Turner and replaced by linebackers coach Ron Rivera.[65] While he refused to point fingers specifically, Cottrell attributed the .500 record to "injuries and attitude problems among the players." However, the defensive coordinator did admit that the attitude problems originated "at the top." "It was a divided team, and when you have a divided team, you can't win consistently," he added.[66] Bradley was more candid.

"Norv Turner was a rookie head coach in 2007, and he was manipulated by Ron Rivera, who was actively campaigning to become the defensive coordinator," insisted Bill. "Rivera ingratiated himself with Turner and convinced him that the team's decline from 11-5 in 2007 to 8-8 in 2008 was due to Ted's defensive scheme. In fact, the reason we were able to return to the playoffs with a .500 team in 2008 was because of Ted's defense. The offense was just not as strong as it should have been because of so many injuries to key players." Instead, Bill believes that his friend was fired because he "told it like it was" and that Turner and Rivera "didn't want to listen to him." To this day, Bradley insists that Cottrell, an African American, was the "most intelligent and creative coach [he] ever worked with" and that he "should've been the first Black head coach in the NFL."[67] Instead, Cottrell went to the United Football League, where he became head coach of the New York Sentinels.[68]

San Diego was Bradley's final stop in the NFL. While he believes the "internal politics" that got him and Cottrell fired remain the same, Bill also thinks the game has "gotten soft."

"I have mixed emotions about the league," he said. "For example, today's NFL is more offensively minded. The rules protect the receivers and the quarterbacks. When I played, we had a saying: 'Offense wins games, but defense wins championships.' Today, the philosophy seems to be that offense wins both games and championships in a league that has gone pass happy. Defense is less important, and it shouldn't be. I also have mixed feelings about other changes. When I played, for example, we had six preseason games, and the starters played in just about all of them. Today, there are three preseason games, and you're lucky to see a starter play more than a single quarter. Similarly, today's preseason practices are nothing like they were when I played back in the 1970s. We were in pads and hitting twice a day. Not today—the players don't have nearly as much contact as we did."

Bradley concedes that some of the changes have also "reduced the number of injuries among the players." He wishes, for example, that there had been a rule against helmet-to-helmet contact when he played. "If we'd have had that rule, we wouldn't have had as many concussions. Nor would we have had as many deaths from CTE [chronic traumatic encephalopathy] as we've had among the players of my generation."[69]

It's a concern that Bill deals with daily in the twilight years of his life. He struggles with memory loss and the fear that he may very well become a victim of the same disease that has claimed the lives of a growing number of NFL veterans.

10

Faith, Hope, and Love

The Bradleys settled full-time in Spring Branch, Texas, about thirty miles north of San Antonio, in 2004 while Bill was still coaching with the New York Jets. He wanted to plant roots in his native state. Susan, an interior decorator by nature, was busy overseeing the construction of the new ranch house and, later, refurbishing it. Carissa was a freshman at nearby Smithson Valley High School and Matthew, a junior. He would later matriculate to American River College in Sacramento, California, in part to be closer geographically to his father. Life was good for the Bradleys. Everyone was happy, healthy, and looking forward to the future—until the summer of 2009.

That June, Matthew, the starting quarterback at his college, and four of his teammates went on a rafting trip on the American River near Sacramento. Stopping at a local park, they came across a rowdy group of young men. One of them began getting rough with his girlfriend. Matt, fearing for her safety, told him to back off. A fight ensued between the two groups.

"Matt was a good fighter," recalled Bill. "Apparently, he was beating up the other guy pretty bad until the culprit retreated. Matt thought the fight was over, but the guy went to his car, got a heavy metal flashlight, and blindsided Matthew, striking him on the back of his head. Then, after Matt fell to the ground unconscious, the guy kicked him in the face and broke his jaw."[1]

While the offending group scattered, Matt's friends dialed 911. He was flown by helicopter to the Medical Center Hospital at University of California, Davis. Rushed to the head trauma unit, Matthew was bleeding so profusely that doctors were forced to perform a partial resection of the cerebellum to release the pressure caused by all the swelling.[2]

At 2:00 a.m. Susan received the phone call that every parent dreads. Her son had been severely injured in a fight. He was now in a coma. And he might not live. “Initially, I was angry that he had gotten into a fight,” she admitted. “But when I flew up there and saw his condition, I knew how serious the situation was. Of course, the doctors told me he was in a coma. But when I looked into Matthew’s eyes, I could see he was *not* in a coma. Call it a mother’s intuition if you will, but looking into my son’s eyes, I could see that he was still there. I could also see the terror in his eyes. Despite his condition, which was critical, there was never any question in my mind that I was going to get him back to a normal life. I promised him that he was going to be okay, and that I wasn’t going to leave him.”[3]

True to her word, Susan moved into Matthew’s hospital room and remained there sleeping on a folding cot for the next two weeks. During that period, he was intubated and placed under cooling blankets to regulate his body temperature. He remained in the intensive care unit for another two weeks until doctors stabilized him. Unfortunately, the part of the cerebellum that was removed controlled most of Matthew’s motor skills, so he had difficulty with even the simplest movements. But he did not lose his cognitive abilities. After a while, Matt began to communicate by blinking his eyes—one blink for *yes*, two blinks for *no*.[4]

Approximately 1.5 million people suffer traumatic brain injury (TBI) annually in the United States. Of that number, 52,000 people die, and another 275,000 victims are hospitalized with moderate to severe symptoms.[5] Traumatic brain injuries are not alike, nor is a victim’s experience with traumatic brain damage. Each type of TBI has its own unique consequences, and each rarely exists in isolation. Often the victim will suffer a combination of injuries, each presenting a different level of severity.[6] In Matthew’s case, the direct hit he took to the back of the head resulted in a linear skull fracture that impacted the cerebellum at the back of the brain and the brainstem beneath the cerebellum, which connects the brain with the spinal cord. The swelling that followed required surgical intervention to resection the cerebellum. That operation created most of Matthew's complications because the cerebellum controls motor skills and coordinates both thought and speech.[7] The brainstem is even more critical to life, as it controls automatic functions like breathing, blood pressure, and heartbeat, and the slightest injury there can lead to coma.[8] As a result, Matthew suffered a severe loss of mobility in all four limbs. Essentially, he was a quadriplegic.[9]

Bill had a difficult time accepting Matthew's condition. As a former professional athlete, he had always feared losing his physical ability to play football. Now he was observing first-hand his worst nightmare. "Bill is a very sensitive person," said Susan. "What really bothered him was that Matthew was not just an incredible athlete; he had many other talents like writing, art, and music. Bill could not wrap his mind around the fact that this talented young person who had such a promising future was now bedridden and might never be able to enjoy those abilities, let alone walk again. Bill also hates hospitals. To see Matt suffering like that was just too much for him to take. There were times he'd retreat to the corner of the room and break down."[10]

In late July Matthew was flown to the Texas NeuroRehab Center in Austin, where he remained for a year. He spent another two years at a rehab center in San Antonio, closer to home. Matt's communication skills gradually improved with the use of a letterboard. By tapping on a series of letters, Matt was able to spell out a word. This was a critical step in his recovery. Prior to the letterboard, Matthew was trapped inside his own body. But the letterboard freed him by allowing him to express himself to others.[11]

Other treatments were also effective but very expensive. The estimated cost of TBI in the United States annually exceeds $48 billion.[12] The Bradleys quickly learned just how expensive their son's rehabilitation would be. One of the first therapies Matthew underwent was a series of experimental hyperbaric dives to prevent his neuron cells from going dormant while keeping them oxygenized. The therapy is actually meant for scuba divers suffering from decompression sickness. Matt would make more than two hundred dives at a cost of $125 each, and there was no insurance to pay for them.[13] Susan became a master at cutting through the red tape with medical insurance companies to pay for those treatments, in addition to Matt's two-year stay in rehab centers. "I had to fight with the insurance companies to make sure we could continue Matthew's therapy," said Susan. "I can't tell you how many times I appealed to those companies or how many times Matthew's physicians and therapists had to intervene so he could continue his therapy. Most families do not have the financial resources to pay for the care of a loved one with TBI, and they buckle under the pressure of insurance companies which only cover fourteen days of therapy before the patient is sent home. But we were determined to get Matthew the help he needed. It didn't matter what it cost. If we had to mortgage the house, we were going to do that."[14] There were other difficulties as well.

Matthew still could not lay flat on his back without choking on his own phlegm. Instead, he was strapped onto a reclining board at a 75-degree angle. He also had extremely limited movement and only with his fingers and arms. Traditional therapies could not resolve these problems. Desperate to find a solution, the Bradleys and Jay Wright, Matt's father, pursued stem-cell treatment. Because the U.S. Food and Drug Administration did not recognize this form of therapy as an acceptable treatment, they began doing their homework. They discovered that John Brodie, the former quarterback of the San Francisco 49ers, had successfully undergone stem-cell treatment in Russia after a massive stroke that left him without speech or the ability to walk.[15] "John's recovery was so successful that he became the poster boy for stem-cell treatment in Russia," noted Bradley.[16]

In 2011 the Bradleys made their first trip to Russia so Matthew could receive stem-cell treatments intravenously through the arm. After receiving the first stem-cell treatment, the Bradleys noticed immediate improvement.[17]

"Matthew started looking so much better," said Susan. "He was getting stronger and breathing more easily. His body temperature also began to regulate itself. But greater improvement came in 2012, when we traveled to a clinic in Kazakhstan."[18] There Matthew began receiving neural stem-cell therapy, which had to be done intravenously through the spine. The treatment had an immediate healing effect. Matthew had feeling in nearly all parts of his body. He began to work with a physical therapist to regain his motor skills. Under the supervision of neurologist Dr. Philip Onghai, Matt rode an exercise bike and did aquatic exercises five to six times a week. He also became very close to another physical therapist, Ashley Hayes, a beautiful young lady who was unconditionally devoted to him. She made Matt feel loved and still relevant. Ashley also became instrumental in Matt's recovery by thinking outside the box for ways to rewire his brain.[19]

For twelve years, Susan, Bill, and Carissa cared for Matt. They built him his own cabin on their ranch so he could have some semblance of privacy, though someone was always present to address his needs, and the cabin was equipped with various devices so he could call Susan or Bill in an emergency. Matthew watched a lot of TV, listened to books on tape, and planned to complete his business degree online. But his favorite pastime was listening to music, including rhythm and blues, country, rock 'n' roll, and rap, but especially the alternative rock group Sublime.[20]

When asked if she thought Matthew's recovery was a miracle, Susan conceded that it was "a part of a miracle." But she also insisted that "without the support of his therapists" and "Matthew's own determination" he would "not have gotten better." She also admitted that she could not have cared for Matthew alone.

"Mathew's care required a huge effort," Susan explained. "Carissa, who was attending San Diego State, would often come home of weekends and in the summer to help out. She will never know how much that meant to Matthew and to me. Nor could I have done this without Bill. He was incredible. He will do anything for this family without ever complaining. He loves Matthew and Carissa like they are his own kids."[21] Because the expenses for Matthew's care were astronomical, Bill returned to coaching, first at Baylor University and later at Lamar University, to help pay for his stepson's therapy.[22]

With his family's help, Matt began to defy the odds and regain a better quality of life. "There is a misconception that the victims of brain damage will never improve. But that's not true," insisted Susan. "What I learned from Matthew's case is that over time, the victim can improve if they are provided therapy from the beginning and it continues throughout the recovery period."[23]

While the long-term impact of TBI is notoriously difficult to predict, recent research shows that recovery *is* possible. In one of the largest studies of TBI survivors, only 12.2 percent of the survivors did not regain movement in their limbs.[24] In addition, early-stage and ongoing involvement in neurorehabilitation has also shown to improve long-term outcome.[25] In his book *The Brain That Changes Itself*, Norman Doidge MD rejects the longtime belief that brain-damaged patients can rarely make full recoveries. His research shows that "neuroplastic treatments enable the brain to change its very structure with each different activity it performs, perfecting its circuits so it is better suited to the task at hand. . . . If certain parts of the brain fail," argues Doidge, "then other parts can sometimes take over." Thus, the damaged brain can "often reorganize itself," and many "circuits" and "even basic reflexes that we think are hardwired are not."[26]

Matthew's recovery confirms the research. Within a decade of his injury, he had not only regained communication skills but some large motor skills as well.[27] It was clear to the Bradleys that their son's cerebellum had become rewired through the stem-cell treatment. The improvement was so evident that he was planning to complete his business degree from American River College online.[28] Susan and Bill were also confident that with continued therapy, Matthew would be able to walk on his own again. Indeed, things were looking up for the Bradleys—until November 14, 2020.[29]

The night before, Matthew was in considerable pain. The discomfort began in his left torso but eventually moved up to his shoulder and became much worse. Ashley, his physical therapist, massaged Matt's left shoulder. But the pain continued. Because Matthew did not like going to a hospital, where people stared at him, Susan promised that she would keep him at home if he agreed to go to an outpatient facility. He did. The doctor took some X-rays and diagnosed a rib contusion. Then he gave Matt some morphine to stop the pain and sent him home.[30]

The next morning, when Susan gave Matthew a shower, he was still in a lot of pain. She gave him some codeine and then went to the pharmacy to purchase a lidocaine patch. Before she left, Susan checked on Matt and said, "Call me if you need me." But he didn't say anything. It was the last time she saw him alive. Twenty minutes later, when she returned to his cabin, Matthew had passed peacefully. The autopsy indicated that his entire left lung had collapsed and that he died of pneumonia.[31]

"For the longest time, I blamed myself because I thought I gave him too much codeine and that I left him when he passed," Susan confessed. "There was all this guilt. It's still hard for me to accept. I thought we really had it down after twelve years of caring for him. We hired some wonderful people to take care of Matthew. But it was mostly Carissa, Ashley, and me. Matthew showed signs of improvement too. He really didn't want to die. He kept his faith, and he tried to be strong so I wouldn't worry about him. I don't know how he did it. How he was able to live that way. That's what's so upsetting to me."[32]

Carissa also struggled to come to terms with Matthew's death. She was a junior at San Diego State when Matt was injured, so she spent the next decade traveling back and forth between Southern California and Spring Branch to help her mother care for him. During that period, Carissa completed a degree in child development and had planned to work with children who had suffered traumatic brain damage but decided that that field was "too close to home because of Matthew's condition." Instead, she completed a master's degree in applied behavior analysis at Arizona State University and went to work as a behavioral specialist for children with autism, trying to "help those kids discover their strengths as well as their place in this world." Over the years since Matthew passed, Carissa, who still misses her brother dearly, found a silver lining in her belief that Matthew "led a very full life in the short time he had on this earth."[33] She also gained an even greater appreciation for her mother.

"My mom is my best friend," said Carissa, who is now married and the mother of three children. "She raised Matthew and me while running a preschool and daycare in our house because she wanted to be there for us. She worked so hard to give us a good upbringing. My mother was not only a parent but the breadwinner, a chef, and an inspiration. She was all that and more for Matthew after his accident. I don't think any parent would do what Mom did to care for Matthew. She is the ultimate caregiver. And Bill was right there by her side. He went back to coaching to help pay for my brother's therapies and to support our family. But when he was at home Bill was 100 percent present for Mom and Matthew."[34]

Matt's injury, the decade he spent recovering from it, and ultimately his death would test the faith of most people. Many would reject their religion and even God Himself, who is supposed to be of a good and loving nature. Why, after all, should they turn for comfort to the same God who made the tragedy happen? Harold Kushner, author of the highly acclaimed book *When Bad Things Happen to Good People*, offers a wise and compassionate answer to that question. "While God is benevolent, he is *not* all-powerful to prevent evil and the suffering it causes," according to Kushner, a Jewish rabbi who wrote the book after losing his own son. "God would like people to get what they deserve in life, but He cannot always arrange it. When we suffer, He is also saddened by our suffering. Still God's love for us is unlimited and His ultimate wish is to have people live fully, bravely and meaningfully in a less-than-perfect world."[35]

Such a finite view of God begs the question *How does one find faith and courage in the midst of unbearable tragedy?* Kushner's answer is for us to accept that "much of the time, we cannot control what happens to us." "But we can *always* control how we respond to what happens to us," he adds. "If we cannot choose to be lucky, to be talented, to be loved, we can choose to be grateful, to be content with who we are and what we have, and to act accordingly."[36] This is how Susan and Bill have chosen to deal with Matthew's death.

Susan, who was raised a Catholic, and Bill, who was raised in three different Christian denominations, left the church many years ago. But they still regard themselves as very spiritual people. "How can I lose my faith when Matthew kept his throughout his recovery?" Susan asked rhetorically. "He was incredibly spiritual and very knowledgeable about the Bible. Watching Matthew struggle daily and never lose his faith was so inspirational for me." Susan's belief that Matthew was "chosen because he was such a gifted young man and loved by so many different kinds of people" has enabled her to come to terms with his death. She has even been able to forgive the young man who injured her son. "I was angry with him at first," she admitted, "but his life was ruined too. He's a felon who spent time in jail. The last time I saw him, he did not look good. I felt bad for him and for his family."[37]

Similarly, Bill, who believes "in a loving and charitable Supreme Being," has also been able to put Matthew's death in perspective without losing his faith. "When we suffer a tragedy, it's not God's fault," he explained. "I believe that God gives all people free will, and they can choose to do good or to do evil. In Matthew's case, another person caused his injury, it sure wasn't God. I was just grateful that we still had Matthew with us for as long as we did after he was injured. I can only believe that Matthew's death was the Lord's will. I've learned to make the best of life since then. All I can do is try to be the best person, the best husband, and the best friend I can be."[38]

Since Matthew's death, Bill wears a chain around his neck containing his stepson's ashes. It hangs close to his heart where his love for Matt remains eternal. Bradley also has another, more sobering reminder of the brain damage Matthew suffered. It has come primarily in the form of memory loss but includes the confusion, anxiety, and anger Bill struggles with daily.

Although no two brain injuries are the same, the Bradleys are convinced that Bill's cognitive impairment is the result of five major concussions and many more subconcussive hits he suffered while playing football. They also fear that he will become yet another victim of chronic traumatic encephalopathy (CTE), a brain disorder linked to repeated trauma to the head.[39]

According to the Mayo Clinic, the predominant American academic medical center focused in integrated health care, education, and research, CTE is a neurodegenerative disease causing the death of nerve cells in the brain. It's related to repeated head injuries, often occurring in contact sports or military combat. CTE has also been associated with second impact syndrome, in which a second head injury happens before the initial head-injury symptoms have fully resolved.

Researchers are still trying to determine how repeated head injuries might contribute to the changes in the brain that result in CTE. They also continue to explore how the number of head injuries someone experiences and how bad the injuries are may affect the risk of CTE. What is known is that CTE does get worse over time, there is at present no cure for the disorder, and the only way to definitively diagnosis it is after death, during an autopsy of the brain.

A constellation of symptoms seems to indicate the existence of the disorder. Cognitive impairment includes trouble thinking, memory loss, and problems planning, organizing, and carrying out tasks. Behavioral changes include impulsiveness and aggression. Mood disorders include depression, emotional instability, and suicidal thoughts or behavior. Among the motor symptoms are problems with walking and balance, parkinsonism, and motor neuron disease, which destroys cells that control walking, speaking, swallowing, and breathing.[40]

The most publicized type of CTE is related to boxing and the punch-drunk state of seasoned fighters. It was first diagnosed as dementia pugilistica in 1928 by Dr. Harrison Martland, the chief medical examiner of Essex County, New Jersey. More than seventy years later, in 2002, Dr. Bennet Omalu, an associate medical examiner in Allegheny County, Pennsylvania, identified CTE in professional football players.[41] The discovery was consistent with the punishing and incredibly brutal culture of the NFL. Each week the game wears down these modern-day gladiators, slowly but surely destroying their bodies and minds. It wasn't always that way, though.

Smashmouth football became the rule in the 1970s, which ushered in an era where both the violence of the sport as well as the glory were celebrated. *Monday Night Football*, which began in 1970, captured the tension between these two extremes, as tens of millions tuned in to their TV sets.[42] Their obsession transformed the NFL into a multi-billion-dollar industry. Fans flocked to the sport to watch their favorite team score touchdowns and revel in the end zone hijinks. Some of the biggest cheers, however, were elicited by bone-crushing tackles, glamorized hits that also resulted in concussions.[43]

In 2002 Bennet Omalu's research linked chronic brain disease with the NFL during an autopsy of Mike Webster, a deceased retired Pittsburgh

Steeler and one of the best centers in the history of the game.[44] After sectioning Webster's brain, Omalu found a unique disease entity with a distinctive neuropathology associated with repetitive blows to the head, subconcussions, and concussions. Omalu's work showed that no amount of padding could protect the human brain from the vicious force generated by modern football. But instead of working with scientists and doctors to better understand the damaging effect of repeated concussions and how the league could improve the game to reduce head injuries, the NFL went after the reputations of Omalu and the other scientists who subsequently worked on CTE. Within a year's time, the NFL reconvened its Mild Traumatic Brain Injury Committee (MTBIC) to investigate the impact of football on the brain and to attack Omalu's findings.[45] Chaired by Dr. Elliot Pellman, a trained internist and rheumatologist who served as a team physician for the New York Jets, the MTBIC was composed of other team physicians, none of whom were neurologists.[46]

In their best-selling book *League of Denial: The NFL, Concussions, and the Battle for Truth*, Mark Fainaru-Wada and Steve Fainaru chronicle the ways the NFL used the MTBIC, as well as the league's power and resources, to attack Omalu and other scientists to promote its own flawed research and protect their $10 billion industry. Beginning in 2003, MTBIC published research in a series of papers in the journal *Neurosurgery* that gave definitive denials, downplaying the breadth and severity of concussions.[47] In 2005 the committee called for a retraction of Omalu's research findings, also published in the journal *Neurosurgery, stating that those findings were "completely wrong."* Omalu and his coauthors beat the attempt at retraction when they published a second paper in the same journal, this one relating to the discovery of CTE in the brain of former Pittsburgh Steelers offensive lineman Terry Long. Again, the NFL attacked Omalu's research, saying "it's not appropriate science" and that his work was "purely speculative."[48]

The NFL's efforts to reject concussion science by harassing Omalu and other scientists continued until 2009, when the league finally acknowledged that "the medical research that's been done shows that concussions can lead to long-term problems."[49] By that time, hundreds of autopsies of former NFL players revealed CTE.[50] Under mounting pressure from the medical community and the league's sponsors, Roger Goodell, Tagliabue's replacement as NFL commissioner, disbanded MTBIC and promised to support research by its most vocal critics. To that end, the NFL, in 2012, donated $30 million to the National Institutes of Health (NIH) for brain research.[51] Four years later, in 2016, the league added new concussion rules and a $100 million initiative that would be "earmarked for independent medical research, diagnosis and treatment of head injuries" and to "enhance medical protocols."[52] In addition, the NFL initiated a $1 billion plan to settle more than twenty thousand concussion lawsuits filed by former players or their estates.[53] To be eligible for compensation, the former player had to take a series of neurological tests administered by the league and meet the baseline requirement.[54] Still, concussions remain a major problem for those like Bradley whose hard-nosed play helped to build the multi-billion-dollar industry that the NFL is today.

Bradley struggles with a constellation of cognitive impairments associated with CTE, including short-term memory loss, repetition, and difficulties with organizing, planning, and completing tasks. As a result of these problems, he also suffers from anxiety. "Bill is very frustrated over his cognitive impairment," said Susan. "He doesn't like feeling as if he's lost control." The anxiety is just as bad. "Some days you'd never know that he is struggling. Other days, he has very little patience, and he gets angry easily. There was even a period when he'd get up in the middle of the night because of all the anxiety."[55]

Because Bradley is seventy-seven years old as of this writing in 2024, the short-term memory loss might be attributed to aging. But the other symptoms are more indicative of the concussions he had during his NFL career. Bill suffered five major concussions during his nine years in the league when helmet-to-helmet contact was legal, even encouraged. The first concussion in the NFL came in 1971 on a punt return against the New York Giants. "I went helmet-to-helmet against a lineman and everything went dark," he recalled. "Then, when I started to come around, I felt like my head was vibrating, like someone banged a giant cymbal." The last concussion Bradley suffered came in 1975 against the St. Louis Cardinals when their tight end forearmed him on the side of the helmet and his neck snapped back. Those two concussions were so severe that Bradley was taken to the hospital for an electroencephalogram. Bill also suffered three major concussions in college, in addition to the many subconcussive hits he absorbed throughout his high school, college, and pro careers. "There is no question that my football career is behind the problems I'm suffering today," insists Bradley. "If it wasn't for my wife, I'd be homeless, living on the streets of Austin, and sleeping under a bridge at night."[56]

Susan, who is fifteen years younger than Bill, not only is responsible for the couple's finances but also serves as a sounding board for him. "I look out for Bill," she explains. "While I don't try to mother him, I make it safe for him to vent. There's a lot of frustration when he can't remember things. Once I suggested that he try antidepressants. But Bill is old school. He doesn't believe in taking any kind of pill. I finally convinced him to see a doctor to explore the possibility that an antidepressant might help him. I think the fact that I had to go on an antidepressant after Matthew's death made him feel it was okay."[57]

Now that Bradley's parents, sister, and brother have passed, he focusses more on family. Susan; Carissa; her husband, Jon Carter; and their children mean the world to him. He revels in the exploits of his young grandsons, who call him "Paps" and love being around him. True to form, Bradley has nicknamed them after his interests in country music and baseball. Thus, Henry, the eldest grandson, is called "Hank Williams," Casey is "Casey at the Bat," and the youngest, Wyatt, has a name that is country by nature.[58] Unfortunately, Bill's memory loss and the anxiety that accompanies it limits the amount of time he spends with Carissa and her family, who live in San Diego. The unfamiliarity of being away from home heightens his anxiety. "I accept the fact that there are times that Bill doesn't want to go to San Diego to visit the grandchildren," admits Susan, who travels to Southern California once a month with or without Bill. "I also realize that he feels more comfortable staying here at home in Spring Branch. He feels that he has more control over himself here than in San Diego, where he is out of his element." At the same time, Susan worries about Bill being alone. But the Bradleys are fortunate that they have good friends and neighbors who will stop in to visit Bill and make sure he is doing okay.[59]

Bradley also treasures the time he spends with his nephews, Kelly and Brodie Hoppers, and Brodie's wife, Kym, and their two daughters, Konner and Kendall, who love singing and dancing with their great uncle. Bradley's friends are also extremely important to him, especially his high school teammates. In fact, there is another small medallion he wears around his neck: the medal the Palestine Wildcats football team was awarded for capturing the state title in 1964. It reminds him of the impenetrable bond of friendship he forged with his teammates, a bond that is just as strong as family. Bradley refers to them as the "posse," and they get together several times a year for a few days at someone's home. These so-called shindigs are a time to party and reminisce about the good old days. "Over the years, our group gets a little smaller, but we still get together and tell the same old stories," said Mickey Hubert, a retired sheriff and a tight end on the 1964 championship team. "One guy remembers a play that I forgot about. And it's nice to relive it."[60]

"You go through an experience like winning a state title, and you have a lifelong bond," adds Jackie Cherry, a retired high school athletic director and Bradley's back-up at quarterback in high school. "I also think we're close because we came from a small town. I don't think you have that kind of bond in a place like Houston or Dallas."[61]

Bill shines at those gatherings. He is not only the smalltown boy who became an NFL star but also the one who never forgot where he came from. He returns to Palestine often to express his appreciation to those who helped him along the way. "Billy's still got that mischievous kid in him," said Curtis Fitzgerald, his best friend. "Doesn't matter how old he gets. He's still a slappy!"[62]

Bradley agrees. Self-deprecating to a fault, he always downplays the moniker "Super Bill" whenever someone addresses him that way. Instead, he tells the admirer, "You got it wrong. It's 'Stupid Bill'!" He never viewed himself as an NFL hero but rather an actor. "I was in the entertainment business," he explains. "Pro football is one of the biggest entertainment industries in this country, and my theater-in-the-round, was [Philadelphia's] Veterans Stadium, with a weekly audience of sixty thousand people or more.

"I think the real heroes of my generation are the guys who went to Vietnam and especially those who sacrificed their lives fighting for what they believed in. They were guys on my high school football team who went to war. Some came back, like Curtis [Fitzgerald], wounded in action. Others came back struggling with posttraumatic stress disorder. Still others didn't make it back. They were killed in action. Guys like that went over there to fight so guys like me could have a pro football career. For me, those are the real heroes."[63]

Bradley does want to be remembered for his achievements as a football player, though. Some of his happiest days are those when he receives fan mail. Often the fan will send a football card and ask Bill to sign it. And he *always* complies. It's the process of receiving and responding to the fan mail that is so meaningful to him. He does not need to worry about being remembered by his coaches and teammates. Not only was Bill inducted into the Texas High School Hall of Fame, the University of Texas Hall of Fame, and the Texas Sports Hall of Fame but also the Philadelphia Eagles Hall of Fame.[64] In fact, the only Hall of Fame that's missing on Bradley's resume is in Canton, Ohio. Perhaps that will change one day too.

Bill Bradley has done a lot more living than most folks in his seventy-seven years on God's green earth—dutiful son, doting brother, high school super athlete, Texas Longhorn, NFL star, male fashion model, gas station owner and operator, hay farmer, cruise-ship host, respected thirty-year coach, husband, father, and friend to all. Bradley has befriended so many people that Forrest Gump has nothing on him. But for those of us who saw him play, he will always be Super Bill: No. 28 in the program and No. 1 in our hearts.

For more information on traumatic brain injuries, contact the National Resource Center for Traumatic Brain Injury (NRCTBI) at https://tbi.vcu.edu, or call (804) 828-3703.

APPENDIX A Bill Bradley's NFL Career Statistics, 1969–77

William Calvin "Bill" Bradley
Position: DB
Height: 5 feet 11
Weight: 190 lb.
Born: January 24, 1947, in Palestine, Texas
High School: Palestine (TX)
College: Texas
Draft: Philadelphia Eagles in the third round (sixty-ninth overall) of the 1969 NFL draft

KEY

No.: Jersey number
Games: Games played
GS: Games started
Int: Interceptions
Yds: Yards
TD: Touchdowns
Long: Longest yard gain
Fmb: Fumbles
FR: Fumble returns
Y/P: Yards per punt
Y/R: Average yards per run
*: Selected to Pro Bowl
+: First Team, Associated Press All-Pro
Bold: NFL leader

Punting

YEAR	AGE	TEAM	POS.	NO.	GAMES	GS	PUNT	YDS	Y/P	LONG
1969	22	PHI	DB	28	14	0	74	2,942	39.8	60
1970	23	PHI	DB	28	12	1	61	2,246	36.8	56
1971*+	24	PHI	FS	28	14	14	2	76	38	45
1972*+	25	PHI	FS	28	14	14	56	2,250	40.2	60
1973*	26	PHI	FS	28	14	14	18	735	40.8	61
1974	27	PHI	FS	28	14	14	2	67	33.5	35
1975	28	PHI	FS	28	14	10	0	0	0	0
1976	29	PHI	FS	28	14	12	0	0	0	0
1977	30	STL	DB	30	4	1	0	0	0	0
Totals					114	80	213	8,316	39	61

Defense

YEAR	AGE	TEAM	POS.	NO.	GAMES	GS	INT	YDS	TD	LONG	FMB	FR	YDS	TD	SACKS
1969	22	PHI	DB	28	14	0	1	56	1	56	2	0	0	0	0
1971*+	24	PHI	FS	28	14	14	**11**	**248**	0	51	2	2	15	0	0
1972*+	25	PHI	FS	28	14	14	**9**	73	0	21	1	2	0	0	1
1973*	26	PHI	FS	28	14	14	4	21	0	18	2	1	17	0	0
1974	27	PHI	FS	28	14	14	2	19	0	10	0	1	0	0	0
1975	28	PHI	FS	28	14	10	5	56	0	20	0	1	0	0	0
1976	29	PHI	FS	28	14	12	2	63	0	52	0	2	0	0	0
1977	30	STL	DB	30	4	1	0	0	0	0	0	0	0	0	1
Totals					98	79	34	536	1	56	7	9	32	0	2

Punt and kick returns

YEAR	AGE	TEAM	POS.	NO.	GAMES	GS	PUNT RET	YDS	TD	LONG	Y/R	KICK RET	YDS	TD	LONG	Y/R
1969	22	PHI	DB	28	14	0	28	181	0	37	6.5	21	467	0	42	22.2
1971*+	24	PHI	FS	28	14	14	18	118	0	33	6.6					
1972*+	25	PHI	FS	28	14	14	22	155	0	60	7.0	2	22	0	20	11.0
1973	26	PHI	FS	28	14	14	8	106	0	43	13.3					
1974	27	PHI	FS	28	14	14	22	248	0	22	11.3					
1975	28	PHI	FS	28	14	10	4	4	0	6	1.0					
1976	29	PHI	FS	28	14	12	9	64	0	23	7.1					
1977	30	STL	DB	30	4	1	11	77	0	14	7.0	4	75	0	28	18.8
Totals					102	79	122	953	0	60	7.8	27	564	0	42	20.9

APPENDIX B Bill Bradley's College Career Statistics, 1966–68

William Calvin "Bill" Bradley
Positions: QB, DB
Height: 5 feet 11
Weight: 180 lb.
Born: January 24, 1947, in Palestine, Texas
High School: Palestine (TX)
College: Texas

KEY

G: Games
Cmp: Completions
Att: Attempts
Pct: % completions
Yds: Yards gained
Y/A: Average yards
TD: Touchdowns
Int: Interceptions
Rate: Quarterback rating
Rec: Receptions

Passing

YEAR	SCHOOL	CONF.	CLASS	POS.	G	CMP	ATT	PCT	YDS	Y/A	TD	INT	RATE
1966	Texas	SWC	So.	QB	9	36	76	47.4	535	7	4	9	100.2
1967	Texas	SWC	Jr.	QB	10	72	153	47.1	1,181	7.7	4	13	103.5
1968	Texas	SWC	Sr.	QB	2	2	12	16.7	17	1.4	0	4	-38.1
Totals					21	110	241	45.6	1,733	7.2	8	26	95.4

Rushing and receiving

						Rushing				*Receiving*				*Scrimmage*			
YEAR	SCHOOL	CONF.	CLASS	POS.	G	ATT	YDS	AVG	TD	REC	YDS	AVG	TD	PLAYS	YDS	AVG	TD
1966	Texas	SWC	So.	QB	9	124	335	2.7	6	1	13	13	0	125	348	2.8	6
1967	Texas	SWC	Jr.	QB	10	172	443	2.6	10					172	443	2.6	10
1968	Texas	SWC	Sr.	QB-WR	2	24	86	3.6	0	4	40	10	1	28	126	4.5	1
Totals					21	320	864	2.7	16	5	53	10.6	1	325	917	2.8	17

Scoring

YEAR	SCHOOL	CONF.	CLASS	POS.	G	RUSHING	REC	POINTS
1966	Texas	SWC	So.	QB	9	6	0	36
1967	Texas	SWC	Jr.	QB	10	10	0	60
1968	Texas	SWC	Sr.	QB-WR	2	0	1	6
Totals					21	16	1	102

NOTES

Introduction

1. "Palestine's 4th Quarter Rally Tops Hirschi," in *King Football: Greatest Moments in Texas High School Football History*, ed. Mike Bynum (Birmingham AL: Epic Sports Classics, 2003), 184.
2. Jim Dent, *The Kids Got It Right: How the Texas All-Stars Kicked Down Racial Walls* (New York: Thomas Dunne Books, 2013). Dent's best-selling book tells the story of Bill Bradley and Jerry LeVias, whose friendship broke the chain of racism that had existed for more than half a century in Texas football. Bradley, gregarious and free-spirited, and LeVias, one of just three Black players on the Texas All-Stars, met in the summer of 1965 at the Big 33 game in Hershey, Pennsylvania. When no one else would room with LeVias, Bradley stepped forward, and the two teammates became close friends and remain so today.
3. Dent, *Kids Got It Right*, 111–16, 145.
4. "Bill Bradley," Football (College), Sports Reference, accessed April 24, 2022, https://www.sports-reference.com/cfb/players/bill-bradley-1.html.
5. "College Football Preview," *Sports Illustrated*, September 11, 1967, 34–44.
6. Bobby Hawthorne, *Longhorn Football: An Illustrated History* (Austin: University of Texas Press, 2007), 123; and "Bill Bradley," Sports Reference.
7. Hawthorne, *Longhorn Football*, 123, 128.
8. Jenna Hays McEachern, *DKR: The Royal Scrapbook* (Austin: University of Texas Press, 2012), 192. The quote is often attributed to Royal, but Royal himself attributed the saying to another run-first coach, Woody Hayes of Ohio State. Todd Jones, "Royal Took Longhorns from Oblivion to No. 1," *Columbus Dispatch*, September 9, 2006.
9. Bill Bradley, in discussion with the author, Spring Branch TX, March 4, 2021.
10. Bill Bradley, discussion, March 4, 2021.
11. John Flynn, "Intercepting Bill Bradley," *Today: The Philadelphia Inquirer Sunday Magazine*, November 19, 1972, 18.
12. Jack Agness, "Even Steers Surprised," *Houston Post*, November 29, 1968.
13. Ray Didinger and Robert S. Lyons, *The Eagles Encyclopedia: Champions Edition* (Philadelphia: Temple University Press, 2018), 428–31.

14. “Bill Bradley,” Defense & Fumbles, Pro Football Reference, accessed April 22, 2022, https://www.pro-football-reference.com/players/B/BradBi00.htm.
15. Didinger and Lyons, *Eagles Encyclopedia*, 30–31. Bradley’s team record for most career interceptions was later tied by Eric Allen (1988–94) and Brian Dawkins (1996–2008), but he still holds team records for most interceptions in a season, most interception return yardage in a season, and most interception return yardage in a career. Didinger and Lyons, *Eagles Encyclopedia*, 483–84.
16. Joe Zagorski, *The NFL in the 1970s: Pro Football’s Most Important Decade* (Jefferson NC: McFarland, 2016), 4–7, 146–47.
17. Bill Bradley, in discussion with author, Spring Branch TX, April 11, 2022.
18. Flynn, “Intercepting Bill Bradley,” 17.
19. Ray Didinger, “Bill Bradley OK’s 3-Year Eagle Pact,” *Philadelphia Evening Bulletin*, September 14, 1972; and Flynn, “Intercepting Bill Bradley,” 20.
20. “Hair Today, Gone Tomorrow; Bill Bradley Cuts It Close in Making All-Pro,” *San Antonio Express-News*, September 22, 1972.
21. Gordon Forbes, “22 Eagles Picket as Birds Open Rookie Camp,” *Philadelphia Inquirer*, July 10, 1974.
22. Among the Eagles’ star players who crossed the picket line were quarterback Roman Gabriel and linebacker Bill Bergey, a free agent who had been recently acquired by the Eagles. Gordon Forbes, “Freedom Issues Soured Gabriel on NFL Strikers,” *Philadelphia Inquirer*, July 17, 1974; and Gordon Forbes, “Eagle Vets to Pickett Falcon Game,” *Philadelphia Inquirer*, August 4, 1974.
23. Jerry LeVias, in discussion with the author, Houston TX, March 15, 2021.

1. Palestine

1. “About Us,” The City of Palestine, accessed April 30, 2022, https://www.cityofpalestinetx.com/348/About-Us; Brian Anderson, “Micham Main,” Historical Marker Database, last modified January 21, 2019, https://www.hmdb.org/m.asp?m=128935.
2. *Texas Almanac for 1861* (Galveston TX: Richardson, 1860), 292, https://texashistory.unt.edu/ark:/67531/metapth123767/m1/292/?q=palestine.
3. Hugh Chisholm, ed., *Encyclopedia Britannica*, s.v. “Palestine, Texas,” 1910, https://www.studylight.org/encyclopedias/eng/bri/p/palestine-texas.html.
4. “Palestine TX,” Union Pacific 150, accessed April 30, 2022, https://web.archive.org/web/20160327163026/http://up150.com/towns/Palestine/TX.
5. In 1924 the New Orleans, Texas and Mexico Railway (NOT&M) bought IGN, along with several former subcompanies of the Gulf Coast Lines. The next year, Missouri Pacific Railroad purchased NOT&M, and IGN reverted to its original independent mode of operation within Missouri Pacific Lines. In 1933 Missouri Pacific Lines entered receivership. Twenty-three years later, in 1956, plans for its reorganization were agreed upon. All of the railroad companies operating in Texas within Missouri Pacific Lines

were merged into the new Missouri Pacific Railroad. This included IGN, but not the Texas & Pacific Railway, which merged with Missouri Pacific Railroad in 1976. In 1997 the Missouri Pacific became part of the Union Pacific Railroad. "Palestine's Railroad History," Texas State Railroad Society, accessed April 30, 2022, https://www.tsrrsociety.com/ign-to-up-rr-history#:~:text=.

6. Lester Hamilton, "Palestine TX (Anderson County)," Texas State Historical Association, last modified January 14, 2021, https://www.tshaonline.org/handbook/entries/palestine-tx-anderson-county.
7. James Hulse, "I&GN Railroad in Palestine," Historical Marker Database, last modified August 30, 2020, https://www.hmdb.org/m.asp?m=155447. The historical marker is located at 105 West Spring Street, Palestine TX 75801.
8. "Joe Hill Bradley," 1930, Palestine, Anderson, Texas, enumeration district 0005, FHL microfilm 2342021, 17A, accessed May 2, 2022, Ancestry.com.
9. Bill Bradley, in discussion with the author, Spring Branch TX, February 24, 2021.
10. "Omega Thomas Rainey," 1940, Houston, Harris, Texas, roll m-t0627-04194, enumeration district 258-149, 16A, accessed May 2, 2022, Ancestry.com.
11. Bill Bradley, discussion, February 24, 2021.
12. Dent, *Kids Got It Right*, 74.
13. Bill Bradley, discussion, February 24, 2021.
14. Bill Bradley, discussion, February 24, 2021.
15. Bill Bradley, discussion, February 24, 2021
16. Bill Bradley, discussion, February 24, 2021.
17. Bill Bradley, discussion, February 24, 2021.
18. Bill Bradley, discussion, February 24, 2021.
19. Harold Sumrall, in discussion with the author, Palestine TX, April 12, 2022.
20. Sumrall, discussion.
21. Curtis Fitzgerald, in discussion with the author, Palestine TX, April 12, 2022.
22. Sumrall, discussion.
23. Bill Bradley, in discussion with the author, Palestine TX, April 12, 2022.
24. Dent, *Kids Got It Right*, 85.
25. Brian Anderson, "Robert (Bob) Knight," Historical Marker Database, last modified January 22, 2019, https://www.hmdb.org/m.asp?m=128977. This historical marker was erected in 2009 and is located at 400 South Micheaux Street, Palestine TX 75801.
26. Sumrall, discussion.
27. Danny Westmoreland, in discussion with the author, Palestine TX, April 13, 2022.
28. Bill Bradley, discussion, April 12, 2022.
29. Bob Stephenson, in discussion with the author, Palestine TX, June 12, 2022.
30. Fitzgerald, discussion.
31. Sumrall, discussion.
32. Bill Bradley, discussion, February 24, 2021.

33. Bill Bradley, discussion, February 24, 2021.
34. Fitzgerald, discussion.
35. Dent, *Kids Got It Right*, 78.
36. Fitzgerald, discussion.
37. Stephenson, discussion.
38. Dent, *Kids Got It Right*, 78–79.
39. Dent, *Kids Got It Right*, 79.
40. Dent, *Kids Got It Right*, 79.
41. Mickey Hubert, in discussion with the author, Palestine TX, April 13, 2022; and Westmoreland, discussion.
42. Hubert, discussion.
43. Barrett Broyles, in discussion with the author, Palestine TX, April 13, 2022.
44. Westmoreland, discussion.
45. Westmoreland, discussion.
46. Dent, *Kids Got It Right*, 80.
47. "James Saxton," in *What It Means to Be a Longhorn: Darrell Royal, Mack Brown and Many of Texas's Greatest Players*, ed. Bill Little and Jenna McEachern (Chicago: Triumph Books, 2007), 68–72. After graduating from UT, Saxton was selected in the tenth round of the 1962 American Football League draft by the Dallas Texans. He saw limited playing time during the '62 season, which ended with the Texans winning their first and only AFL championship with a 20–17 win over the Houston Oilers in a seventy-seven-minute, fifty-four-second, two-overtime game. It was the longest game ever played up to that time. After that season, Saxton quit pro football and became a successful banker in Austin.
48. Bill Bradley, discussion, February 24, 2021.
49. Dent, *Kids Got It Right*, 80.
50. Dent, *Kids Got It Right*, 81.
51. Dent, *Kids Got It Right*, 81.
52. Westmoreland, discussion.
53. Dent, *Kids Got It Right*, 81.
54. Westmoreland, discussion.
55. "Razorback Greats Named to 2010 UA Sports Hall of Honor Class," KARK.com, August 8, 2019, https://www.kark.com/news/razorback-greats-named-to-2019-ua-sports-hall-of-honor-class/.

2. Friday Night Lights

1. Bill Bradley, discussion, April 12, 2022.
2. H. G. "Buzz" Bissinger, *Friday Night Lights: A Town, a Team, and a Dream* (New York: Da Capo Press, 1990). *Friday night lights* refers to the giant floodlights that rise above high school football fields. The term was made popular in 1990 by Bissinger's best-selling

book, which followed the Permian High School Panthers' 1988 high school football season in Odessa, Texas. That year, Permian tied for their district championship with just one loss and got into the Texas state playoffs due to a coin flip. It made it to the semifinals before giving up a fourth-quarter lead to Dallas Carter.

Although the 1988 Panthers team was not the most remarkable high school football team in Texas, Permian does enjoy a prestigious program that has won six Texas state championships. The team plays at Ratliff Stadium, which sits over nineteen thousand people, and has produced several NFL players, including Bront Bird (San Diego Chargers), Stoney Case (Arizona Cardinals), Britt Hager (Philadelphia Eagles), Roy Williams (Detroit Lions), and Daryl Hunt (Houston Oilers).

Bissinger's book captures the obsessive culture of high school football, which gives rise to both social celebration and tremendous pressure. He focuses on Permian to explore the larger social issues of racial and economic divides and the economic reliance on oil in small-town Texas.

3. Mike Bynum, ed., *King Football: Greatest Moments in Texas High School Football History* (Birmingham AL: Epic Sports Classics, 2003), 26–29.
4. Albert Lasker, "Ball High Falls to the Rugbys," *Galveston Daily News*, December 25, 1892.
5. Ty Cashion, *Pigskin Pulpit: A Social History of Texas High School Football Coaches* (Austin: Texas State Historical Association, 1998), 52.
6. Bynum, *King Football*, 34.
7. Bynum, *King Football*, 30, 36–38.
8. Bynum, *King Football*, 30–31.
9. Joe Lee Smith, "Season Records: N–Plainview," Texas High School Football History, accessed May 24, 2022, https://www.texashighschoolfootballhistory.com/season_records__n.
10. "Luke McKinney Thornton," historical plaque, Palestine High School, 1600 South Loop 256, Palestine TX; and Joe Lee Smith, "Coaches Records by Seasons: Sullivan–Whitehall," Texas High School Football History, accessed May 24, 2022, https://www.texashighschoolfootballhistory.com/coaches_-_stumbaugh.
11. Bill Bradley, discussion, April 12, 2022.
12. Jackie Cherry, in discussion with the author, Palestine TX, April 13, 2022.
13. Westmoreland, discussion.
14. Fitzgerald, discussion; Hubert, discussion; and Westmoreland, discussion.
15. "Thornton Likes 'Cats' Fight," *Palestine (TX) Herald-Press*, August 29, 1964.
16. Fitzgerald, discussion; Hubert, discussion; and Sumrall, discussion.
17. Hubert, discussion.
18. Fitzgerald, discussion.
19. "Thornton Likes 'Cats' Fight," *Palestine (TX) Herald-Press*.
20. "'Cats to Test Rating against Tough Athens," *Palestine (TX) Herald-Press*, September 11, 1964.

21. Westmoreland, discussion.
22. "'Cats Lose to Tough Athens, 28–7; Drop to 7th in Polls," *Palestine (TX) Herald-Press*, September 12, 1964.
23. Hubert, discussion.
24. Westmoreland, discussion.
25. Stephenson, discussion.
26. Bill Bradley, discussion, April 12, 2022.
27. Bill Bradley, discussion, April 12, 2022; Fitzgerald, discussion; Hubert, discussion; and Westmoreland, discussion.
28. "Tough Terrell Here Tonight," *Palestine (TX) Herald-News*, September 18, 1964.
29. "Wildcats Rip Terrell, 26–8," *Palestine (TX) Herald-News*, September 19, 1964.
30. "Wildcats Roll Over Ennis, 34–6," *Palestine (TX) Herald-News*, October 3, 1964.
31. "Cats Shake Off Slow Start to Capture District Opener," *Palestine (TX) Herald-News*, October 10, 1964.
32. Fitzgerald, discussion; Hubert, discussion; and Sumrall, discussion.
33. Fitzgerald, discussion.
34. "Crippled Wildcats Hang Up Second Victory in District," *Palestine (TX) Herald-News*, October 17, 1964.
35. "Wildcats No. 5 in Texas Poll," *Palestine (TX) Herald-News*, October 17, 1964.
36. "Cats Bombard Center, 34–0," *Palestine (TX) Herald-News*, October 17, 1964.
37. Blackie Sherrod, "Palestine's Bradley Has Hot Hand at QB," *Dallas Times Herald*, October 18, 1964.
38. Stephen Missildine, in discussion with the author, Palestine TX, April 12, 2022.
39. Hubert, discussion.
40. Cherry, discussion.
41. Bill Bradley, discussion, February 24, 2021.
42. Fitzpatrick, discussion.
43. Bill Bradley, discussion, April 12, 2022.
44. Cherry, discussion.
45. Fitzgerald, discussion.
46. Bill Bradley, discussion, February 24, 2021.
47. Hubert, discussion; and Westmoreland, discussion.
48. Sumrall, discussion.
49. "'Cats Squeeze by Kilgore," *Palestine (TX) Herald-News*, October 31, 1964; and "'Cats Roll by Nacogdoches," *Palestine (TX) Herald-News*, November 7, 1964.
50. Cherry, discussion.
51. "Wildcats Nudge Pine Tree, Meet Jacksonville for Title," *Palestine (TX) Herald-News*, November 14, 1964; and "Palestine Fifth, Jacksonville 10th in State Rankings," *Palestine (TX) Herald-News*, November 15, 1964.
52. Stephenson, discussion.

53. Bill Bradley, discussion, April 12, 2022.
54. "Palestine Unseats Jacksonville, 8–7," *Palestine (TX) Herald-News*, November 21, 1964.
55. "Palestine Moves to Fourth Place in State Rating," *Palestine (TX) Herald-News*, November 22, 1964.
56. "Yeager Praises Scrappy Linemen," *Palestine (TX) Herald-News*, November 27, 1964.
57. Fitzgerald, discussion; Bill Bradley, discussion, April 12, 2022; and Cherry, discussion.
58. "Wildcats Whip Athens in Bi-District, 8–0," *Palestine (TX) Herald-News*, November 28, 1964.
59. "Wildcats Whip Athens," *Palestine (TX) Herald-News*.
60. Missildine, discussion.
61. "Thornton Hails 'Cats' Defense," *Palestine (TX) Herald-News*, November 28, 1964.
62. Westmoreland, discussion.
63. Hubert, discussion.
64. Fitzgerald, discussion.
65. Duff Daniels, "Palestine Breezes to 22–0 Win," *Dallas Morning News*, December 5, 1964; and "Wildcats Bounce Warriors," *Palestine (TX) Herald-News*, December 5, 1964.
66. Dent, *Kids Got It Right*, 102; and Joe Lee Smith, "Season Records: Weatherford–Z," Texas High School Football History, accessed May 24, 2022, https://www.texashighschoolfootballhistory.com/seasons_-_weatherford_-_z.
67. Harold V. Ratliff, "AP Scribe Predicts Hirschi to Win over 'Cats in Upset," *Dallas Morning News*, December 10, 1964.
68. "'Cats Whip Hirschi on Rally, 28–23," *Palestine (TX) Herald-News*, December 13, 1964; and Missildine, discussion.
69. Westmoreland, discussion.
70. Fitzgerald, discussion.
71. Fitzgerald, discussion.
72. Bill Bradley, discussion, April 12, 2000; Fitzgerald, discussion; and Westmoreland, discussion.
73. "'Cats Whip Hirschi," *Palestine (TX) Herald-News*.
74. Fitzgerald, discussion.
75. Duff Daniels, "Palestine Comeback Stuns Hirschi, 28–23," *Dallas Morning News*, December 13, 1964.
76. Fitzgerald, discussion.
77. "'Cats Whip Hirschi," *Palestine (TX) Herald-News*.
78. Stephenson, discussion.
79. Dent, *Kids Got It Right*, 102.
80. Bill Bradley, discussion, April 12, 2022.
81. "'Cats Whip Hirschi," *Palestine (TX) Herald-News*.
82. Dent, *Kids Got It Right*, 103; and Bill Bradley, discussion, April 12, 2022.
83. Fitzgerald, discussion.

84. Bill Bradley, discussion, April 12, 2022.
85. Fitzgerald, discussion; and Bill Bradley, discussion, April 12, 2022.
86. Daniels, "Palestine Comeback Stuns Hirschi."
87. Blackie Sherrod, "Bradley Leads Palestine over Hirschi, 28–23," *Dallas Times Herald*, December 13, 1964.
88. Daniels, "Palestine Comeback Stuns Hirschi"; and Gene Wilson, "From Hare to Eternally," *Dallas Times Herald*, December 16, 1964.
89. Wilson, "From Hare to Eternally."
90. Stephenson, discussion.
91. Bill Duncan, "Palestine Winner, 24–15, in State AAA Title Game," *Dallas Times Herald*, December 19, 1964; and "Wildcats Charm Rattlers, 24–15," *Palestine (TX) Herald-News*, December 19, 1964.
92. "Seven Wildcats on All-District," *Palestine (TX) Herald-News*, December 19, 1964. In addition to Bradley, the other Wildcats who received District 7-AAA honors were Eddie Bentley, Curtis Fitzpatrick, Stephen Missildine, Jerry Reeder, Bob Stephenson, and Danny Westmoreland.

3. Blue-Eyed Soul Brother

1. James Smith, *African American Heritage: Legends and Legacies* (Palestine TX: Palestine Historical Preservation Commission, 1997).
2. Smith, *African American Heritage.*
3. Fitzpatrick, discussion; Sumrall, discussion; and Westmoreland, discussion.
4. Bill Bradley, discussion, February 24, 2021.
5. Dent, *Kids Got It Right*, 143.
6. Bill Bradley, discussion, February 24, 2021.
7. Bill Bradley, discussion, February 24, 2021.
8. Dent, *Kids Got It Right*, 143.
9. Bill Bradley, discussion, February 24, 2021.
10. Fitzpatrick, discussion; Sumrall, discussion; and Westmoreland, discussion.
11. Smith, *African American Heritage*; and Bill Bradley, discussion, February 24, 2021.
12. Cherry, discussion. According to Jackie Cherry, a Wildcats quarterback who went on to become principal of Palestine's Westwood High School, "three Black students enrolled in Palestine High School and played on the football team in [his] senior year of 1965. Five years later, when [he] returned to Palestine to teach and coach at the new Westwood High School, A. B. Story was integrated and turned into a junior high. The Black high school students either went to Westwood or to Palestine, and both of those high schools were fully integrated."
13. Robert D. Jacobus, *Black Man in the Huddle: Stories from the Integration of Texas Football* (College Station: Texas A&M University Press, 2019), xv.
14. Jacobus, *Black Man in the Huddle*, xv.

15. Jacobus, *Black Man in the Huddle*, xv, 9–11. Jacobus points out that Texas can be considered "a model for integration for the former Confederacy" because the process of integration began in the 1950s and continued over the next decade, compared to more rigidly segregated states like Alabama, Georgia, Louisiana, and Mississippi.
16. Jacobus, *Black Man in the Huddle*, 12–13.
17. Bill Bradley, discussion, February 24, 2021. Contrary to popular belief, Jerry LaVias was not the first African American Texas high school football player to be selected for an All-State team. That distinction belongs to Bobby Smith, a halfback from Corpus Christi's Miller High School. Smith was the first Black athlete from a University Interscholastic League team to be named All-State, in 1959. David Flores, "Bobby Smith: A Trailblazer to Remember," in *King Football*, ed. Mike Bynum (Birmingham AL: Epic Sports Classics, 2003), 542–45.
18. Cashion, *Pigskin Pulpit*, 172; and "What Is the Big 33 Game?" PSFCA Big 33, accessed June 17, 2022, https://big33.org/about/. While the game was originally played with the best thirty-three players in each state (hence its name), the organizers added a thirty-fourth player to include kickers. If selected players were unable to play, the staff of the team and the Big 33 would select other players to fill their places on the roster.
19. Van Thomas, "Terry Don Phillips to Play in Texas-Pennsylvania Game," *Longview (TX) News-Journal*, August 2, 1965. Today, the Big 33 game features the best high school seniors from Pennsylvania against those from Maryland.
20. Cashion, *Pigskin Pulpit*, 172.
21. Robert H. Boyle, "Beef, Bones and Hershey Bars," *Sports Illustrated*, August 10, 1964, 18.
22. "Texas Hopes for Revenge," *Fort Worth Star-Telegram*, August 14, 1965. Such Texas high school football stars as Warren McVea, Linus Baer, and Ronnie Pipes did not compete in the 1964 Big 33 All-Star Game, electing to remain in the Lone Star State to play in the North and South All-Star contest. Had they played at Hershey, the outcome might very well have been in Texas's favor.
23. "Big 33 Grid Game Tonight," *San Antonio Express-News*, August 14, 1965.
24. Bill Bradley, discussion, February 24, 2021.
25. Harold V. Ratliff, "Big 33 Game Next on Tap for Texas Schoolboy Stars," *Standard Times* (San Angelo TX), August 6, 1965. The North and South All-Star Game had been integrated by the Texas Football Coaches Association a year earlier in 1964, when halfback Warren McVea of San Antonio Brackenridge was selected to play. Dent, *Kids Got It Right*, 135.
26. Dent, *Kids Got It Right*, 135.
27. Dent, *Kids Got It Right*, 35–37.
28. Dent, *Kids Got It Right*, 35–37.
29. Morton Sharnik, "Too Small to be Overlooked," *Sports Illustrated*, November 29, 1970, 26.
30. Jacobus, *Black Man in the Huddle*, 211.
31. Dent, *Kids Got It Right*, 59.

32. Sharnik, "Too Small," 26; and Jacobus, *Black Man in the Huddle*, 210.
33. LeVias, discussion.
34. Bill Bradley, discussion, February 24, 2021.
35. LeVias, discussion.
36. Peter King, "Searching for Bobby Layne," *Sports Illustrated*, November 25, 2010, https://vault.si.com/vault/2009/03/02/searching-for-bobby-layne.
37. Martin D. Kohut, "Robert Lawrence Layne (1926–1986)," Texas State Historical Association, last modified May 12, 2021, https://www.tshaonline.org/handbook/entries/layne-robert-lawrence.
38. Randy Harvey, "Bobby Layne: 1926–1986; Football Legend Dies at 59 of Heart Failure," *Los Angeles Times*, December 2, 1989.
39. Dent, *Kids Got It Right*, 28.
40. Dent, *Kids Got It Right*, 29.
41. Dent, *Kids Got It Right*, 152.
42. Dent, *Kids Got It Right*, 157.
43. Bill Bradley, discussion, February 24, 2021.
44. Dent, *Kids Got It Right*, 147–50.
45. LeVias, discussion.
46. LeVias, discussion.
47. Dent, *Kids Got It Right*, 136.
48. "Texas High School Football Hall of Fame Inductees: Norm Bulaich," Dave Campbell's Texas Football, accessed July 27, 2022, https://www.texasfootball.com/hof-norman-bulaich.
49. Norm Bulaich, in discussion with the author, Hurst TX, July 28, 2022.
50. Bill Bradley, discussion, February 24, 2021.
51. LeVias, discussion.
52. Dent, *Kids Got It Right*, 176.
53. Dent, *Kids Got It Right*, 173–74.
54. Corby Robertson, in discussion with the author, Houston TX, October 20, 2022.
55. Dent, *Kids Got It Right*, 192.
56. Dent, *Kids Got It Right*, 193.
57. Bill Bradley, discussion, February 24, 2021.
58. Bill Bradley, discussion, February 24, 2021; LeVias, discussion.
59. LeVias, discussion.
60. LeVias, discussion.
61. Dent, *Kids Got It Right*, 194.
62. Bill Bradley, discussion, February 24, 2021; LeVias, discussion.
63. LeVias, discussion.
64. Robertson, discussion.
65. Robertson, discussion.

66. Dent, *Kids Got It Right*, 195–96.
67. Robertson, discussion.
68. Dent, *Kids Got It Right*, 195–96.
69. Dent, *Kids Got It Right*, 206, 209.
70. Associated Press, "Big 33 Grid Game Tonight," *San Antonio (TX) Express*, August 14, 1965. Scranton bet Connally 1,061 Pennsylvania apples in 1965.
71. Associated Press, "Big 33 Grid Game Tonight."
72. Associated Press, "Texas, Pennsylvania Clash in Big 33 Grid Tilt Tonight," *Morning Call* (Allentown PA), August 14, 1965; and Dave Leherr, "Pennsylvania Puts Perfect 'Big 33' Mark on Line Against Texans," *Daily Item* (Sunbury PA), August 14, 1965.
73. Bulaich, discussion.
74. For starting lineups, see Dent, *Kids Got It Right*, 208. For high schools, see Texas High School Football History, https://www.texashighschoolfootballhistory.com/won-loss_records; and "1965 Team Pennsylvania Roster," PSFCA Big 33, accessed July 7, 2022, https://big33.org/the-game/history/pennsylvania/1965-roster/. For colleges, see rosters of "1965 Southwest Conference Year Summary," Sports Reference, accessed February 15, 2024, https://www.sports-reference.com/cfb/conferences/swc/1965.html. To search for players to see NFL teams played for, see "List of All Pro Football Players," Pro Football Reference, accessed July 7, 2022, https://www.pro-football-reference.com/players/.
75. John Underwood, "Texas Teeners Strike Back," *Sports Illustrated*, August 23, 1965, 20–21.
76. Dent, *Kids Got It Right*, 210–11; and LeVias, discussion.
77. Bill Bradley, discussion, February 24, 2021.
78. Associated Press, "Coal Crackers Learn Lesson; Big 33 Texans Win, 26–10," *San Antonio Express*, August 16, 1965; and Underwood, "Texas Teeners Strike Back," 21.
79. Dent, *Kids Got It Right*, 217; Bill Bradley, discussion, February 24, 2021; and LeVias, discussion.
80. Underwood, "Texas Teeners Strike Back," 21.
81. LeVias, discussion.
82. Bulaich, discussion.
83. Underwood, "Texas Teeners Strike Back," 21, 23; and Associated Press, "Coal Crackers Learn Lesson."
84. Underwood, "Texas Teeners Strike Back," 23; and Associated Press, "Coal Crackers Learn Lesson."
85. Underwood, "Texas Teeners Strike Back," 23.
86. Little and McEachern, *What It Means to Be a Longhorn*, 94. Bobby Layne had vindicated himself. He would win two more Big 33 games, routing the Pennsylvania All-Stars by scores of 34–2 in 1966 and 45–14 in 1967. After that, his Texas All-Stars were disinvited to Hershey, and the Big 33 would devolve into just another high school gridiron All-Star

contest. Cashion, *Pigskin Pulpit*, 172–73; and "Scores: 1960's," PSFCA Big 33, accessed June 17, 2022, https://big33.org/the-game/scores/1960s/.

4. Longhorns

1. "All-Time Results," Football, Texas Sports, last modified January 19, 2023, https://texassports.com/sports/2013/7/21/FB_0721134841.aspx.
2. Dan Jenkins, "Pride and Field Position," in *Sports Illustrated Presents Texas Longhorns Football* (New York: Sports Illustrated, 2009), 47–48.
3. Gene Schoor, *The Fightin' Texas Aggies: 100 Years of A&M Football* (Dallas TX: Taylor Publishing, 1994), 121; Jim Dent, *The Junction Boys: How Ten Days in Hell with Bear Bryant Forged a Championship Team* (New York: Thomas Dunn Books, 1999); and Carolyn Mason, "Life on the Ranch: Gene Stallings May Live in Texas, but He's Taken a Piece of Alabama with Him," *Tuscaloosa Magazine*, September 7, 2006.
4. Bill Bradley, discussion, March 4, 2021.
5. Bill Bradley, discussion, March 4, 2021.
6. Bobby Hawthorne, *Longhorn Football: An Illustrated History* (Austin: University of Texas, 2007), 83–89, 100, 111–13, 146. Several Longhorns players identified Royal's ability to hire good coaches, delegate responsibility to them, and make them accountable as a key to his success. Bradley, discussion, April 11, 2022; Tom Campbell, in discussion with the author, Austin TX, July 29, 2022; Bill Hall, in discussion with the author, Austin TX, November 12, 2022; Bob McKay, in discussion with the author, Austin TX, September 2, 2022; Ted Koy, in discussion with the author, Georgetown TX, October 23, 2022; and Robertson, discussion.
7. Bill Bradley, discussion, March 4, 2021.
8. Little and McEachern, *What It Means to Be a Longhorn*, 113–14.
9. Little and McEachern, *What It Means to Be a Longhorn*, 94.
10. McKay, discussion.
11. Dean of Admissions Henry Y. McCown to UT President Logan Wilson, "Confidential Memorandum," November 10, 1959, Dolph Briscoe Center for American History, University of Texas, Austin; Asher Price, "Memo Shows UT Coaches Wanted to Keep Black Players off Their Teams," *Texas Monthly*, August 30, 2021, https://www.texasmonthly.com/arts-entertainment/ut-sports-memo-integration/?pagewanted=all&_r=0.
12. Hawthorne, *Longhorn Football*, 137; Price, "Memo Shows"; and Asher Price, "A Secret 1950s Strategy to Keep Out Black Students," *The Atlantic*, September 19, 2019, https://www.theatlantic.com/ideas/archive/2019/09/how-ut-used-standardized-testing-to-slow-integration/597814/.
13. Bill Bradley, discussion, March 4, 2021; and Marc Ramirez, "Julius Whittier, UT's First Black Football Letterman and Former Dallas County Prosecutor, Dies at 68," *Dallas Morning News*, September 29, 2018.
14. McKay, discussion.

15. Monique Brand, "Former Killeen High Star Became the First Black to Get a Football Athletic Scholarship at UT," *Killeen Daily Herald*, February 28, 2015; and Hawthorne, *Longhorn Football*, 137.
16. Ramirez, "Julius Whittier."
17. "Legendary Coach Darrell K. Royal Dies at Age 88," *UT News*, November 7, 2012, https://news.utexas.edu/2012/11/07/legendary-coach-darrell-k-royal-dies-at-88/.
18. Campbell, discussion.
19. United Press International, "Frank Erwin, Jr., the Controversial 'Emperor' of the University of Texas," *Austin American-Statesman*, October 1, 1980; and Mitchell Lerner, "Erwin, Frank Craig, Jr. (1920–1980)," Handbook of Texas Online, Texas State Historical Association, last modified May 29, 2020, https://www.tshaonline.org/handbook/entries/erwin-frank-craig-jr.
20. United Press International, "Erwin, the Controversial 'Emperor'"; and Deborah Lynn Bay, "The Influence of Frank Erwin on Texas Higher Education" (PhD diss., University of Texas at Austin, 1988), Barker Texas History Center, University of Texas, Austin.
21. Joe Drape, "Changing the Face of Texas Football," *New York Times*, December 23, 2005.
22. Hawthorne, *Longhorn Football*, 137.
23. Robertson, discussion.
24. Robertson, discussion.
25. Bulaich, discussion.
26. Bill Bradley, discussion, March 4, 2021
27. Little and McEachern, *What It Means to Be a Longhorn*, 111, 113.
28. Tai Kreidler, "Greg Lott, a Longhorn from Lubbock," *Lubbock (TX) Avalanche-Journal*, September 25, 2020.
29. Kreidler, "Greg Lott, a Longhorn."
30. Kreidler, "Greg Lott, a Longhorn."
31. Bill Bradley, discussion, March 4, 2021.
32. Lou Maysel, "Trojans Mash Steers' Surge," *Austin American-Statesman*, September 18, 1966.
33. Maysel, "Trojans Mash Steers' Surge."
34. Fred Sanner, "Royal Pinpoints Loss," *Austin American-Statesman*, September 18, 1966.
35. George Breazeale, "Lonnghorns Dispel Raiders' 'Year' With 31–21 Victory," *Austin American-Statesman*, September 25, 1966.
36. Carlton Stowers, "Injuries Dim UT Win," *Austin American-Statesman*, September 25, 1966.
37. Bill Bradley, in discussion with the author, Lake Silkworth PA, October 6, 2022.
38. Stowers, "Injuries Dim UT Win."
39. Lou Maysel, "Bradley's Knee Injured," *Austin American-Statesman*, October 2, 1966.
40. Bradley, discussion, March 4, 2021.
41. Maysel, "Bradley's Knee Injured."

42. Richard Boldt, "OU Fans Run Amok in Cotton Bowl," *Austin American-Statesman*, October 9, 1966.
43. Lou Maysel, "Porkers Uncork 12–7 Haymaker to Grab Bumble-Packed Contest," *Austin American-Statesman*, October 16, 1966.
44. Fred Sanner, "Lott Will Be Out for Year," *Austin American-Statesman*, October 16, 1966; and Kreidler, "Greg Lott, a Longhorn."
45. Bill Bradley, discussion, March 4, 2021; and Hall, discussion.
46. Gregory Curtis, "How Farrah Fawcett Changed the World," *Texas Monthly*, April 1982, https://www.texasmonthly.com/arts-entertainment/how-farrah-fawcett-changed-the-world/.
47. Caroline Graham, "Revealed: Farrah Fawcett Had Secret End-of-Life 11-Year Affair," *Daily Mail* (United Kingdom), August 30, 2009.
48. Curtis, "How Farrah Fawcett Changed World"; and "Farrah Fawcett," Biography.com, last modified November 5, 2021, https://www.biography.com/actor/farrah-fawcett.
49. Bill Bradley, discussion, March 4, 2021.
50. Graham, "Revealed: Farrah Fawcett"; and Kreidler, "Greg Lott, a Longhorn."
51. Richard Bolt, "Robuck Got 2nd Wind on 90-Yard Interception Return," *Austin American-Statesman*, October 23, 1966.
52. Dick Collins, "Texas Goal Defense Too Tough for Rice," *Austin American-Statesman*, October 23, 1966.
53. Morton Sharnik, "Too Small to Be Overlooked," *Sports Illustrated*, November 30, 1970, 26.
54. Bill Bradley, discussion, March 4, 2021. For more details on the discrimination LeVias faced during his college football career, see Jacobus, *Black Man in the Huddle*, 210–16.
55. Lou Maysel, "Ponies Boot Orange Out of Title Race," *Austin American-Statesman*, October 30, 1966.
56. LeVias, discussion; and Bill Bradley, discussion, March 4, 2021.
57. Sharnik, "Too Small to Be Overlooked," 26.
58. Lou Maysel, "Gilbert Stars as UT Downs Baylor, 26–14," *Austin American-Statesman*, November 6, 1966.
59. Dick Collins, "Longhorns Pin 13–3 Thrashing on Fiery Frogs," *Austin American-Statesman*, November 13, 1966.
60. Bill Bradley, discussion, February 24, 2021.
61. Courtney Fox, "The Best Little Whorehouse in Texas: The Real Story That Inspired the Dolly Parton Film," Wide Open Country, January 27, 2022, https://www.wideopencountry.com/the-best-little-whorehouse-in-texas-real-story/. The brothel closed in 1973, abandoning an inconsolable clientele.
62. John Nova Lomax, "The Road to the Chicken Ranch," *Texas Monthly*, May 3, 2016, https://www.texasmonthly.com/the-daily-post/road-chicken-ranch/.
63. Bill Bradley, discussion, April 12, 2022.

64. Lou Maysel, "Longhorns Turn Back Aggies, 22–14, Accept Bluebonnet Bowl Offer," *Austin American-Statesman*, November 25, 1966.
65. Lou Maysel, "'Horns Kick Dixie Out of Mississippi," *Austin American-Statesman*, December 18, 1966.
66. George Breazeale, "'Texas Beat Us in Every Way,' Says Johnny Vaught," *Austin American-Statesman*, December 18, 1966.
67. Hawthorne, *Longhorn Football*, 123.
68. Dick Collins, "Win Fitting Climax, Preview of Next Year," *Austin American-Statesman*, December 18, 1966.
69. Bill Bradley, discussion, February 24, 2021.
70. Kevin Boyle, *The Shattering: America in the 1960s* (New York: W. W. Norton, 2021), 316–17; and Randolph B. Campbell, *Gone to Texas: A History of the Lone Star State*, 3rd ed. (New York: Oxford University Press, 2018), 400.
71. Bill Bradley, discussion, March 4, 2021.
72. Bill Bradley, discussion, October 6, 2022.
73. Bill Bradley, discussion, October 6, 2022.
74. Jim Nicar, "The Battle of Waller Creek," UT *History Center* (blog), November 11, 2013, https://jimnicar.com/2013/11/11/the-battle-of-waller-creek/.
75. Nicar, "Battle of Waller Creek."
76. Nicar, "Battle of Waller Creek."
77. Bill Bradley, discussion, October 6, 2022. On October 22, 1969, the so-called Battle of Waller Creek reached a climax. On that day, UT's Board of Regents, at the insistence of chairman Frank Erwin, went ahead with their plan to bulldoze several hundred feet of the local creek. This time, student protesters chained themselves to the trees. Erwin, without the approval of university president Norman Hackerman, called in campus, city, and state law enforcement, along with a fire truck with an extended ladder, to remove the students from the trees as quickly as possible. Hundreds gathered to watch the police bodily remove the tenacious protesters. Erwin, complete with hard hat and bullhorn, personally oversaw the removals. "Arrest all the people you have to," he ordered. "Once the trees are down, there won't be anything to protest."

    Working their way up to higher branches, police using the extended ladder of the fire truck removed the last few holdouts. They even sawed limbs with protesters still clinging to the branches. The final dissenter was a female student perched on the end of a branch atop an estimated fifty-foot-tall cypress tree. When the police got to her, they almost knocked her off the branch. She dangled for several minutes by her hands until they pulled her safely onto the ladder. Amazingly, no one got killed. In all, twenty-seven people were arrested. Nicar, "Battle of Waller Creek"; and Lerner, "Erwin, Frank Craig, Jr."

    Erwin, in a blatant abuse of power, had broken the nonviolent tradition on UT's campus for the first time by using police force. In so doing, he had not only dismissed student and faculty concerns but also ignored the proper chain of authority that began and ended with the university administration. Bradley was no longer at the University of Texas when the showdown at Waller Creek occurred. He was in the National Football League playing for the Philadelphia Eagles.

78. The phrase *speak truth to power* was coined by Stephen G. Cary in a 1955 book published by the American Friends Service Committee. Cary defines the phrase as "using truth as a person understands it as well as a non-violent approach to oppose acts of oppression by any civil authority that has the power to punish people in some way, shape or form." Those who act on the principle understand that there are grave consequences for doing so. Speaking truth to power takes the kind of courage and conviction that Martin Luther King Jr. demonstrated during the modern civil rights movement. Stephen G. Cary, *Speak Truth to Power: A Quaker Search for an Alternative to Violence* (Philadelphia: American Friends Service Committee, 1955).
79. Mike Jones, "The Life and Times of Darrell Royal," *Chicago Tribune*, November 9, 1986.
80. Country music was managed by record labels in the 1960s, which decided what sound was appealing, handed out assignments to artists, and dictated their appearance and public image. The Nashville sound, with its string arrangements and background singers, had been instituted in the late 1950s to differentiate and protect country music from the commercial threat of rock and roll. For artists like Jennings, Jones, Owens, and Nelson, the Nashville sound was stifling. They envied their rock and roll peers, who could write and record their own music with a degree of creative control. Jacob Shelton, "Outlaw Country: How Willie, Waylon and Others Broke Free," Groovy History, April 11, 2019, https://groovyhistory.com/outlaw-country-music/4.
81. Jones, "Life and Times of Darrell Royal."
82. Bill Bradley, discussion, March 4, 2021.

5. Reality Check

1. Robertson, discussion.
2. Dave Meggyesy, a former NFL player who attended Syracuse University, wrote about the corrupt practices of boosterism at Division I schools in *Out of Their League* (Berkeley CA: Ramparts Press, 1970; Lincoln: University of Nebraska Press, 2005), 38–39, 44–45. Page numbers refer to the 2005 edition.
3. Southern Methodist University was investigated and punished for repeated violations of National Collegiate Athletic Association (NCAA) rules and regulations over several years between the late 1970s and mid-1980s. The most serious violation was the maintenance of a slush fund used for under-the-table payments to players and their families to entice them to come to SMU to play. As a result of SMU's repeated violations, the NCAA instituted a rule change to stiffen penalties for multiple rule violations over a certain period. Today, the NCAA is now required to consider canceling a school's

season—a death penalty—if a school's violations are severe enough. Dave Whitford, *A Payroll to Meet: A Story of Greed, Corruption and Football at SMU* (Lincoln: University of Nebraska Press, 1989).

4. Tommy Asaff, in discussion with the author, Austin TX, April 11, 2022; and Bill Bradley, discussion, April 11, 2022.
5. Bill Bradley, discussion, April 11, 2022.
6. Asaff, discussion; and Bradley, discussion, April 11, 2021.
7. Asaff, discussion; and Bill Bradley, discussion, April 11, 2021.
8. Hawthorne, *Longhorn Football*, 123, 128.
9. Bradley, discussion, April 11, 2022.
10. Dan Jenkins, "College Football 1967: The Top 20, and Why They Are Better Than All the Rest," *Sports Illustrated*, September 11, 1967, 48.
11. Jenkins, "College Football 1967," 48.
12. Dick Collins, "Longhorns Lose Opener to USC, 17–13," *Austin American-Statesman*, September 24, 1967.
13. Lou Maysel, "Scovell Guides TT to 19–13 Upset Win," *Austin American-Statesman*, October 1, 1967.
14. Lou Maysel, "'Horns Cross Virgin OSU Goal Thrice," *Austin American-Statesman*, October 8, 1967.
15. "1967 Texas Longhorns Football Team," American Football Database, accessed November 6, 2022, https://americanfootballdatabase.fandom.com/wiki/1967_Texas_Longhorns_football_team.
16. Fred Sanner, "Pass-Minded Bears Laud Bradley's Arm," *Austin American-Statesman*, November 12, 1967.
17. For Bradley's passing statistics, see *Austin American-Statesman*, October 8, 15, 22, 29, 1967, and November 5, 12, 1967.
18. Bill Bradley, discussion, April 11, 2022.
19. Bill Bradley, discussion, April 11, 2022.
20. Bill Bradley, discussion, April 11, 2022.
21. Lou Maysel, "TCU Rally Clips 'Horns," *Austin American-Statesman*, November 19, 1967; and George Breazeale, "No Bowl for UT," *Austin American-Statesman*, November 24, 1967.
22. Dick Collins, "Just Remember That Next Year," *Austin American-Statesman*, November 24, 1967.
23. Dick Collins, "No Bowl Games for this 6–4 Texas Team," *Austin American-Statesman*, November 24, 1967.
24. Koy, discussion; Bill Bradley, discussion, April 11, 2022; Campbell, discussion; McKay, discussion; and Robertson, discussion.
25. Bill Bradley, discussion, April 11, 2022; Campbell, discussion; Koy, discussion; McKay, discussion; and Robertson, discussion.

26. Little and McEachern, *What It Means to Be a Longhorn*, 118.
27. Bill Bradley, discussion, April 11, 2022.
28. McKay, discussion.
29. Robertson, discussion.
30. Gary Shaw, *Meat on the Hoof: The Hidden World of Texas Football* (New York: St. Martin's Press, 1972). Shaw, an All-State tackle at Denton High School, arrived at the University of Texas in 1963. He struggled for four seasons trying to break into the Longhorns' starting lineup as a guard. But injuries and his relatively small size (6 feet, 196 pounds in his first year) kept him low on the depth chart. He quit the team in the fall of 1966. All of the Longhorns players I interviewed discredited Shaw's allegations.

    Shaw became homeless in the 1980s, wandering the streets of Dallas. In 1990 he was diagnosed as a paranoid schizophrenic. With the aid of his family and mental-disability payments, he was able to live the last nine years of his life away from the dangers of the street. He died on June 21, 1990, of an apparent heart attack in his hometown of Denton, Texas. Mike Butts, "Tarnished Legends," *Austin Chronicle*, July 9, 1999, https://www.austinchronicle.com/news/1999-07-09/522343/.
31. Koy, discussion; McKay, discussion; and Robertson, discussion.
32. Robertson, discussion.
33. McKay, discussion.
34. Koy, discussion.
35. Koy, discussion.
36. Jake Trotter, "Texas' Iconic Wishbone Offense, at 50, Still Influential in College Football," ESPN.com, July 24, 2018, https://www.espn.com/college-football/story/_/id/24175747/texas-iconic-wishbone-offense-50-influential-college-football. *Houston Post* sportswriter Mickey Herskowitz is often credited for giving the new formation its name, but he actually made the observation that it looked like a "pulley bone" when he first saw Texas run it in September 1968. Royal agreed but gave the new offense the name Wishbone. Hawthorne, *Longhorn Football*, 128.
37. Larry Carlson, "Texas Wishbone Offense Fondly Remembered 50 Years after Debut," Horns247.com, August 25, 2018, https://247sports.com/college/texas/LongFormArticle/Texas-Longhorns-Football-Wishbone-offense-50-years-later-Ted-Koy-Darrell-Royal-Emory-Bellard-121024976/#121024976_5. Bellard won five Southwest Conference crowns and two national titles during his collegiate career as an assistant coach at the University of Texas and as a head coach at Texas A&M and Mississippi State. He discusses how he invented the Wishbone offense in his autobiography: Emory Bellard and Al Pickett, *Wishbone Wisdom: Emory Bellard: Texas Football Visionary* (Buffalo Gap TX: State House Press, 2010).
38. Koy, discussion.
39. Hawthorne, *Longhorn Football*, 123, 128.
40. Bill Bradley, discussion, April 11, 2022.

41. Little and McEachern, *What It Means to Be a Longhorn*, 114.
42. Mickey Herskowitz, "Texas Holds Fired-Up Cougars to 20–20 Tie," *Houston Post*, September 22, 1968; and Jack Agness, "UT Stall Defended: 'Let 'Em Boo,' Says Royal," *Houston Post*, September 22, 1968.
43. Ed Fowler, "After Defeat by Texas Tech, Longhorns Reshuffle for OSU," *Austin American-Statesman*, September 29, 1968; and Little and McEachern, *What It Means to Be a Longhorn*, 114.
44. Bill Bradley, discussion, March 4, 2021.
45. Hall, discussion.
46. Hall, discussion.
47. Hall, discussion.
48. Bill Bradley, discussion, March 4, 2021.
49. Bill Bradley, discussion, March 4, 2021; Campbell, discussion; Hall, discussion; Koy, discussion; McKay, discussion; and Robertson, discussion.
50. McKay, discussion.
51. Campbell, discussion; Koy, discussion; McKay, discussion; and Robertson, discussion.
52. Koy, discussion.
53. Lou Maysel, "Steers Rebound, Rout OSU," *Austin American-Statesman*, October 6, 1968.
54. Ed Fowler, "Royal Says New UT Quarterback Knows Team," *Austin American-Statesman*, October 6, 1968.
55. Dan Cook, "The Bradley Story," *San Antonio Express-News*, October 8, 1968.
56. Koy, discussion.
57. Ed Fowler, "Texas Had So Many Key Plays, So Many Heroes," *Austin American-Statesman*, October 13, 1968.
58. Lou Maysel, "Longhorn Stampede Annihilates Porkers," *Austin American-Statesman*, October 20, 1968.
59. Robertson, discussion.
60. Leon Cross to Bill Bradley, October 15, 1968, Norman OK, private collection. Bill sent Cross's letter home to his parents, Joe and Mildred Bradley, who kept scrapbooks of newspaper articles, letters, and paper awards of their son's athletic achievements. But before she added the letter, Mildred shared it with a few neighbors. One, Ron Alexander, wrote an essay about how proud the citizens of Palestine were of their native son and quoted Cross. Then he submitted the essay to the *Daily Texan*, UT's student newspaper, which ran the piece in early November. Ron Anderson, "A Tribute to Bill Bradley," *Daily Texan*, November 4, 1968.
61. Bill Bradley, discussion, March 4, 2021.
62. Steve Zabel, in discussion with the author, Edmond OK, December 15, 2022.
63. Fowler, "Texas Had So Many Key Plays."
64. Little and McEachern, *What It Means to Be a Longhorn*, 95.

65. Campbell, discussion.
66. Andy Yemma, "'Game Got Outta Hand in 4th Quarter'—Hagan," *Austin American-Statesman*, October 27, 1968.
67. Yemma, "'Game Got Outta Hand.'"
68. Yemma, "'Game Got Outta Hand.'"
69. Lou Maysel, "Longhorns Pluck Owls," *Austin American-Statesman*, October 27, 1968.
70. Bill Bradley, in discussion with the author, Philadelphia, August 19, 2023.
71. Freddie Steinmark, *I Play to Win* (Boston: Little Brown, 1971); Jim Dent, *Courage Beyond the Game: The Freddie Steinmark Story* (New York: St. Martin's Press, 2012); and Bower Yousse and Thomas J. Cryan, *Freddie Steinmark: Faith, Family, Football* (Austin: University of Texas Press, 2017). Steinmark is also the subject of the 2015 movie *My All-American*, starring Finn Wittrock and Aaron Eckhart.
72. National Cancer Act of 1971, Public L. No. 92-218, 85 Stat. 778, https://www.cancer.gov/news-events/nca50/commemorate-national-cancer-act-50-years.
73. Bill Little, "Freddie Steinmark Scoreboard," Texassports.com, November 23, 2005, https://texassports.com/sports/2013/8/1/facilities_0801130203.
74. Lou Maysel, "Explosive Steers Saddle Mustangs with 38–7 Loss," *Austin American-Statesman*, November 3, 1968; and Ed Fowler, "Surprise Play Put in Thursday," *Austin American-Statesman*, November 3, 1968.
75. Maysel, "Explosive Steers Saddle Mustangs."
76. Lou Maysel, "Steers Crush Bears, 47–26," *Austin American-Statesman*, November 10, 1968; and Lou Maysel, "Steers Spank Frogs, 47–21," *Austin American-Statesman*, November 17, 1968.
77. Carlson, "Texas Wishbone Offense Fondly Remembered."
78. Stephenson, discussion.
79. Paul Kristynik, in discussion with the author, Austin TX, April 11, 2022.
80. Little and McEachern, *What It Means to Be a Longhorn*, 95–96.
81. Jack Agnes, "Even Steers Surprised," *Houston Post*, November 29, 1968.
82. Agnes, "Even Steers Surprised."
83. Robertson, discussion.
84. "Texas 36, Tennessee 13," The Classics, CottonBowl.com, accessed November 15, 2022, https://www.cottonbowl.com/documents/2019/10/14//1969_Classic_Recap.pdf?id=57.
85. Campbell, discussion.
86. "1968 College Football Polls," AP Polls, Sports Reference, accessed November 16, 2022, https://www.sports-reference.com/cfb/years/1968-polls.html.
87. Carlson, "Texas Wishbone Offense Fondly Remembered."
88. Little and McEachern, *What It Means to Be a Longhorn*, 99–100.
89. Hawthorne, *Longhorn Football*, 128.
90. Koy, discussion; McKay, discussion; Robertson, discussion; and Stephenson, discussion.

91. A *servant leader* is an individual who understands the larger obligation that he or she has to serve other people with a common goal. Robert Greenleaf, *The Servant as Leader: Corporate Ethics and Corporate Governance* (New York: Paulist Press, 2007), 79–85. Bradley learned to make serving his teammates his main priority after the demotion. He did that by setting an example of how to win.

6. Penthouse to Shithouse

1. Bill Bradley, in discussion with the author, Lake Silkworth PA, September 12, 2022.
2. Bill Bradley, discussion, September 12, 2022.
3. Ray Didinger and Robert S. Lyons, "Bert Bell and the Birth of the Eagles," in *The Eagles Encyclopedia: Champions Edition* (Philadelphia: Temple University Press, 2018), 13–14. The entry fee paid by Bell and Wray is equal to $58,990 in 2024. The other expansion teams to join the NFL in 1933 were the Pittsburgh Steelers and the now-defunct Cincinnati Reds.
4. Didinger and Lyons, "Bert Bell and the Birth of Eagles," 14–15; and Les Bowen, *Philadelphia Eagles: The Complete Illustrated History* (Minneapolis MN: MVP Books, 2011), 6–15.
5. Didinger and Lyons, *Eagles Encyclopedia*, 188.
6. Matthew Algeo, *Steagles: Last Team Standing. How the Steelers and the Eagles Saved Pro Football During World War II* (Chicago: Chicago Review Press, 2006).
7. Didinger and Lyons, "The Postseason," in *Eagles Encyclopedia*, 250–55; and Bowen, *Philadelphia Eagles*, 16–33.
8. Didinger and Lyons, *Eagles Encyclopedia*, 189.
9. Didinger and Lyons, *Eagles Encyclopedia*, 190.
10. Eli Kowalski, *1960 NFL Champions: Relive the Philadelphia Eagles 1960 Championship Season* (Philadelphia: Sports Challenge Network, 2010); and Didinger and Lyons, *Eagles Encyclopedia*, 255–58.
11. Didinger and Lyons, *Eagles Encyclopedia*, 424.
12. Didinger and Lyons, *Eagles Encyclopedia*, 424.
13. Theodore N. Beitchman, "Why JFK Loved Philly," *Philly Sport*, November/December 2013, 9; and Frank Fitzpatrick, "Kennedys' Flight of Fancy? According to Some, Brothers Wanted to Buy Eagles," *Philadelphia Inquirer*, November 20, 2013.
14. Didinger and Lyons, *Eagles Encyclopedia*, 191.
15. Didinger and Lyons, *Eagles Encyclopedia*, 165–66.
16. Stan Hochman, "Santa Pelted in Ugly Ending to Ugly Season," *Philadelphia Daily News*, December 16, 1968; and Frank Dolson, "Only the Name Is Changed," *Philadelphia Inquirer*, December 16, 1968.
17. Didinger and Lyons, *Eagles Encyclopedia*, 193.
18. Didinger and Lyons, *Eagles Encyclopedia*, 194.

19. Tom Woodeshick, in discussion with the author, Blakeslee PA, September 21, 2021.
20. Bradley, discussion, September 12, 2022.
21. Bradley, discussion, September 12, 2022.
22. Didinger and Lyons, *Eagles Encyclopedia*, 428; and Gordon Forbes, "Eagles Rout Steelers for First Victory," *Philadelphia Inquirer*, September 29, 1969.
23. Mike Evans, in discussion with the author, Media PA, December 2, 2022.
24. Bill Bradley, discussion, September 12, 2022.
25. Bill Shefski, "For Bradley, a Rough Homecoming," *Philadelphia Daily News*, October 20, 1969; and Ray Didinger, "A Safety for the Ages," *NFL Game Day Program*, Eagles vs. Giants, November 21, 1993, 4.
26. Bill Bradley, discussion, September 12, 2022.
27. Didinger, "Safety for the Ages," 4.
28. Bill Bradley, discussion, September 12, 2022.
29. Evans, discussion.
30. Bill Bradley, discussion, September 12, 2022.
31. Didinger and Lyons, *Eagles Encyclopedia*, 46.
32. Bill Bradley, discussion, September 12, 2022.
33. Bill Bradley, discussion, September 12, 2022.
34. Bill Bradley, discussion, September 12, 2022.
35. Didinger, *Eagles Encyclopedia*, 428. The NFL's Capitol Division was formed in 1967. The division was so named because it was centered around Washington DC, the U.S. capital. In 1967 and 1969 the teams in the division were Dallas, Philadelphia, Washington, and the expansion New Orleans Saints, which was replaced by the New York Giants for the 1968 season. In 1970, with the NFL merger, the Capitol Division was replaced by the NFC East and retained the same four teams. Although Dallas is not located along the Eastern Seaboard, it remained in the same division as Philadelphia, New York, and Washington because of its long-standing rivalries with those teams. Barry Shuck, "NFC East Beginnings: A Look Back through the Division's History," Big Blue View, July 17, 2015, https://www.bigblueview.com/2015/7/17/8956013/nfc-east-beginnings-giants-cowboys-eagles-redskins.
36. Jim Gallagher and Jim Murray, "Player Profiles: Bill Bradley," *1970 Philadelphia Eagles Yearbook, Press, Radio, TV Guide* (Philadelphia: Eagles Football Club, 1970), 33; and "Bill Bradley," Punting, Kick & Punt Returns, Pro Football Reference, accessed December 15, 2022, https://www.pro-football-reference.com/players/B/BradBi00.htm.
37. Didinger and Lyons, *Eagles Encyclopedia*, 428.
38. Bill Bradley, discussion, September 12, 2022. Years later, Bill would regret his decision to continue punting after the injury. His punting average dropped from 41.8 yards to 39.4 yards, bringing his career average down to below 40 yards. "Bill Bradley," Punting, Pro Football Reference.

39. Bill Shefski, "Bradley Returning to Heart of Texas as No. 1," *Philadelphia Daily News*, November 12, 1971.
40. Gordon Forbes, "Eagles Turn Back Dolphins and Stop Losing Streak at 16," *Philadelphia Inquirer*, November 9, 1970.
41. Bill Shefski, "Eagles Sizzling Show Chills Giants," *Philadelphia Daily News*, November 24, 1970.
42. Evans, discussion.
43. Didinger and Lyons, "Eagles on Monday Night Football," in *Eagles Encyclopedia*, 389.
44. Evans, discussion.
45. Saul Braun, "Cosell—the Voice You Love to Hate," *TV Guide*, August 28, 1971, 22–24.
46. Bruce Newman, "Howard Cosell," *Sports Illustrated*, September 19, 1994, 104.
47. Didinger and Lyons, *Eagles Encyclopedia*, 428.
48. Didinger and Lyons, "Veterans Stadium, 1971–2002," in *Eagles Encyclopedia*, 366–69; and Rich Westcott, *Veterans Stadium: Field of Memories* (Philadelphia: Temple University Press, 2005), 15–26.
49. Harold Jackson, in discussion with the author, Los Angeles CA, December 1, 2022.
50. Didinger and Lyons, *Eagles Encyclopedia*, 72–73. Of the thirty-one wide receivers in the Pro Football Hall of Fame, twenty-two played fewer seasons than Jackson's 16, six played the same number, and three played more; twenty-two played fewer games than Jackson's 208, and nine played more; twelve made fewer receptions than Jackson's 579, and nineteen made more; sixteen gained fewer yards than Jackson's 10,377, and fifteen gained more; and fifteen scored fewer touchdowns than Jackson's 76, one scored just as many, and fifteen scored more. "Harold Jackson," Receiving & Rushing, Pro Football Reference, accessed December 17, 2022, https://www.pro-football-reference.com/players/J/JackHa00.htm; "Pro Football WR Hall of Fame Monitor," Pro Football Reference, accessed December 17, 2022, https://www.pro-football-reference.com/hof/hofm_WR.htm; and Aaron Tallent, "25 Greatest Wide Receivers in NFL History," Athlon Sports, last modified February 18, 2022, https://athlonsports.com/nfl/25-greatest-wide-receivers-nfl-history. The list created by Tallent was modified after 2022, and Jackson is no longer listed.
51. Gordon Forbes, "Defense Takes 2d-Half Holiday, Eagles Bow to Bengals, 37–14," *Philadelphia Inquirer*, September 20, 1971.
52. Gordon Forbes, "Cowboys Pluck Eagles Bald, 42–7," *Philadelphia Inquirer*, September 27, 1971.
53. Gordon Forbes, "Eagles Watch as Brodie Soars," *Philadelphia Inquirer*, October 4, 1971.
54. "Say, Jerry! You Ask, Eagles Coach Answers," *Philadelphia Inquirer*, October 4, 1971.
55. "News Flash: Williams Fired by Eagles," *Philadelphia Daily News*, October 6, 1971.
56. Bill Shefski, "Williams' Dismissal as Coach Draws Criticism of Tose," *Philadelphia Daily News*, October 7, 1971.

57. Bruce Keidan, "Coach Exits with Salvo at Ex-Boss," *Philadelphia Inquirer*, October 7, 1971. Tose directed general manager Pete Retzlaff to offer Williams up to a full year's salary, which was approximately $40,000, in addition to the salary covered by the former coach's contract. Williams considered the offer a bribe to quit.
58. Keidan, "Coach Exits with Salvo."
59. Keidan, "Coach Exits with Salvo."
60. "Players: Raw Deal!" *Philadelphia Daily News*, October 7, 1971.
61. Bill Bradley, discussion, September 12, 2022.
62. Didinger and Lyons, "Ed Khayat," in *Eagles Encyclopedia*, 168.
63. Ed Khayat, in discussion with the author, Nashville TN, December 2, 2022.
64. W. J. Rorabaugh, *American Hippies* (New York: Cambridge University Press, 2015), 11–13; Skip Stone, *Hippies from A to Z: Their Sex, Drugs, Music and Impact on Society from the Sixties to the Present* (New York: W. W. Norton, 1994); and Emerald Pellot, "The History of Hippie Fashion in the 70s," Leaf (website), last modified May 3, 2017, https://www.leaf.tv/articles/the-history-of-hippie-fashion-in-the-70s/.
65. Zagorski, *NFL in the 1970s*, 5–6.
66. Bill Bradley, discussion, September 12, 2022.
67. John Underwood, "He's Burning to Be a Success," *Sports Illustrated*, September 20, 1971, 90–93, 96–98, 100–104, 107–8.
68. *The New Breed*, produced by Steve Sabol (Philadelphia: NFL Films, 1971), video, 25:30, https://www.youtube.com/watch?v=9RYCj1nzgp4.
69. *New Breed.*
70. Woodeshick, discussion.
71. Bill Bradley, discussion, September 12, 2022.
72. Underwood, "He's Burning to Be a Success," 100.
73. Barbara "Cis" Rundle, in discussion with the author, Reading PA, December 19, 2022. Rundle served as a stand-in for Farrah Fawcett in 1976, and later for Cheryl Ladd, on *Charlie's Angels*. Rundle is better known for her work on *Hunter* (1984), *Matt Houston* (1982), and *Star 80* (1983). "Cis Rundle," *TV Guide*, accessed December 19, 2022, https://www.tvguide.com/celebrities/cis-rundle/credits/3030429976/; and "Cis Rundle Biography," IMDb, accessed December 19, 2022, www.imdb.com/name/nm0750223/bio.
74. Underwood, "He's Burning to Be a Success," 97–97; and Frank Dolson, "Khayat's Li'l Shavers Gain Clean Victory," *Philadelphia Inquirer*, October 25, 1971.
75. Bill Bradley, discussion, September 12, 2022.
76. Bill Shefski, "Eagles' Shutout a 'Noble' Effort," *Philadelphia Daily News*, October 11, 1971.
77. Chuck Newman, "'We Played Like Williams Was Still Our Coach'—Zabel," *Philadelphia Inquirer*, October 11, 1971.
78. Gordon Forbes, "Vikings Ruin Khayat's Debut," *Philadelphia Inquirer*, October 11, 1971.

79. Shefski, "Eagles' Shutout 'Noble' Effort."
80. Newman, "'We Played Like Williams Was Still Our Coach.'"
81. Chuck Newman, "Arrington Learned Lesson So Well He Was Injured," *Philadelphia Inquirer*, October 18, 1971; and Gordon Forbes, "Raiders Stun Eagles on 3 Quick Scores; Arrington Is Injured," *Philadelphia Inquirer*, October 18, 1971.
82. Evans, discussion.
83. Harold Carmichael, in discussion with the author, Glassboro NJ, October 18, 2021; Zabel, discussion; Bill Bradley, discussion, September 12, 2022; Jackson, discussion; and Evans, discussion.
84. Jackson, discussion.
85. Carmichael, discussion.
86. Bill Bradley, discussion, September 12, 2022; Carmichael, discussion; Jackson, discussion; and Zabel, discussion.
87. Jackson, discussion; and Bill Bradley, discussion, September 12, 2022.
88. Jackson, discussion.
89. Ray Didinger, in discussion with the author, Philadelphia PA, February 9, 2022. Didinger became a beloved figure among Eagles fans over a fifty-year career as a sports journalist in Philadelphia. His most recent book is a compilation of his favorite columns, some of which are autobiographical in nature: Ray Didinger, *Finished Business: My Fifty Years of Headlines, Heroes, and Heartaches* (Philadelphia: Temple University Press, 2021). His *One Last Read: The Collected Works of the World's Slowest Sportswriter* (Philadelphia: Temple University Press, 2023), originally published in 2007, came out in paperback in 2023.
90. Didinger, discussion, February 9, 2022.
91. Bill Bradley, discussion, September 12, 2022.
92. Bill Bradley, discussion, September 12, 2022.
93. Gordon Forbes, "Eagles Playbook a 1st-Grade," *Philadelphia Inquirer*, October 25, 1971.
94. Dolson, "Khayat's Li'l Shavers."
95. Bill Shefski, "A Super Success for Eagles' Defense," *Philadelphia Daily News*, November 1, 1971.
96. Gordon Forbes, "Bradley Steals Two Passes in Wild 4th Period," *Philadelphia Inquirer*, November 1, 1971.
97. Shefski, "Super Success for Eagles' Defense."
98. Shefski, "Super Success for Eagles' Defense."
99. Forbes, "Bradley Steals Two Passes."
100. Shefski, "Super Success for Eagles' Defense."
101. Bill Bradley, discussion, September 12, 2022.
102. Gordon Forbes, "Eagles Tie as Clock Rescues Redskins," *Philadelphia Inquirer*, November 8, 1971.

103. Bill Bradley, discussion, September 12, 2022.
104. Forbes, "Eagles Tie as Clock Rescues Redskins."
105. Bill Shefski, "Liske Cautious, Eagles Fit to Be Tied," *Philadelphia Daily News*, November 8, 1971. Unless the receiver steps out of bounds, the clock continues to run in the NFL. The Redskins also knew that they could run out the clock as long as they didn't make it obvious that they were trying to consume time in accordance with the league rule book (rule 4, section 3, article 4, item 2).
106. Shefski, "Liske Cautious."
107. Shefski, "Bradley Returning to Heart of Texas."
108. Didinger and Lyons, *Eagles Encyclopedia*, 52–53.
109. Ryan Autullo, "Happy Feller's Timely Kicks Left Longhorn Fans Smiling," *Austin American-Statesman*, November 5, 2014. Feller, who kicked the Texas Longhorns to back-to-back national championships in 1969 and 1970, was drafted in the fourth round of the 1971 NFL draft by the Philadelphia Eagles and was the first kicker selected. Of the six out of twenty field goals made during his rookie season, his longest was from 50 yards out. In his second season, after being traded to the Saints, he went six for eleven in field goals, with his longest at 46 yards. In the 1973 season, his last in the NFL, he connected on four for twelve attempts, with his longest 18 yards.
110. Shefski, "Bradley Returning to Heart of Texas."
111. Shefski, "Bradley Returning to Heart of Texas."
112. Shefski, "Bradley Returning to Heart of Texas."
113. Gordon Forbes, "Eagles Lost in Texas," *Philadelphia Inquirer*, November 15, 1971; and Bill Shefski, "Negative Strategy Nets Negative Result," *Philadelphia Daily News*, November 15, 1971.
114. "Bradley Ties Eagle Record," *Philadelphia Inquirer*, November 22, 1971.
115. Gordon Forbes, "Birds Climb Out of Last Place with 37–20 Win," *Philadelphia Inquirer*, November 22, 1971.
116. Ray Didinger, "Bill Bradley—League Leading Interceptor and Pressure Breaker," *Philadelphia Evening Bulletin*, December 6, 1971.
117. Associated Press, "'Super Bill' Tag Fits Bradley Now," *Philadelphia Inquirer*, December 9, 1971.
118. Gordon Forbes, "Dempsey's 4 Field Goals Help Eagles Win," *Philadelphia Inquirer*, December 13, 1971.
119. Ray Didinger, "Super Bill Lies Down on Job but Gets 11th Steal," *Philadelphia Evening Bulletin*, December 12, 1971.
120. Associated Press, "Eagles Place Super Bill Bradley as Free Safety on All-Pro Team," *Philadelphia Inquirer*, December 30, 1971.
121. Bill Shefski, "Khayat, Retzlaff Rehired," *Philadelphia Daily News*, December 20, 1971.
122. Shefski, "Khayat, Retzlaff Rehired."

7. Billy Bo Bitch

1. Gordon Forbes, "Bradley a Free Safety with Free Spirit," *Philadelphia Inquirer*, December 9, 1972.
2. Forbes, "Bradley a Free Safety with Free Spirit."
3. Bill Bradley, discussion, September 12, 2022.
4. Bill Bradley, discussion, September 12, 2022.
5. Ray Didinger, "A Hairy Situation," *Evening Bulletin*, July 17, 1972; and Ray Didinger, "Tim, Bill Put Pinch on Eagles," *Evening Bulletin*, July 29, 1972.
6. Jack McKinney, "Vince McNally about Sammy Glick: 'That's an Agent?'" *Philadelphia Daily News*, August 24, 1972.
7. Retzlaff was correct in not trusting Mark Stewart. In 1982 Stewart was investigated by the FBI for bankruptcy fraud and money laundering. By that time, he was operating nearly forty businesses, including a sports arena, a recording company, and a record-promotion company that were all involved in the conspiracy. Barbara Webster and Michael S. McCampbell, "International Money Laundering: Research and Investigation Join Forces," *National Institute of Justice Research in Brief*, U.S. Department of Justice, September 1992, 7, https://www.ojp.gov/pdffiles1/Digitization/135942NCJRS.pdf.
8. Gordon Forbes, "Retzlaff Is Firm on Bradley and Rossovich; Reaction of Teammates Is Mixed," *Philadelphia Inquirer*, July 19, 1972.
9. Richard C. Crepeau, *NFL Football: A History of America's New National Pastime* (Urbana: University of Illinois Press, 2020), 3–7.
10. Gerald Eskenazi, "Red Grange, Football Hero of 1920s, Dead at 87," *New York Times*, January 29, 1991.
11. Crepeau, *NFL Football: A History*, 135–36, 140.
12. Zagorsky, *NFL in the 1970s*, 118–19.
13. Bill Bradley, discussion, September 12, 2022.
14. Bill Bradley, discussion, September 12, 2022.
15. Forbes, "Retzlaff Is Firm."
16. Ray Didinger, "Bobby May Be Major Problem for Bradley," *Evening Bulletin*, July 27, 1972.
17. Woodeshick, discussion.
18. Forbes, "Bradley a Free Safety with Free Spirit."
19. Zabel, discussion.
20. Gordon Forbes, "Sacrificial Eagle?" *Philadelphia Inquirer*, August 2, 1972.
21. Gordon Forbes, "Back to Conformity for Birds' Bradley," *Philadelphia Inquirer*, August 6, 1972.
22. Bill Bradley, discussion, September 12, 2022.
23. Bill Shefski, "Tim's Good-Bye Brings Tears," *Philadelphia Daily News*, August 2, 1972.

24. John Flynn, "Eagles Should Be Able to Win Despite Khayat, Rossovich Says," *Philadelphia Inquirer*, October 25, 1972.
25. Gordon Forbes, "The Deft Mr. Retzlaff Puts It All Together and Earns His Spurs," *Philadelphia Inquirer*, August 3, 1972.
26. Ray Didinger, "Bradley Oks 3-Year Eagle Pact," *Evening Bulletin*, September 14, 1972.
27. Bill Bradley, discussion, September 12, 2022.
28. Forbes, "Back to Conformity for Bradley."
29. Bill Shefski, "Bradley's Attitude Super Again," *Philadelphia Daily News*, August 18, 1972.
30. Bill Shefski, "Woody's Goal: Make Khayat Expendable," *Philadelphia Daily News*, September 12, 1972.
31. Gordon Forbes, "Ed Khayat," *Philadelphia Inquirer*, September 10, 1972.
32. Zabel, discussion.
33. Forbes, "Eagles' Bradley a Free Safety with Free Spirit."
34. John Bunting, in discussion with the author, Wilmington NC, December 15, 2022.
35. Bill Shefski, "Cowboys Put Eagles on the Carpet," *Philadelphia Daily News*, September 18, 1972.
36. Shefski, "Cowboys Put Eagles on Carpet"; and Jack McKinney, "Sizzing Eagles: Were They Unready to Stand the Heat?" *Philadelphia Daily News*, September 18, 1972.
37. McKinney, "Sizzling Eagles."
38. Bill Shefski, "Blooper Bill Bradley Thwarts Super Bill," *Philadelphia Daily News*, September 1972.
39. Shefski, "Blooper Bill Bradley Thwarts Super Bill."
40. Bill Bradley, discussion, September 12, 2022.
41. Shefski, "Blooper Bill Bradley Thwarts Super Bill."
42. Shefski, "Blooper Bill Bradley Thwarts Super Bill."
43. Shefski, "Blooper Bill Bradley Thwarts Super Bill."
44. John Flynn, "Dempsey Off Target with Old Holder 3,000 Miles Away," *Philadelphia Inquirer*, September 25, 1972; and Shefski, "Blooper Bill Bradley Thwarts Super Bill."
45. Gordon Forbes, "Reaves Fails in First Start," *Philadelphia Inquirer*, October 3, 1972.
46. Stan Hochman, "Howard Cosell Fumbles Another Night in Philly," *Philadelphia Daily News*, October 3, 1972.
47. Bill Shefski, "Jurgy: Just Like George Washington," *Philadelphia Daily News*, October 9, 1972.
48. Gordon Forbes, "Eagles (0-4) Lose to Redskins, 14–0," *Philadelphia Inquirer*, October 9, 1972.
49. John Flynn, "Eagle Defender Bradley Earns Respect of 'Skins," *Philadelphia Inquirer*, October 9, 1972.
50. Flynn, "Eagle Defender Bradley Earns Respect."
51. Bill Bradley, discussion, September 12, 2022.

52. Gordon Forbes, "Eagles Beaten by Rams, 34–3, for 5th Loss," *Philadelphia Inquirer*, October 16, 1972.
53. John Flynn, "Khayat Didn't Hear Fans Sing, 'Good-Bye, Eddie,'" *Philadelphia Inquirer*, October 16, 1972.
54. Ray Didinger, in discussion with the author, Philadelphia PA, November 26, 2022. NFL Films captured the incident of Bradley knocking over the trainer's table in an eight-minute highlight film narrated by John Facenda. *Bill Bradley, Philadelphia Eagles Returner/Defensive Back/Punter 1969–1976*, NFL Films, video, 8:11, https://www.youtube.com/watch?v=ZHiuWb1VCKk.
55. Bradley, discussion, September 12, 2022.
56. Gordon Forbes, "Liske Hits on 3 TD Passes," *Philadelphia Inquirer*, October 23, 1972.
57. Bruce Keidan, "Eagles and Saints Agree: No Embarrassment Intended," *Philadelphia Inquirer*, October 30, 1972.
58. Bruce Keidan, "Even Fate Helps Downtrodden Eagles Muff This One," *Philadelphia Inquirer*, November 6, 1972.
59. Gordon Forbes, "Eagles Win on 6 Field Goals," *Philadelphia Inquirer*, November 13, 1972.
60. Bill Bradley, discussion, September 12, 2022.
61. Bill Bradley, discussion, September 12, 2022.
62. Bill Bradley, discussion, September 12, 2022.
63. Bill Bradley, discussion, September 12, 2022.
64. Gordon Forbes, "Cowboys Rally to Jar Eagles, 28–7," *Philadelphia Inquirer*, November 20, 1972.
65. Gordon Forbes, "Redskins Defeat Eagles, 23–7, to Win Eastern Division Crown," *Philadelphia Inquirer*, December 4, 1972.
66. John Flynn, "The Worst Defeat; Even Giants Feel Pity for Birds," *Philadelphia Inquirer*, November 27, 1972. The only other defeat that compared to the 62–10 loss was also inflicted by New York. It came on October 15, 1933, when the Giants shutout the Birds, 56–0. Based on point differential, the 1933 loss was the worst defeat in Eagles history. "Philadelphia Eagles at New York Giants—October 15, 1933," Pro Football Reference, accessed February 14, 2023, https://www.pro-football-reference.com/boxscores/193310150nyg.htm.
67. Ray Didinger, "Giants Embarrass Eagles, 62–10," *Philadelphia Evening Bulletin*, November 27, 1972.
68. Gordon Forbes, "Eagles Lose to Bears, Finish Winless at Home," *Philadelphia Inquirer*, December 11, 1972.
69. Bill Bradley, discussion, September 12, 2022. For a film clip of the muff and Bradley slapping the ball away, see Old Time Football, "Bad snap on the PAT," X (Twitter), October 12, 2019, video, 0:16, https://twitter.com/Ol_TimeFootball/status/1182882031371345920.
70. Gordon Forbes, "Cards Shade Eagles, 24–23," *Philadelphia Inquirer*, December 18, 1972.

71. Ray Didinger, "Super Ghost Looks for More Picks," *Evening Bulletin*, October 10, 1973.
72. Associated Press, "Eagles' Bill Bradley Is All-Pro Selection," *Philadelphia Evening Bulletin*, January 5, 1973.
73. Gordon Forbes, "Powerful One-Man Rule May Be in Store for Eagles," *Philadelphia Inquirer*, December 19, 1972.
74. Bill Bradley, discussion, September 12, 2022.
75. Ray Didinger, "Bradley May Laugh During Season, Too," *Philadelphia Evening Bulletin*, July 17, 1973.
76. Kevin Reilly, in discussion with the author, Wilmington DE, January 23, 2023.
77. Evans, discussion.
78. Didinger and Lyons, *Eagles Encyclopedia*, 169–70.
79. Didinger and Lyons, *Eagles Encyclopedia*, 430.
80. Didinger, "Bradley May Laugh."
81. Carmichael, discussion.
82. Didinger and Lyons, *Eagles Encyclopedia*, 430.
83. Didinger, "Super Ghost Looks for More Picks."
84. Didinger, "Super Ghost Looks for More Picks."
85. Didinger, "Super Ghost Looks for More Picks."
86. Gordon Forbes, "McCormack: 'It Was a Long Time Coming, Wasn't It?'" *Philadelphia Inquirer*, October 15, 1973.
87. Gordon Forbes, "Birds Win First Here Since '71," *Philadelphia Inquirer*, October 29, 1973.
88. Bunting, discussion.
89. Gordon Forbes, "Dempsey's FG, Zabel's Block, Make Eagles 24–23 Winners," *Philadelphia Inquirer*, November 5, 1973.
90. Gordon Forbes, "Eagles Lose, 31–10; Gabriel Is Injured," *Philadelphia Inquirer*, November 19, 1973.
91. Bruce Keidan, "Bradley Specializes in Versatility for Home Fans," *Philadelphia Inquirer*, November 19, 1973.
92. Keidan, "Bradley Specializes in Versatility."
93. Keidan, "Bradley Specializes in Versatility."
94. Keidan, "Bradley Specializes in Versatility."
95. Reilly, discussion.
96. Bill Bradley, discussion, September 12, 2022.
97. Bunting, discussion.
98. Didinger and Lyons, *Eagles Encyclopedia*, 430.
99. Gordon Forbes, "Brown Stars in 38–29 Win," *Philadelphia Inquirer*, December 17, 1973.
100. Bill Bradley, discussion, September 12, 2022.
101. Bill Bradley, discussion, September 12, 2022.

102. Bill Shefski, "Taylor-ing the Eagles to a Winner," *Philadelphia Daily News*, December 4, 1972.
103. Didinger and Lyons, *Eagles Encyclopedia*, 430.
104. Bunting, discussion.
105. Coult Aubrey, "Eagles Better Stick to Football," *Allentown Morning Call*, March 31, 1974.
106. Reilly, discussion.
107. Bill Bradley, discussion, September 12, 2022.
108. Julie Bacanskas, "The House That the Shamrock Shake Built," *Philadelphia*, March 17, 2017, https://express.adobe.com/page/IEK4sZ2HSvoQc/.
109. Bill Bradley, discussion, September 12, 2022.
110. Bill Bradley, discussion, September 12, 2022.
111. Reilly, discussion.

8. Bamboozled

1. Didinger and Lyons, *Eagles Encyclopedia*, 429–30.
2. Didinger and Lyons, *Eagles Encyclopedia*, 28.
3. Bill Bergey, in discussion with the author, Chadds Ford PA, November 2, 2021.
4. Bergey, discussion.
5. Chick McElrone, ed., *The 1975 Philadelphia Eagles Yearbook* (Philadelphia: Philadelphia Eagles, 1975), 79.
6. Bergey, discussion.
7. Bill Bradley, discussion, September 12, 2022.
8. Bunting, discussion.
9. United Press International, "N.F.L. Players Strike," *New York Times*, July 1, 1974; and Ray Kennedy, "Star-Struck Canton," *Sports Illustrated*, August 5, 1974, 12.
10. Richard C. Crepeau, *NFL Football: A History of America's New National Pastime* (Urbana: University of Illinois Press, 2020), 134–42; and Ed Garvey, "No Freedom, No Football—1974," in *Never Ask "Why": Football Players' Fight for Freedom in the NFL*, ed. Chuck Cascio (Philadelphia: Temple University Press, 2023).
11. Bill Bradley, discussion, September 12, 2022.
12. United Press International, "N.F.L. Players Strike."
13. United Press International, "N.F.L. Players Strike."
14. Stan Hochman, "Eagles Wives Lead Pickets' Charge," *Philadelphia Daily News*, July 11, 1974.
15. United Press International, "N.F.L. Players Strike."
16. Chuck Gardner, "World Football League—a Brief History," World Football League (website), accessed June 24, 2023, http://wfl.charlottehornetswfl.com/pages_wfl/history.php. By early June 1974 the WFL claimed it had some sixty NFL players under contract.

Most of the defections came in the form of futures contracts. The players would play out their existing deals with the NFL, then jump to the WFL when those deals expired. For example, quarterback Ken Stabler planned to stay with the Oakland Raiders through 1975, then would have joined Birmingham in 1976 had the team and league survived that long.

17. Gordon Forbes, "Gabriel Quits Strike, Joins Eagle Camp," *Philadelphia Inquirer*, July 26, 1974.
18. Gordon Forbes, "Bergey Reports to Eagle Camp," *Philadelphia Inquirer*, July 28, 1974.
19. Jerry Sisemore, in discussion with the author, Lake Travis TX, April 11, 2022.
20. "NFL Strike Halted," *New York Times*, August 12, 1974.
21. Gordon Forbes, "14 Veterans Enter Camp at Widener," *Philadelphia Inquirer*, August 13, 1974.
22. Didinger and Lyons, *Eagles Encyclopedia*, 430.
23. Discussion with Philadelphia Eagles player, Dover DE, January 24, 2023; and Jack McKinney, "Roman Gabriel Lost the Team When He Crossed the Picket Line," *Philadelphia Daily News*, December 22, 1975. When center Jerry Sisemore was asked if the offensive linemen purposely missed their blocks to get revenge on Gabriel, he insisted that it "never happened." Sisemore, discussion.
24. Didinger and Lyons, *Eagles Encyclopedia*, 65, 431.
25. Frank Dolson, "McCormack's Stocking Comes Up Empty," *Philadelphia Inquirer*, December 23, 1975.
26. Bill Bradley, discussion, September 12, 2022.
27. Bulaich, discussion.
28. Bunting, discussion.
29. Gordan Forbes, "Eagles Trade Dempsey to Rams," *Philadelphia Inquirer*, April 23, 1975.
30. Bill Bradley, in discussion with the author, Philadelphia, October 10, 2022.
31. Bill Bradley, discussion, October 10, 2022
32. Frank Fitzpatrick, "In Life, the Eagles' Tim Rossovich Bit Off More Than He Could Chew," *Philadelphia Inquirer*, December 14, 2018.
33. Rundle, discussion.
34. Bill Bradley, discussion, October 10, 2022.
35. Rundle, discussion.
36. Ray Didinger, "Tim Rossovich, a Wild Man Burning to Make a Difference," Philadelphia Eagles, December 9, 2018, https://www.philadelphiaeagles.com/news/didinger-tim-rossovich-a-wild-man-burning-to-make-a-difference.
37. Gary Smith, "A New Life: Dick Vermeil," *Sports Illustrated*, March 28, 1983, 63–65. For the most complete account of Vermeil, see Gordon Forbes, *Dick Vermeil: Whistle in His Mouth, Heart on His Sleeve. A Biography* (Chicago: Triumph Books, 2009).
38. Didinger and Lyons, *Eagles Encyclopedia*, 170.

39. Dick Vermeil, in discussion with the author, East Fallowfield Township PA, March 24, 2022.
40. Gordon Forbes, "Eagle 'War' Drills Take Toll," *Philadelphia Inquirer*, July 15, 1976; Bradley, discussion, October 10, 2022; Bergey, discussion; Bunting, discussion; Carmichael, discussion; and Sisemore, discussion.
41. Phil Jasner, "Vermeil Sees Red over Lavender," *Philadelphia Daily News*, July 28, 1976.
42. Phil Jasner, "Lavender Wants In if Vermeil Wants Him," *Philadelphia Daily News*, July 30, 1976; and Dick Weiss, "Manny Likes Trade," *Philadelphia Daily News*, August 6, 1976. In addition to Sistrunk, a 6-foot-5, 274-pound defensive tackle, general manager Jim Murray was able to wrest a sixth-round draft pick in 1977, a fifth in 1978, and a fourth in 1979 from the Washington Redskins
43. Phil Jasner, "One Bird Who Never Left the Nest," *Philadelphia Daily News*, October 21, 1976.
44. Bergey, discussion.
45. Bergey, discussion.
46. Carmichael, discussion.
47. Didinger and Lyons, *Eagles Encyclopedia*, 431. Papale was a fine example of how head coach Dick Vermeil began to change the culture of the team when he arrived in Philadelphia. In 1976, his first year with the Eagles, Vermeil held an open tryout, where he discovered Papale, a thirty-year-old bartender who never played college football. Instead, Papale had attended St. Joseph's University on a track scholarship. Still, he was the only one Vermeil signed from the open tryout and kept on the roster. As a rookie, Papale excelled on special teams. His underdog story resonated with Philadelphia's fans because it played out in 1976, the same year the Hollywood film *Rocky* won the Oscar for Best Picture. The similarities between the stories of the two Philly underdogs, Italian Stallions, were played up in newspapers and magazines and later became a feature film, *Invincible*, starring Mark Wahlberg as Papale and Greg Kinnear as Vermeil.
48. Didinger and Lyons, *Eagles Encyclopedia*, 431.
49. Didinger and Lyons, *Eagles Encyclopedia*, 170–71.
50. Vermeil, discussion.
51. Bill Bradley, discussion, October 10, 2022.
52. Gordon Forbes, "Trade to Vikings Brightens Bradley's Future," *Philadelphia Inquirer*, June 21, 1977.
53. Forbes, "Trade to Vikings."
54. Phil Jasner, "Vikings Brighten Bradley's Future," *Philadelphia Daily News*, June 21, 1977.
55. Bill Bradley, discussion, October 10, 2022.
56. "To You, 'the People,'" advertisement, *Philadelphia Daily News*, June 21, 1977.
57. Bill Bradley, "Game Face Forever: A Poem to the Fans of Philadelphia," *Philadelphia Daily News*, June 21, 1977.

58. Phil Jasner, "Say Goodbye to Bill Bradley," *Philadelphia Daily News*, July 13, 1977.
59. Glenn Sheeley, "Bradley Back in Time to Renew Feud?" *Pittsburgh Press*, November 16, 1977.
60. Bradley set the Eagles' franchise record for career interceptions with thirty-four in 1976. Unfortunately, he is not given as much credit as he deserves for that achievement because Eric Allen (1988–94) and later Hall of Fame safety Brian Dawkins (1996–2008) tied the record, and both of those Eagles played on winning teams. Didinger and Lyons, *Eagles Encyclopedia*, 483.
61. Bradley's franchise record of 111 career punt returns was broken by Wally Henry (148 returns between 1977 and 1982), DeSean Jackson (131 between 2008 and 2013), Brian Mitchell (117 between 2000 and 2002), and John Sciarra (117 between 1978 and 1983). Didinger and Lyons, *Eagles Encyclopedia*, 484.
62. Bradley was the first player to lead the NFL in interceptions in consecutive seasons (1971 and 1972). Everson Walls of the Dallas Cowboys tied Bradley by leading the league in interceptions for two straight years in 1981 (11 interceptions) and 1982 (7). In 1985 Walls set the record for most NFL-leading seasons in interceptions with three when he had 9 picks. Ed Reed of the Baltimore Ravens matched Walls by leading the NFL in interceptions in 2004 (9), 2008 (9), and 2010 (8). "Bill Bradley," Pro Football Reference; "Everson Walls," Pro Football Reference, accessed July 4, 2023, https://www.pro-football-reference.com/players/W/WallEv00.htm; and "Ed Reed," Pro Football Reference, accessed July 4, 2023, https://www.pro-football-reference.com/players/R/ReedEd00.htm.
63. The Eagles were 35-72-5 during Bradley's tenure in Philadelphia. Didinger and Lyons, *Eagles Encyclopedia*, 428–31.
64. Mark Eckel considers Bradley one of the two best free safeties in Eagles history, with the other being Brian Dawkins. Mark Eckel, *The Big 50: The Men and Moments That Made the Philadelphia Eagles* (Chicago: Triumph Books, 2016), 312. Robert W. Cohen believes that Bradley is among the top twenty Eagles players of all time. Robert W. Cohen, *The 50 Greatest Players in Philadelphia Eagles History* (Guilford CT: Lyons Press, 2019), 135–40.
65. Ray Didinger, "Eagles Fell Out of Love with Bradley," *Philadelphia Evening Bulletin*, June 21, 1977.
66. Forbes, "Trade to Vikings Brightens Bradley's Future."
67. Associated Press, "Viking Bradley Finds 'a New Love Affair,'" *Philadelphia Inquirer*, July 6, 1977; United Press International, "Vikings' Bradley Is Among Axed NFL Vets," *Philadelphia Daily News*, September 14, 1977; and Bill Bradley, discussion, October 10, 2022. Krause completed his sixteen-year NFL career with eighty-one interceptions to become the all-time leader in that category. "Paul Krause," Pro Football Reference, n.d., https://www.pro-football-reference.com/players/K/KrauPa00.htm.

68. Doug Grow, "Big Red's Newest Battler in the Swing of Things," *St. Louis Post-Dispatch*, November 28, 1977.
69. Gordon Forbes, "Eagles Cut Will Wynn, Tee Parker," *Philadelphia Inquirer*, September 14, 1977.
70. "Mark Mitchell," Pro Football Reference, n.d., https://www.pro-football-reference.com/players/M/MitcMa21.htm. Martin also went by "Mark."
71. "Herm Edwards," Pro Football Reference, n.d., https://www.pro-football-reference.com/players/E/EdwaHe20.htm.
72. "Where Are They Now? DB John Sciarra," Philadelphia Eagles, May 13, 2015, https://www.philadelphiaeagles.com/news/where-are-they-now-db-john-sciarra-15284037.
73. Bill Bradley, in discussion with the author, Spring Branch TX, March 10, 2023.
74. Phil Jasner, "Bradley Out to Prove He's No Has-Been," *Philadelphia Daily News*, September 20, 1977.
75. Bill Bradley, discussion, March 10, 2023.
76. Associated Press, "NFL Mourns Passing of Raiders Owner Al Davis," *Deseret News*, October 8, 2011, https://www.deseret.com/2011/10/8/20221658/nfl-mourns-passing-of-raiders-owner-al-davis/.
77. Associated Press, "NFL Mourns Passing."
78. "Bill Bradley," Pro Football Reference.
79. Bill Bradley, discussion, March 10, 2023.
80. Sheeley, "Bradley Back in Time?"
81. Bill Bradley, discussion, March 10, 2023.
82. Bill Curry, "Avant Garde Group Sets Up Shop Here," *Philadelphia Inquirer*, August 24, 1976.
83. Bill Bradley, discussion, March 10, 2023. According to Bradley, Larry Wilson's offer was precipitated by Jim Hanifan, St. Louis's offensive line coach. Hanifan went to the owner, Bill Bidwell, and the head coach, Don Coryell, and recommended that they sign Bill if they hoped to get into the playoffs.
84. Phil Jasner, "Bradley: Joining Cards Is Strange," *Philadelphia Daily News*, November 23, 1977.
85. Grow, "Big Red's Newest Battler."
86. Daphne Hurford, "'I'll Do Anything I Can Get Away With,'" *Sports Illustrated*, July 25, 1977, 30.
87. Grow, "Big Red's Newest Battler."
88. Bill Bradley, discussion, March 10, 2023.
89. "1977 St. Louis Cardinals Rosters, Stats, Schedule, Team Draftees," Pro Football Reference, n.d., https://www.pro-football-reference.com/teams/crd/1977.htm.
90. Didinger and Lyons, *Eagles Encyclopedia*, 430.
91. Didinger and Lyons, *Eagles Encyclopedia*, 430–31.

92. Bill Bradley, discussion, March 10, 2023.
93. Ken Belson, "Fight for Cash Goes On for NFL's Longtime Retirees," *New York Times*, September 7, 2018; and Zach Miller, "The NFL Retirement Plan: Everything You Need to Know," *Athlete Wealth Management*, November 11, 2021.
94. Bill Bradley, discussion, March 10, 2023.
95. *Bill Bradley, Philadelphia Eagles*, NFL Films.

9. Teacher-Coach

1. Raymond A. Partsch III, "Like a Movie: Bill Bradley's Life Reads Like a Screenplay," *Beaumont (TX) Enterprise*, April 16, 2014.
2. Bill Bradley discussion, August 19, 2023.
3. Partsch, "Like a Movie."
4. Douglas Martin, "Clinton Manges, Volatile Texas Oilman and Rancher, Dies at 87," *New York Times*, September 28, 2010.
5. Vinnie Vinzetta, "SA's USFL Team Lives On with Gunslingers Players," KENS5.com, November 12, 2017, https://www.kens5.com/article/sports/sas-usfl-team-lives-on-with-gunslingers-players/273-490989033.
6. Bill Bradley, discussion, August 19, 2023.
7. Shaun Powell, "A USFL Team That Played for the Love of the Game," *New York Times*, April 18, 2009.
8. Billy Schott, in discussion with the author, Austin TX, April 11, 2022.
9. Bill Bradley, discussion, August 19, 2023.
10. Powell, "USFL Team."
11. Powell, "USFL Team." In 1995 Manges was sentenced to twenty-seven months in prison for his role in a bribery scandal.
12. Ben Bolch, "Pepper Rodgers, Whose Long Coaching Career Included UCLA Stint, Dies at 88," *Los Angeles Times*, May 14, 2020, https://www.latimes.com/sports/ucla/story/2020-05-14/pepper-rodgers-obit-college-football-coach-ucla-dies-88.
13. Bill Bradley, discussion, August 19, 2023.
14. Bill Bradley, discussion, August 19, 2023.
15. Bill Bradley, discussion, August 19, 2023.
16. Bill Bradley, discussion, August 19, 2023.
17. Drew Jubera, "How Donald Trump Destroyed a Football League: An Oral History of the Rise and Fall of the USFL," *Esquire Magazine*, January 13, 2016, https://www.esquire.com/news-politics/a41135/donald-trump-usfl/.
18. "CFL History," in *Canadian Football League: Guide & Record Book*, ed. Steve Daniel (Winnipeg MB: CFL Publications, 2017), 153, https://d3ham790trbkqy.cloudfront.net/wp-content/uploads/2017/07/CFL-Book-2017-Perfect-Bind.pdf#page=153.
19. "Former Stampeders, Lions Coach Lary Kuharich Dies at the Age of 70," *Canadian Press*, November 15, 2016.

20. Bill Bradley, discussion, August 19, 2023.
21. Bill Bradley, discussion, August 19, 2023.
22. Chuck Cox, "Palestine Native Bradley Likes San Antonio," *Palestine (TX) Herald-Press*, September 3, 1995; and Partsch, "Like a Movie."
23. Susan Bradley, in discussion with the author, Spring Branch TX, April 9, 2022.
24. Bill Bradley, discussion, April 9, 2022.
25. Susan Bradley, discussion.
26. Susan Bradley, discussion.
27. Carissa Carter, in discussion with the author, Spring Branch TX, April 9, 2022.
28. Susan Bradley, discussion.
29. Susan Bradley, discussion.
30. Bill Bradley, discussion, April 9, 2022.
31. Susan Bradley, discussion.
32. Bill Bradley, discussion, April 9, 2022.
33. For the most complete account of Wade Phillips's NFL career, see Wade Phillips and Vic Carucci, *Son of Bum: Lessons My Dad Taught Me about Football and Life* (New York: Diversion Books, 2017).
34. Bill Bradley, discussion, August 19, 2023.
35. Wade Phillips, in discussion with the author, Grand Prairie TX, August 17, 2023.
36. Phillips, discussion.
37. Kobe Scales, "Ted Cottrell: Find Your Calling," in "Stories of Service: Former Falcons Detail Life as a Black Athlete, Living in Atlanta during the 1960s, 1970s," by Kobe Scales and SeMaj Musco, AtlantaFalcons.com, February 27, 2023, https://www.atlantafalcons.com/news/stories-of-service-former-falcons-detail-life-as-a-black-nfl-athlete-living-in-a.
38. Ted Cottrell, in discussion with the author, Tyrone GA, August 18, 2023.
39. Cottrell, discussion.
40. Phillips, discussion.
41. Kurt Schulz, in discussion with the author, Kirkland WA, August 18, 2023.
42. "Kurt Schulz," Pro Football Reference, accessed September 2, 2023, https://www.pro-football-reference.com/players/S/SchuKu20.htm.
43. Schulz, discussion.
44. "1998 Buffalo Bills Rosters, Stats, Schedule, Team Draftees," Pro Football Reference, accessed September 1, 2023, https://www.pro-football-reference.com/teams/buf/1998.htm.
45. "1999 Buffalo Bills Rosters, Stats, Schedule, Team Draftees," Pro Football Reference, accessed September 1, 2023, https://www.pro-football-reference.com/teams/buf/1999.htm.
46. Schulz, discussion.
47. Tyler Dunn, "Fifteen Years Later, the 'Miracle' Lingers On for the Bills," *Buffalo News*, October 10, 2015.

48. Phillips and Carucci, *Son of Bum*, 172–73. Seventeen years later, Phillips defended the decision to start Johnson in his autobiography, writing: "It wasn't a bad idea, considering the Titans were unbeaten at home and won all their games there by big scores. We had just played one of our best games of the whole season, and Rob played tremendously. Plus, if we weren't playing well, Flutie could come in and give us a spark."
49. "2000 Buffalo Bills Rosters, Stats, Schedule, Team Draftees," Pro Football Reference, accessed September 1, 2023, https://www.pro-football-reference.com/teams/buf/2000.htm.
50. Cottrell, discussion.
51. "2001 New York Jets Rosters, Stats, Schedule, Team Draftees," Pro Football Reference, accessed September 1, 2023, https://www.pro-football-reference.com/teams/nyj/2001.htm.
52. "2002 New York Jets Rosters, Stats, Schedule, Team Draftees," Pro Football Reference, accessed September 1, 2023, https://www.pro-football-reference.com/teams/nyj/2002.htm.
53. Bill Bradley, discussion, August 19, 2023; Cottrell, discussion.
54. Bill Bradley, discussion, August 19, 2023.
55. Cottrell, discussion.
56. "2002 New York Jets," Pro Football Reference.
57. "2003 New York Jets Rosters, Stats, Schedule, Team Draftees," Pro Football Reference, accessed September 1, 2023, https://www.pro-football-reference.com/teams/nyj/2003.htm.
58. Bill Bradley, discussion, August 19, 2023.
59. Susan Bradley, discussion.
60. Carter, discussion.
61. Carter, discussion.
62. Carter, discussion.
63. "2007 San Diego Chargers Rosters, Stats, Schedule, Team Draftees," Pro Football Reference, accessed September 2, 2023, https://www.pro-football-reference.com/teams/sdg/2007.htm.
64. "2008 San Diego Chargers Rosters, Stats, Schedule, Team Draftees," Pro Football Reference, accessed September 2, 2023, https://www.pro-football-reference.com/teams/sdg/2008.htm.
65. Associated Press, "Chargers Fire Cottrell, Name Rivera New Defensive Coordinator," ESPN.com, October 28, 2008, https://www.espn.com/nfl/news/story?id=3669441.
66. Cottrell, discussion.
67. Bill Bradley, discussion, August 19, 2023.
68. Bob Grotz, "Despite Disappointments, Ted Cottrell Helped Plant a Seed of Diversity in NFL," *Delaware County (PA) Daily Times*, June 22, 2020.
69. Bill Bradley, discussion, August 19, 2023.

10. Faith, Hope, and Love

1. Bill Bradley, in discussion with the author, Spring Branch TX, April 10, 2022.
2. Jim Dent, "The Bradley Family Comeback," in Dent, *Kids Got It Right*, 269.
3. Susan Bradley, discussion.
4. Dent, "Bradley Family Comeback," 270.
5. Leon Edward and Anum Khan, *Concussion, Traumatic Brain Injury, MTBI: The Ultimate TBI Rehabilitation Guide* (New York: self-pub., 2019), 13–14.
6. Edward and Khan, *Concussion*, 16–17.
7. Susan Bradley, discussion.
8. Vani Rao and Sandeep Vaishnavi, *The Traumatized Brain: A Family Guide to Understanding Mood, Memory, and Behavior after Brain Injury* (Baltimore: Johns Hopkins University Press, 2015), 1, 15–18.
9. Susan Bradley, discussion.
10. Susan Bradley, discussion.
11. Susan Bradley, discussion.
12. Edward and Khan, *Concussion*, 14.
13. Dent, "Bradley Family Comeback," 270–71.
14. Susan Bradley, discussion.
15. Dent, "Bradley Family Comeback," 270–71.
16. Bill Bradley, discussion, April 10, 2022.
17. Susan Bradley, discussion.
18. Susan Bradley, discussion.
19. Dent, "Bradley Family Comeback," 273.
20. Susan Bradley, discussion.
21. Susan Bradley, discussion.
22. Partsch, "Like a Movie."
23. Susan Bradley, discussion.
24. D. T. Stuss et al., "The Acute Period of Recovery from Traumatic Brain Injury: Posttraumatic Amnesia or Posttraumatic Confusional State?" *Journal of Neurosurgery* 90, no. 4 (April 1999): 638–40, https://doi.org/10.3171/jns.1999.90.4.0635.
25. Trandur Ulfarsson, *Predictors of Long-Term Outcome after Severe Traumatic Brain Injury* (Department of Clinical Neuroscience and Rehabilitation, Institute of Neuroscience and Physiology, Sahlgrenska Academy at University of Gothenberg, 2013), https://www.semanticscholar.org/paper/Predictors-of-long-term-outcome-after-severe-brain-Ulfarsson/8dfa96ff619177598bf4a13d1832c4d210637f8f.
26. Norman Doidge, *The Brain That Changes Itself* (New York: Viking Press, 2007; New York: Penguin Life, 2007), xviii–xix. Citations refer to the Penguin edition.
27. Susan Bradley, discussion.
28. Susan Bradley, discussion.
29. Bill Bradley, discussion, April 10, 2022; and Susan Bradley, discussion.

30. Susan Bradley, discussion.
31. Susan Bradley, discussion.
32. Susan Bradley, discussion.
33. Carter, discussion.
34. Carter, discussion.
35. Harold S. Kushner, *When Bad Things Happen to Good People* (New York: Schocken Books, 1981; New York: Avon Books, 1981), 113–31. Citations refer to the Avon Books edition.
36. After the catastrophic events of September 11, 2001, Kushner's meditation on Psalm 23 became a bestseller, offering guidance on how to find faith and courage in the midst of unbearable tragedy. Harold S. Kushner, *The Lord Is My Shepherd: Healing Wisdom of the Twenty-Third Psalm* (New York: Anchor, 2004), 172.
37. Susan Bradley, discussion.
38. Bill Bradley, discussion, April 10, 2022.
39. Bill Bradley, discussion, April 10, 2022; and Susan Bradley, discussion.
40. "Chronic Traumatic Encephalopathy," Mayo Clinic, last modified November 18, 2023, https://www.mayoclinic.org/diseases-conditions/chronic-traumatic-encephalopathy/symptoms-causes/syc-20370921.
41. For Martland's research, see Harrison S. Martland, "Punch Drunk," *Journal of American Medical Association* 91, no. 15 (October 13, 1928): 1103–7. For Omalu's research, see Bennet I. Omalu et al., "Chronic Traumatic Encephalopathy in a National Football League Player," *Neurosurgery* 57, no. 1 (July 2005): 128–34; Bennet I. Omalu et al., "Chronic Traumatic Encephalopathy in a National Football League Player: Part II," *Neurosurgery* 59, no. 5 (November 2006): 1086–92; and B. I. Omalu et al., "Chronic Traumatic Encephalopathy in a National Football League Player: Case Report and Emerging Medico-Legal Practice Questions," *Journal of Forensic Nursing* 6, no. 1 (Spring 2010): 40–46.
42. Zagorski, *NFL in the 1970s*, 15–16.
43. Mark Fainaru-Wada and Steve Fainaru, *League of Denial: The NFL, Concussions, and the Battle for Truth* (New York: Crown Archetype, 2013; New York: Three Rivers Press, 2014), 4–6. Citations refer to the Three Rivers Press edition.
44. Bennet Omalu, *A Historical Foundation of CTE in Football Players: Before the NFL, There Was CTE* (self-pub., 2014), 11.
45. High-profile concussion-related retirements and injuries in the early 1990s prompted reluctant NFL commissioner Paul Tagliabue to create the NFL-run Mild Traumatic Brain Injury Committee (MTBI).
46. Fainaru-Wada and Fainaru, *League of Denial*, 126–27.
47. Fainaru-Wada and Fainaru, *League of Denial*, 164–65, 167–68.
48. Fainaru-Wada and Fainaru, *League of Denial*, 189–92.

49. Alan Schwartz, "NFL Acknowledges Long-Term Concussion Effects," *New York Times*, December 20, 2009. The quote belongs to Greg Aiello, an NFL spokesman.
50. The number of former NFL players with CTE grew to 345 by 2023. "Researchers Find CTE in 345 of 376 Former NFL Players Studied," Boston University Chobanian and Avedisian School of Medicine, February 6, 2023, https://www.bumc.bu.edu/camed/2023/02/06/researchers-find-cte-in-345-of-376-former-nfl-players-studied/.
51. Mark Maske, "NFL Donating $30 Million to NIH for Brain Injury Research," *Washington Post*, September 5, 2012. The relationship between the NFL and the NIH was fraught with problems. According to a 2016 congressional report, the league attempted to influence the research, causing the NIH to leave $16 million of the NFL's donation on the table. John Branch, "NFL Tried to Influence Concussion Research, Congressional Study Finds," *New York Times*, May 23, 2016.
52. Ken Belson, "NFL to Spend $100 Million to Address Head Trauma," *New York Times*, September 14, 2016.
53. "NFL Players' Concussion Injury Litigation," Seeger Weiss, February 6, 2023, https://www.seegerweiss.com/catastrophic-injury/nfl-concussion-settlement/. For the official NFL concussion settlement website, visit https://www.nflconcussionsettlement.com.
54. Ryan Wood, "Delay, Denial: NFL's Landmark Concussion Settlement Leaves Some Former Players Struggling for Relief," Packers News (website), last modified January 6, 2022, htpps://www.packersnews.com/in-depth/sports/nfl/2021/10/27/nfl-concussion-settlement-leaves-former-players-struggling-relief/6010087001/.
55. Susan Bradley, discussion.
56. Bill Bradley, discussion, April 10, 2022.
57. Susan Bradley, discussion.
58. Bill Bradley, discussion, April 10, 2022.
59. Susan Bradley, discussion.
60. Hubert, discussion.
61. Cherry, discussion.
62. Fitzgerald, discussion.
63. Bill Bradley, discussion, April 10, 2022.
64. John Werner, "Ex-Longhorn, NFL Star Bradley: 'This Is My Canton,'" *Waco Tribune-Herald*, February 13, 2009; David Flores, "Bradley's Induction into Texas Hall of Fame Was Long Overdue," *San Antonio Express-News*, March 6, 2009; Chuck Cox, "From Prep to Pros: Palestine Native Bradley Likes San Antonio," *Palestine (TX) Herald-Press*, September 3, 1995; and Didinger, "Safety for the Ages," 4–5.

SELECTED BIBLIOGRAPHY

Bissinger, Buzz. *Friday Night Lights: A Town, a Team, and a Dream*. New York: Da Capo Press, 1990.

Boyle, Kevin. *The Shattering: America in the 1960s*. New York: W. W. Norton, 2021.

Bynum, Mike, ed. *King Football: Greatest Moments in Texas High School Football History*. Birmingham AL: Epic Sports Classics, 2003.

Campbell, Randolph B. *Gone to Texas: A History of the Lone Star State*. 3rd ed. New York: Oxford University Press, 2018.

Cashion, Ty. *Pigskin Pulpit: A Social History of Texas High School Football Coaches*. Austin: Texas State Historical Association, 1998.

Cohen, Robert W. *The 50 Greatest Players in Philadelphia Eagles History*. Guilford CT: Lyons Press, 2019.

Crepeau, Richard C. *NFL Football: A History of America's New National Pastime*. Urbana: University of Illinois Press, 2020.

Dent, Jim. *The Kids Got It Right: How the Texas All-Stars Kicked Down Racial Walls*. New York: Thomas Dunne Books, 2013.

Didinger, Ray. *Finished Business: My Fifty Years of Headlines, Heroes, and Heartaches*. Philadelphia: Temple University Press, 2021.

Didinger, Ray, and Robert S. Lyons. *The Eagles Encyclopedia: Champions Edition*. Philadelphia: Temple University Press, 2018.

Doidge, Norman. *The Brain That Changes Itself: Stories of Personal Triumph from the Frontiers of Brain Science*. New York: Penguin Life, 2007. First published 2007 by Viking Press (New York).

Eckel, Mark. *The Big 50: The Men and Moments That Made the Philadelphia Eagles*. Chicago: Triumph Books, 2016.

Edward, Leon, and Anum Khan. *Concussion, Traumatic Brain Injury, MTBI: The Ultimate TBI Rehabilitation Guide*. Self-published, 2019.

Fainaru-Wada, Mark, and Steve Fainaru. *League of Denial: The NFL, Concussions, and the Battle for Truth*. New York: Three Rivers Press, 2014. First published 2013 by Crown Archetype (New York).

Forbes, Gordon. *Dick Vermeil: Whistle in His Mouth, Heart on His Sleeve. A Biography.* Chicago: Triumph Books, 2009.

Garvey, Ed. *Never Ask "Why": Football Players' Fight for Freedom in the NFL.* Edited by Chuck Cascio. Philadelphia: Temple University Press, 2023.

Hawthorne, Bobby. *Longhorn Football: An Illustrated History.* Austin: University of Texas Press, 2007.

Jacobus, Robert D. *Black Man in the Huddle: Stories from the Integration of Texas Football.* College Station: Texas A&M University Press, 2019.

Little, Bill, and Jenna McEachern, eds. *What It Means to Be a Longhorn.* Chicago: Triumph Books, 2007.

Omalu, Bennet I. *A Historical Foundation of CTE in Football Players: Before the NFL, There Was CTE.* Self-published, 2014.

Rao, Vani, and Sandeep Vaishnavi. *The Traumatized Brain: A Family Guide to Understanding Mood, Memory, and Behavior after Brain Injury.* Baltimore: Johns Hopkins University Press, 2015.

Shaw, Gary. *Meat on the Hoof: The Hidden World of Texas Football.* New York: St. Martin's Press, 1972.

Westcott, Rich. *Veterans Stadium: Field of Memories.* Philadelphia: Temple University Press, 2005.

Zagorski, Joe. *The NFL in the 1970s: Pro Football's Most Important Decade.* Jefferson NC: McFarland, 2016.

INDEX